ALONE

LOST OVERBOARD IN THE INDIAN OCEAN

BRETT ARCHIBALD

ROBINSON

ALONE

BRETT ARCHIBALD is a businessman and entrepreneur. Over the course of 35 years he has built an illustrious global career, with various directorship positions in Durban, Johannesburg, Sydney, London and Hong Kong. He now lives in Cape Town with his wife Anita and his two children, Zara and Jamie. He is currently the chairman of an events and hospitality company, as well as an inspirational speaker on the national and international circuits.

ROBINSON

First published in South Africa in 2016 by Mercury, an imprint of Burnet Media

This edition published in Great Britain in 2016 by Robinson

Copyright © Brett Archibald, 2016

Maps copyright © FreeVectorMaps.com

1 3 5 7 9 8 6 4 2

ISBN: 978-1-47213-935-1 (paperback)

Design and typesetting by Hewer Text
Printed and bound in Great Britain by Clays Ltd, St Ives plc
Papers used by Robinson are from well-managed forests and other responsible sources

MIX
Paper from
responsible sources
FSC® C104740

Robinson
is an imprint of
Little, Brown Book Group
Carmelite House
50 Victoria Embankment
London EC4Y 0DZ

An Hachette UK Company
www.hachette.co.uk

www.littlebrown.co.uk

This book is dedicated to my 3 'F's.

This is a true story.

SOMEWHERE IN THE MENTAWAI STRAIT
WEDNESDAY, 17 APRIL 2013
2.15AM

From the shelter of the upper deck, I stumble out to the port railing of the *Naga Laut* and into the full brunt of the storm. The sea is heaving. A surge of Coke and bile rockets up my throat and I spew it out over the side, only for the wind to toss it back in my face. I've barely wiped my mouth when another projectile fires up through my diaphragm and I lurch over the side once more.

My head is pounding, my stomach a corkscrew of pain. I vomit a third time. I feel dizzy looking down at the white water churning beneath me. Then there is an explosion in my skull, as if an electric current has run up from the base of my spine and clouted me on the back of my head.

My last conscious thought is, *If I vomit like that again, I'm going to pass out.*

A great weight forces my chin to my chest. I'm somersaulting, tumbling, turning as if in a washing machine. Why didn't we play this game as kids, I think to myself. Fill the washing machine up with soap, climb in and switch on! What a cool game that would've been!

My knees are suddenly thrust towards my chest, my feet crumpling into my backside, foetal-like. Momentarily, it's exhilarating. Bubbles crowd around my face, bursting against my cheeks and closed eyes. I hear a gurgle as they froth from my ears and nose. I try to fix on another sound; it's distant and indistinct. I realise I'm hearing voices, hollow and thin. They remind me of the tin-can telephones we used to make as kids.

'Arch, wake up! Wake up, we're there. We're going for a surf. Wake up!'

Tony and JM sound relentlessly upbeat, giggling as they pour water over my head. Man-child pranks; fifty-year-olds behaving like schoolboys – normal behaviour on our surf trips.

'Don't splash water on my bed!' I hear myself shouting at them. I am meticulous about my bunk being clean and tidy. 'This cabin has no portholes. The sheets won't dry.'

Their laughter recedes and is replaced with a roar that fills my head. I'm suddenly aware of water all around my body, warm contracting pressure against my arms and legs, my chest and neck. Walls of water emerge from the surrounding darkness to swamp my face, flood my nose and wash down my throat.

I cough violently and open my eyes. I wipe away the water to find no cabin, no cohorts. The dream instantly evaporates.

I'm in the ocean, fully awake and alert. The wind is howling and the surf boiling around me. Perhaps thirty metres ahead, the *Naga Laut*, its upper and lower deck lights pulsating through the storm, is moving slowly away from me.

Incredulity hits like a crowbar, my heart hammering in my chest. Is this really happening? It must be some kind of out-of-body experience. I'll snap out of it in a second and somehow be back on deck.

But this is no dream.

Instead, I'm in the ocean, in the centre of a storm.

I hear the diesel engine of the boat grinding against the roar of the wind, and for a moment its acrid fumes reach my nostrils, bringing a further surge of vomit into my mouth. This is real all right, and an unseen wave hits me from behind as if to confirm it.

'Hey!' I scream. My throat is thick, as though I've swallowed a tennis ball. My voice doesn't sound like my own. 'Hey! Hey! Hey!' I scream so loud my lungs feel as if they're going to burst. I propel my upper body as far as I can out of the water in a water polo lift, waving both arms wildly above my head.

'Baz, over here! Baz!' I yell about five or six times as hard as I can. Baz, the Indonesian engineer, does not hear me.

I shout again. And again. My throat begins to burn from the effort. But the sound is stolen away by the waves and the wind and the rain, now beginning to obscure my vision. Calling for help is futile. I'm simply wasting energy trying to get them to hear me.

I can't see anyone else on the back of the boat, but I can make out Banger lying on the upper deck, face down with his head in a bowl.

No-one has seen me fall overboard.

The reality hits me and my mind starts racing. Instinctively, I start swimming after the boat.

You know it's pointless.

I don't know if I think this or say it out loud.

The boat's moving – at what? Probably about six-and-a-half-knots in this storm? You'll never catch them.

Disbelief. Desperation. A slow-spreading sense of dread.

Then something that is for me a little rusty – I begin to pray. 'Please, God. Please. Please, let someone have seen me. Please make the boat turn around and come back for me.'

I can't make out any activity on the *Naga Laut* as the boat forges on into the night, the stern getting smaller and smaller. The muscles in my throat are like lead pipes as I watch it recede. I will the boat to turn but it keeps going. Leaving me behind.

'Please...'

It comes out as a whisper. My stomach has begun to contract beneath my ribcage and I'm finding it hard to breathe.

I know. Inside, I know. *This is where I die.*

Still, I start counting.

I'm a qualified sailor and know the rules of Man Overboard. You practise it a hundred times when you get your skipper's ticket. If someone falls overboard, you throw him a life-ring and start counting – *One-thousand-and-one, one-thousand-and-two, one-thousand-and-three...* – to measure the distance until the captain turns the boat around.

... one-thousand-and-fifteen, one-thousand-and-sixteen, one-thousand-and-seventeen...

Was there a chance? A hope? Could someone have seen me go over?

... one-thousand-and-twenty-three, one-thousand-and-twenty-four...

The boat begins to lose its shape in the blackness; the lights become increasingly dimmer, then they're just a blur. I watch the boat go, a toy in the distance. It looks so vulnerable in the angry storm and yet it's my retreating refuge.

I wait, stunned, desperately treading water. My outstretched arms pull great circles in the swirling foam as I fight to take breaths between the waves. My soaked T-shirt, constricted across my chest, feels like it's trying to suffocate me.

I'm in the ocean, unwittingly abandoned.

'I'm going to die out here,' I say to no-one in particular. 'Alone.'

THE MENTAWAIS

It started with an email, a tantalising invitation to surf the world's best waves in a magnificent tropical paradise. The idea was fuelled by blokey banter and talked up over time and more than the occasional beer.

Just cause was found – 'What better way to celebrate a fiftieth birthday?' – and taken up by Tony Singleton, who called on his circle of ten closest friends to sign up. The lure? A dream surf charter trip to the Mentawai Islands in Indonesia.

The ten men, all South Africans in their early fifties, had been mates since school. A couple had started out together as five-year-olds in Class One; others had known one another since primary school. But most had forged their friendships as tousled-haired teenagers in the corridors and on the sports fields of Durban's Westville Boys' High.

'Boys,' Tony wrote in the email, 'the time has come. *Kry daardie gevoel!*'*

He explained that he'd made a tentative booking on the *Naga Laut*, the same boat that a few of them had used the previous year, and he outlined dates and costs.

'This is fairly early season, but the trip is over full moon, so crowds should not be too bad and we will get waves. Guys, I know things are tight now but will be easing up, so let's look ahead and get this going. You in?'

By that Sunday evening Niall Hegarty, Craig Killeen, Mark Ridgway, Mark Snowball, Jean-Marc Tostee, Benoit

---

* Get the feeling!

Maingard, Brett Archibald, Eddie Pickles and Tony himself had all confirmed. Weyne Mudde needed a little more time to convince his wife and children that time away with the boys was a fitting way to celebrate his fiftieth birthday.

They were to leave behind their boardroom meetings and business pressures, relationship niggles and cumbersome mortgages to escape on a trip that they would later christen the 'Ten Green Bottles Tour', referring to Bintangs, the thin, watery lager consumed in Indonesia.

Indonesian surf charters are expensive in anyone's language and consequently are most often made up of the middle-aged and more well-to-do. They also frequently comprise disparate groups, people from different countries who don't know one another. But this charter was different. It was to be a reunion of old friends, many of whom had been separated by time and geography for years. They came together again with one unifying desire: their love of riding the sea.

The ten had all surfed since childhood, but now with families and businesses to run surfing had become a more occasional pastime. For those who lived near the sea the opportunity to surf presented itself more often, but it still could never match the addiction of their youth. The days when the warm Indian Ocean off Durban's east coast called them from their Westville Boys' classrooms.

The sea was their playground.

It was 1970s South Africa, a time when surfing champion Shaun Tomson was at the peak of his international fame. Surfing was considered a 'rebel' sport with a mad, bad reputation with which many of the boys identified. It became a bond between them.

As fourteen-year-olds, Tony, Weyne, Ed and Mark 'Ridgy' Ridgway would hitchhike in baggies and T-shirts, boards under arm, down the hilly highway from their Westville North homes to the long sweeps of sand and cooling winds of Durban's city beaches. They'd hook up with the others: the Tostee brothers, Craig, Benoit (known as 'Banger'), Niall and Brett from Westville Central and South, and Mark Snowball ('Snowman') – from the suburb of Glenwood but 'an honorary Westville bloke' – to spend the whole day surfing.

It was a free life in the extreme.

On weekends they'd get up at 4.30am and hitch down to Durban's pristine beaches and perfect rolling waves

For Niall Hegarty, a recent immigrant from England, surfing became a way to make friends. 'There was no more beautiful sight than sitting on your board and watching the sun rise over the waves.'

JM, although a year below the others in school, was equal to them in the water. The Tostee boys were mad about the ocean; JM's younger brother Pierre would go on to become a Springbok surf champion. Tony also surfed with his older brother and would go on surfing family holidays to Southbroom and the wilder Transkei coast.

Over the years, some of the men had gone in search of greater rides; international surf spots had beckoned. Indonesia had become a favourite with its dazzling beaches and unmatchable reef breaks. So when the opportunity for the ten of them to surf in the Mentawais arose, they all leapt at it.

The Ten Green Bottles Tour was set. At the last minute, Ed Pickles had to pull out due to a skin cancer scare, but the nickname stuck because he was there in spirit. And so, in April 2013, the nine men found themselves converging in Indonesia – from their respective cities around South Africa and from the other countries to which some had emigrated – to do what they loved most, in a place they all dreamed about.

THE MENTAWAIS

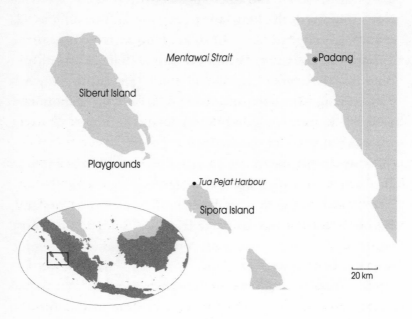

Across the Indian Ocean, in Australia, Perth waste manager Lyall Davieson began a remarkably similar process in January 2013. With a chain of phone calls that darted up and down the Western Australian coastline, he was determined to fulfil the wish of his best friend, Simon Carlin, who wanted to celebrate his fiftieth birthday on a surf charter in the Mentawais.

Lyall had taken weeks to contact Simon's inner circle, a group of nine men who had all been close friends since high school. Many of them had surfed together since they were boys, taking one another on in the waves off Perth's Rottnest Island, up near their neighbourhood Trigg Point, or pitting themselves against the challenging waves at Margaret River.

Apart from Simon, Lyall had, in a flurry of emails, finally secured Colin Chenu, Dave Carbon, Pete Inglis, Jeff Vidler, Justin Vivian, Mark Swan and Gary Catlin. They were all seasoned surfers and many had been on Indonesian charters before, but this time they were looking for a slightly different experience – something a little less run-of-the-mill. They wanted to test their skills and strength in more remote surf spots and take on waves that were more formidable.

As the designated trip organiser, Lyall scoured the internet, trawling the irresistible Mentawai menu for a surf charter that was prepared to do the unconventional. For this they needed a charter captain who was different: someone who knew where to find those fiendish waves, who appreciated their attraction and who respected the danger involved. A man who understood that the hunt for the perfect wave never ends.

Leaving behind their personal and professional concerns, the nine Western Australians left at the end of the first week in April 2013 to fly via Bali to Padang. There they would meet up with one of the most skilled veteran skippers known in the area. A hard man and a good man, someone who was respected as a true man of the sea: Tony 'Doris' Eltherington, Australian expat captain of the *Rajah Elang* and one-time Gold Coast surfing legend.

Indonesia – Indo – is famed for its surf spots. But if Bali is considered the sport's stronghold of money and tourism, the reefs and bays of the Mentawai Island Regency are its Holy Grail. This is an archipelago within an archipelago. Remote, exotic and, alluringly, a little dangerous, it's a collection of around seventy islands in a great ocean expanse, the main ones with beautiful sibilant names such as Siberut, North and South Pagai and Sipura. They're separated from the west coast of Sumatra by a perilous stretch of water, more than one hundred nautical miles wide, called the Mentawai Strait.

If you close your eyes and dream of a perfect island locale, a picture of the Mentawais might come to mind: shimmering, clear blue seas, powder-white beaches with nearby coral reefs and tropical palm forests, wild and undeveloped. However, their beauty has come at a price,

The islands sit on the angry Sunda megathrust, a zone of seismic activity that hosts regular earthquakes and their accompanying deadly tsunamis. The smaller quakes are frequent and come with death tolls, but it's the big ones that hit the headlines, most notoriously in December 2004 when the Boxing Day tsunami, emanating from the northern limits of the Mentawais, resulted in one of recorded history's worst natural disasters. The death toll was estimated at anywhere between 230,000 and 284,000, with half a million injured and entire villages wiped from the earth. More than half of those killed were Indonesian. Some Mentawai Islanders claim that entire villages were wiped out and that the death toll from the area was never fully realised.

The local people have, however, learnt to live with nature's temper. It's meeting the modern world face to face that has been harder to deal with.

Behind the palm trees are the real-life problems: poverty, poor housing, lack of infrastructure, malnutrition and massive health epidemics.

Modern progress has brought these changes – but really only since the early 1900s. Previously, the Islands' contact with the outside world was, bizarrely, quite minimal.

Despite being part of the dynamic eastern trade routes since the 5th century, the Mentawai Islands remained largely isolated for hundreds of years, some claim because of their strong ocean currents, unpredictable winds and natural perimeter defence system: the razor-sharp coral reefs that surround many of the islands.

Today the indigenous Mentawai have mostly forsaken their *umas*, the traditional village houses where clans once lived beneath one roof. They've been resettled in poverty-stricken towns in artificial administrative districts where cholera and hepatitis are rife. And the shamans have cellphones.

Rickety motorcycles comprise the main mode of transport on land, while people get around from village to village on the water, on the rivers and across the bays, in *perahu* or dug-out canoes. Surprisingly, despite being water people, many don't know how to swim.

Notwithstanding the challenges of modern living and the ever-present threat of nature's wrath, the islands are blessed with a sublime natural gift: an unsurpassed sea. Ironically, it's the seismic activity and unstable ocean beds that have over time caused the reefs to rise by several metres and they, in turn, produce every surfer's yen: great thunderous barrels.

Along with Hawaii and Tahiti, the Mentawais have become a surfing Promised Land. The menacing reefs have sifted out the wannabees and it is the more experienced surfers who bring their sunblock and boards from all over the world to surf consistent swells that have been christened with unforgettable names like 'Thunders', 'Macaronis', 'Bat Caves', 'Playgrounds', 'Hollow Trees', 'Bintangs', 'Scarecrows', 'Telescopes', 'E-Bay', 'Bank Vaults' and the titillating 'Nipussi' or 'Pussies'.

Surfing brings tourism – and money – to the islands.

But it has also brought its problems. The industry is still largely unregulated and certain spots can get crowded in surf season. Also, the islands, which were trumpeted as the new surfing Mecca when the sport was nascent in the early 1990s, are remote. There is no international airport to feed tourist traffic. The islands are far away from their provincial capital, Padang in West Sumatra, and the transport, medical and communication infrastructures are pretty much nonexistent. There is a ferry that makes the ten-hour steam over the Strait twice a week, but it doesn't always run. And the only cellphone reception is in port.

The Mentawais are, quite simply, in the middle of nowhere.

The weather can also be moody and fickle.

Because of their isolation, the charter boats that operate throughout the islands from Padang are largely private entities and exist essentially in their own world. Some are entirely locally driven, but most are expat-owned operations, crewed by Indonesians and captained by men (and a few women) of all nationalities.

Guests come for an unforgettable, carefree adventure on a surf charter, but beneath the holiday fun is a very serious undercurrent. All of the charter captains, their surf guides and crew know that things can go wrong, and when they do it's usually in a split second. A dragging anchor can leave a boat stranded on a reef and in an emergency, medical or otherwise, help is not simply a phone call away. So while they try to ensure their guests have a great experience that will encourage them to return, these are not malarkey operations.

Charter boats work within a code. They're generally run according to strict rules and captains are aware of the lines that cannot be crossed. Guides quickly determine the level of their guests' surfing ability and decide what waves they can or can't handle. A breach of safety, they know, can harm the whole industry.

A lack of facilities has meant that they have to be resourceful in times of need. Skippers have become skilful surgeons, ready and able to sew up a surfer torn apart on a reef. Serious injuries do occur, however, and while Padang has two functional hospitals, most charter companies insist that guests have solid medical insurance that can cover the thousands of dollars it will take to medivac them to Singapore for first-class treatment.

In every other case, surf charter operations are forced to rely on one another. And in areas where the stakes are high, where earthquakes and tsunamis hit with unsettling frequency, captains have an implicit mandate: to be knowledgeable and accountable, but most importantly, cautious. A crew member is awake 24/7 – crews sleep in shifts – so that someone is always on watch, and if they're not out at sea, they know all the safe anchorages. In the absence of a formal warning system, the captains have developed an intricate network of satellite phone, and increasingly Facebook, communication to keep track of one another, as well as to put out alerts.

The boats are also the first in line in the wake of disaster to rescue and deliver aid, working with organisations like Doctors Without Borders and charities like SurfAid.

Still, surfers argue that the Mentawais are all the more special because of the inseparable danger, their rough charm and pristine isolation. They're well worth the arduous journey, it is said – the hours of flying, long stopovers, internal flights and then an overnight boat crossing.

They come for the sickle-shaped white-sand beaches, the seemingly unpopulated islands thick with vegetation and the odd ramshackle village hidden amongst the trees, the clear seas and, most of all, the big, clean breaks. They leave with surf scars, sun-stretched skin and endless photos and footage of their greatest rides ever.

The Mentawais are the endless summer of their dreams.

For the nine friends from Westville and the nine from Perth, however, this trip would be something else; the scene of something truly extraordinary. Each would face a colossal test of strength, endurance, gallantry, loyalty and heroism. Their journeys would cross, their lives intersect and the destinies of two men would meet over the course of two unforgettable days.

Two days that would prove to be a spectacular coincidence of fate.

WEDNESDAY, 17 APRIL 2013
THE NAGA LAUT
TUA PEJAT HARBOUR, NORTH SIPURA
8.12AM

Brett's not on the boat.

The thought doesn't hit Jean-Marc with sledgehammer force. It unfolds itself slowly, bringing a strange, spreading disquiet and the feeling of his insides being hollowed out. For a moment he thinks he might be sick. Still, he doesn't say anything. He has to be sure.

From where he's sitting, he can see down the passage that leads into the 'dungeon', the gloomy porthole-less cabin beneath the prow of the boat that he's sharing with his friend of forty-two years, Brett Archibald. He knows that Brett isn't down there.

JM pushes the surf magazine he's been reading a few centimetres forward and quietly gets up from the galley table. Weyne and Craig, first-timers on a surf trip like this, are bent over the coffee machine trying to figure out how it works. Tony and the two Marks sit around the end of the table, stirring coffee and pouring cereal into their bowls.

Conversation is subdued after the rough overnight crossing.

JM unfurls his six-foot frame and walks through the boat's dining area, ducking out onto the *Naga Laut*'s lower deck. He takes a deep breath to suppress a brewing sense of panic and looks up to the sky. It's clogged with heavy bruise-like clouds. The wind, although weakened, still swirls in gusts about the boat.

He scans the jungle outline of the island about 150 metres away, but can barely make out its scruffy palm trees poking out of the thick vegetation. They look like giant upturned

1

bottlebrushes through the thin veil of rain. In the dullness of the morning the island looks gloomy and inhospitable.

JM crosses his arms against the uncharacteristic cold.

Last night was no *sumatra*, the local name given to the flash storms that sweep through these tropics. This weather has set in. The strength of the night's ill temper has eased somewhat, but the storm's prolonged tail will take all day to run its course. Rain continues to fall and the boat is pitching beneath him, despite its protected anchorage in the small bay spread out before the few ramshackle buildings that make up the harbour of Tua Pejat.

It was an awful night, the crossing from Padang ferocious. The storm, the worst JM has seen on his many trips to Indonesia, savaged the boat and left four of the nine friends spending much of the night vomiting – a combination of seasickness, jet lag and suspected food poisoning. The Bintangs they'd had at a roadside bar in Padang probably hadn't helped either.

It isn't a promising start to their talked-up surf trip: their way of celebrating Weyne's fiftieth and, hell, a bloody fine excuse to surf some of the planet's most unbelievable breaks.

A few almost hadn't made the trip. All successful businessmen, they'd had to convince their colleagues and their consciences that there would never be a better time to do something like this, something totally indulgent and personally thrilling. For ten days, all of them would be almost entirely uncontactable.

It's around 8am, JM guesses. He'd packed for the trip in haste and had forgotten his wristwatch. He looks down at the pale tan mark on his left wrist and frowns.

It's the absence of a single voice that unsettles him.

Brett, whom he's known since they were Cubs, then Scouts,

at school, is a conspicuous presence. On the boat. In a room. In life.

He's a man known for his contagious enthusiasm for everything. Boundlessly energetic, Brett is a big personality. Loud, easy-going, good-natured, but with a reputation as a non-conformist and a risk-taker in both his personal and professional life. It's won him adoration and enmity in equal measure.

In younger, wilder days, Brett was notable, even admired, for his high-spirited misbehaviour. His madcap adventures are legendary, even if he's had a hand in making them so.

Brett's talent as a raconteur is well known to his friends. His playfully embroidered storytelling, nicknaming everyone and everything, and frequently dipping into a vast library of jokes, means it's impossible for him to go unnoticed for long.

This morning, no-one has heard the human hurricane that is 'the Arch'.

The silence is unsettling.

Brett had been ill during the night, but even that, JM knew, would not keep him down for long.

JM wipes the raindrops from his face and tentatively climbs the stainless-steel ladder to the upper deck; its steps are slick under foot. As the rain comes down in a fine mist, he looks around the open area on top.

No sign of Brett.

He checks the starboard and port sides of the boat and walks through the swirling drizzle up to the front. Nothing.

'He's not up there. He must be in your cabin,' Tony said when JM casually asked after their friend half an hour ago. Tony had gone up on deck as soon as he'd woken to prep his board for their first day's surf.

Weyne had joined him up there. 'Shit, what happened to paradise?' Weyne had said on seeing the weather.

Tony Singleton, owner of a Durban-based awning company and the trip organiser, is a eight-time veteran of these Indonesian surf charters. 'Things change very quickly here,' he'd replied. 'In fifteen minutes, things could swing around and we could have waves.'

That didn't seem likely now.

The cabin, JM knows, is empty. He'd left it two hours ago and the bunk, though unmade, had not been slept in.

I must have missed him, JM thinks. Perhaps he went to the toilet and is back there now. Or maybe he moved to the spare bunk in one of the other cabins, and I've just forgotten which one it is.

The dungeon, with the anchor winch just above taking up valuable headspace, and with its proximity to the engine room's diesel fumes, is the worst place to be on the boat if you're seasick.

JM returns to the galley and makes his way back past the others, who, apart from Banger and Niall, are now all up and talking in hushed voices. Banger and Niall were also violently ill through the night.

JM turns on the dungeon's lights. They crackle and buzz into action. The ceiling is so low a man can hardly stand upright, so JM crawls on his hands and knees to Brett's bunk and again he lifts the crumpled duvet in case he's missed his friend creeping back there at some point.

Empty.

He throws the pillow across the cabin.

Brett's half-open bag, now the only hint of his presence, has not moved from the end of the bunk. JM noticed it earlier when, as the first one awake, he'd pulled on his boardshorts

4

and a T-shirt in the dim light of his headlamp. His roommate, he presumed, had slept on deck.

The friends had bunked together on previous trips, and since they were both light sleepers Brett often chose to sleep under the stars, especially on hot nights. With Brett moving up and down being sick in the night, JM assumed he'd finally fallen asleep on one of the benches upstairs.

JM climbs the two or three steps to the other cabins and moves slowly backwards through the narrow passage, looking into the two smaller adjacent cabins – one where Weyne is bunking alone and the other where Tony is sharing with Snowman. They're both empty.

He then moves back to glance in on Niall, alone in his cabin and still curled up facing the wall. Opposite, Banger is on the top bunk, the duvet over his head.

Perhaps he's back in the loo, thinks JM. He checks the heads, one on each side of the passage. Both were very busy during the night.

Also empty.

This isn't good. Dread is beginning to rise. There is nowhere else on the boat that Brett could be.

'Hey, has anyone seen Brett this morning?'

It feels like a freight train is running through JM's chest as he comes back through to the galley.

The eyes that meet his are expressionless.

'He was radically sick last night,' Ridgy remarks, 'he must be sleeping.'

'He's not in our cabin.' JM's voice sounds like it's been roughly cut.

'He was on the top deck last night. Did you check upstairs?'

JM suddenly thinks of one last place. He walks briskly through the galley again and clambers up the ladder to the bridge. He hasn't checked the crews' bunks behind the skipper's wheel. Perhaps Brett just bundled into the nearest refuge at some point. Ridgy follows him.

Yanto, the only English-speaking member of the Indonesian crew and the all-round fixer on the surf charter, is chuckling with the captain, an older man whom Brett had immediately christened 'Skippy' after they'd boarded. The crew has remained awake all night to coax the *Naga Laut* through the stormy 12-hour crossing.

Yanto watches curiously as the two men glance around the cabin, ducking their heads between the bunks. Hums and grunts are coming from the engine room beneath.

'Yanto, have you seen Brett?' JM's question is urgent, even a little impatient, a signal of his growing apprehension. 'The loud one with no hair?'

Since the guests had arrived only the day before, name identification isn't reliable.

'He was sick in the night on deck, Mr Jimmy,' Yanto offers.

'Yes, we know,' Ridgy says, 'but did he sleep here last night?'

'No. He's not in his cabin?'

'No,' says JM. 'I've already searched everywhere and Brett is not on board.'

Yanto freezes. All the blood drains instantly from his face. His wide eyes reflect the power of that statement: *Brett is not on board.*

In an instant, all three men register its enormity. A man is overboard. Now obvious and incontrovertible, they all know it will have momentous consequences. In Indonesia, losing someone at sea means a mandatory jail sentence for a boat's captain and his first mate.

Yanto, now shaking, starts a panicked discussion in Bahasa, the local language, with Skippy.

'Okay, we've got a big problem.' JM keeps his composure. 'This is what we are going to do. Yanto, get your crew to the back of the boat. All of them. I will round up our guys and we'll all search the boat again. Brett could have slipped in the storm, he could have fallen somewhere, hurt his ankle. We have to search the boat. Otherwise he's overboard.' He's working hard to stay controlled.

Ridgy turns to make his way to the lower deck. He meets Tony at the ladder. 'Listen, we think Brett's off the boat.'

A chill runs up Tony's spine. 'What do you mean "off the boat"?'

'We can't find him.'

Tony looks up blankly as he assesses the impact of the words.

The change in mood runs through the boat like a powder fuse.

'What? Where's Brett?' Banger, a tall burly man, leaps from his bunk.

Niall, too, quickly joins the others. 'What's going on? Brett's gone?'

Still a little disorientated and detached, the men all look at one another, unable to believe what they're hearing. Dismay, then disbelief settles upon all of them.

JM comes through the door. 'Guys, I need you all at the back of the boat. Now, please.'

Someone laughs nervously. After all, this has the hallmark of one of Brett's adolescent stunts.

'No, seriously,' JM says. 'I've been looking for Brett. He should've been up and he's nowhere to be found. I've checked and rechecked all the cabins. He's not here.'

The relaxed air has been obliterated, and after a momentary stock-take of the situation at the back of the boat, everyone sets into action. The men move off in all directions to begin the search.

'Count the surfboards,' Craig Killeen suggests. 'Perhaps he got up really early and paddled to the beach?' Despite the rain the water is relatively flat.

Tony and Ridgy move to the stacked boards. They're all there.

'He could have got cold last night on deck and slept in one of the board bags?' says Snowman. This is common practice on surf trips. The covers are duly pulled out from under the benches but again the men draw a blank.

Craig and Weyne head down to inspect the cabins yet again. 'I swapped cabins with Brett and JM when we came aboard. He could have been disorientated and gone to the wrong cabin,' says Weyne. He sounds bewildered.

'I've checked them all,' JM insists.

'Maybe he went down to the engine room, it's warm there,' Banger offers. But Yanto's ashen face as he walks up from the bowels of the mono-hull dispels that hope.

Dazed, the men move around the boat. A sense of unreality hangs like a thick fog. These circumstances, each man knows, are far from normal.

'How ridiculous,' Craig mutters to himself as he looks in the galley's kitchen cupboards.

'I know, how bloody stupid! He's not going to be in here.' Weyne closes a drawer.

Shock, confusion and disorientation at searching an unfamiliar, three-storey boat seeps like fast-rising damp through the group. It surely couldn't have been Brett's carelessness that caused him to go overboard. He has his skipper's licence and is an experienced seaman.

'He could have had a heart attack and hit his head as he fell over and went into the water unconscious.' Niall's speculation ratchets up new concerns.

'I'll check the railings for blood.' JM climbs up the ladder to the upper deck. 'Or damage to the rails.'

'I'll check the tender. Jesus, if that hit him in the water...' Ridgy doesn't want to complete the sentence. The tender had been let out about twenty metres behind the *Naga Laut* before the crossing, to prevent it from being smashed against the boat during the storm.

'I reckon he was vomiting so badly over the side that he became exhausted, and with the rocking and rolling of the boat he must've lost his footing. The deck is as slippery as hell up there.' Banger climbs the ladder after JM.

After fifteen minutes the eight friends regroup at the stern of the boat and for a few moments stare at one another in silence.

The terrible truth descends. It feels like a bubble bursting.

'What the fuck! What now?' Tony whispers.

'We have to go back for him.' Ridgy utters what they all know in their hearts. 'We have to find him.'

It's a major undertaking – they all know that intuitively – but no-one questions that it has to be done.

By contrast, the Indonesian crew, scrambling up and down the decks, are frantic. Yanto is speaking quickly and hysterically with the captain, the engineer and deckhands.

'Calm down, Yanto,' says Ridgy, taking him by the shoulders. 'We have to stay calm.'

'They're going to put captain and me in jail, Mr Jimmy. Fifteen years. I have wife. Little girl of three.' He's in great distress. 'Captain go now to harbour master to report that Mr Brett is overboard.'

'You can't go now!' shouts JM. 'We have to go back out there as quickly as we can.'

Yanto interprets this to the captain, who is shouting back. The communication is confused and haphazard, but his fear is palpable. The captain's resistance needs no translation.

'People don't come back from the sea, Mr Jimmy,' says Yanto shaking his head, tears welling in his eyes.

This infuriates JM.

'Listen, Yanto, we've booked and paid for this boat for ten days. If it takes all ten days we're going to go back out there and find him!'

'We have to report it in Tua Pejat!' Yanto almost shrieks.

'Okay, slow down. We must follow the rules.' Ridgy, a credit consultant whose company runs e-toll roads in South Africa, is also a trained pilot and, like some of the others on the *Naga Laut*, was an officer during his national service days in the South African Defence Force. He's a decisive man. 'What's the protocol? What's the course of action?'

Yanto and the crew appear overwhelmed, out of their depth. The South Africans realise that they'll have to gently assume control.

'Okay,' JM says to the young man. 'If we can't start a search mission until it's reported, the captain must hit the tinny and get to the Port Authority on the island. We'll ready the boat and turn it around.'

Orders dispatched, JM starts moving inside, but then he turns back to Yanto.

'We'll find him,' he says firmly. It seems to mollify Yanto temporarily. 'I promise you, we will find him. He's swimming out there. He's swimming.'

SIX HOURS EARLIER
2.30AM TO 3.30AM
FIRST HOUR IN THE WATER

You should be feeling fear, Brett. Panic.
  I'm confused. I don't feel anything.
  Am I in shock? Emotionally cauterised?
  And then like the flick of a switch: logic.

I quickly calculate that it's close to 2.30am. I saw the time glaring up in green from the captain's GPS screen shortly before I fell overboard. I know almost exactly where we are in the Strait.
  Methodically, I replay the evening's events in my head.
  Weyne and I had been the last to go to bed, just before midnight. We'd stayed on deck, drinking a short whisky and catching up on the thirty-five or so years since we'd last seen each other, until the rain and wind had become unbearable.
  I awoke abruptly to the pounding of the boat as it crashed into massive swells, the prow rising and falling into cavernous troughs of water. Checking my Blackberry for the time – 1.30am – I saw to my dismay that a BBM to Anita, my wife, hadn't gone through. I had promised her I would let her know when we were leaving Padang and in the excitement of setting sail it had slipped my mind.
  JM, my cabin mate, was also awake, and we laughed about the rough seas and what a baptism of fire this crossing would be for the three first-timers aboard, Craig, Niall and Weyne. Needing the bathroom, I headed up the small wooden ladder from the depths of the forecabin to find a commotion amidships. Ridgy was busy prying open the door of the first cabin with a screwdriver, and the sight beyond was not a

11

pretty one. Banger, all 6 foot 4 inches and 110 kilos, was green to the gills and emptying his toiletry bag onto the floor from the top bunk, whereupon he promptly vomited into the opened bag. On the bunk below Craig looked up horrified.

On witnessing the scene, I figured to make it to the bathroom before Banger did, so I staggered off down the passage towards the heads. As I started to pee I too was overcome with nausea. Suddenly gripped by crippling stomach cramps, it occurred to me as I ripped down my trousers what the offending dish was: the calzone pizza we'd all looked at so quizzically over dinner, with its encrusted topping of dodgy mince meat.

It was horrific. For what seemed like a lifetime I vomited copiously into the basin in front of me as my bowels emptied behind, my body crackling with sweat. I had never been so violently ill in my life.

Finally, when the worst was past, I hosed down my entire body with the small hose attached to the toilet and made my way out. I glanced at the large clock in the galley, the buckled arms reflecting 2.15am. Needing fresh air, I turned towards the stern of the boat and stumbled out in to the glaring lights of the *Naga Laut*'s aft deck, where I found Banger lying prone on the fibreglass deck, plastic bowl in hand and retching like a dying man.

Diesel fumes from the engine consumed us from below in overpowering waves, constricting my stomach and filling my mouth with saliva. I felt so nauseous, I could hardly breathe.

'Banger!' I managed to croak. 'We've got to move to the upper deck to get more air.'

It was raining steadily. The boat surged headlong into great swells, pitching hard left and right.

Banger made his way up the ladder first, and as I followed I noticed Baz had nodded off in his chair at the boat's edge.

How could anyone sleep in this storm?

'Hey, Baz!' I shouted in as jovial a tone as I could muster given my tender state. 'You must wake up! You're on night duty, bud!'

Up top, I found a place on one of the benches and sat head in hands while Banger lay opposite, on the other side of the table, vomiting intermittently into his bowl.

'Jetman,' he eventually croaked, using his nickname for me, 'please ask the skipper how long we've got to go. I can't carry on like this. If it's much longer I'd rather jump overboard and swim.'

I rose, unsteady on my feet, and made my way to the captain's cabin just in front of the two benches.

'Skippy,' I shouted over the storm, 'how long have we got to go?'

'Mr Brett, big storm.' It was Yanto, the first mate. 'It's still a long time. Maybe we get there 9.30am.'

In good weather we would have arrived at the islands three hours earlier. Could the storm really have put us this far behind schedule?

I squinted down at the little GPS screen, which showed our progress.

'This how far we got to go,' Yanto translated as Skippy pointed out the distance we still needed to cover.

I noticed that the digital clock read 2.21am, and was shocked to realise I had been in the head for nearly forty-five minutes being ill. No wonder I was feeling so fragile.

'We've still got another seven hours of this, my bud,' I told Banger as I stumbled back out to the table. He promptly vomited again into the bowl.

Below decks, I had been wearing a pair of floral cargo shorts, but out in the storm I was getting cold. I grabbed one of my T-shirts, a grey cotton crewneck, out of one of the little deck lockers and pulled it over my head, one arm at a time in order to steady myself against the pitching and yawing of the boat

'We're dehydrating. We should drink something,' I said to Banger. 'Want a Coke?'

He responded to my suggestion with more retching.

I stumbled to the little bar fridge, fully stocked for our post-surf chill sessions. It didn't close properly and needed an enormous stretch band to seal it shut. Back on the bench, I cracked open a small tin of Coca-Cola and drank it down in one gulp – but I could instantly feel it, sugary and effervescent, ready to come back up.

I stood up and moved quickly to the side of the boat. Rain seemed to be coming sideways from my right, as well as straight up off the sea and into my face as the boat careened from side to side. With my left hand I held on to the vertical railing that supported the deck's canvas roofing; with my right I clung to the short deck railing that ran around the boat.

I vaguely noted the life ring within easy reach, not even twenty centimetres from my right hand.

Why hadn't I just put my hand through the strap and secured it to my arm?

I took a deep breath.

This really isn't good, I thought. We are in a really dangerous situation here and the boat is struggling to maintain course in ferocious conditions. Flashbacks from the movie *The Perfect Storm* raced through my mind.

'How are you boys doing?' I could only just hear Ridgy's voice over the wind and pelting rain. He'd popped up his torso from the deck below.

'I'm not well, boss,' I said. 'Never felt so sick in my life.'

He told us the others were also being sick downstairs. 'It's carnage!' he bellowed. 'I'll come back and check on you guys later.'

As he climbed down the ladder, I felt the surge of Coke and bile come rocketing up my throat and I spewed it out over the side, only for the wind to splatter it back in my face. I'd barely wiped my mouth when the second projectile came heaving up through my diaphragm.

It's like a fire hydrant – a distant thought.

My head was pounding, my insides caving in; my stomach was a corkscrew of pain. I vomited a third time. I felt dizzy looking down at the white water churning six metres beneath me – then the explosion in my skull, as if an electric current had run up from the base of my spine into my head.

If I vomit like that again, I'm going to pass out.

That's what happened, I think to myself now, struggling to stay afloat as the ocean pummels me from all sides. I must have blacked out – exhausted, dehydrated, even a little delirious – and hit the water.

And no-one saw it happen.

Darkness deepens, an enveloping black pit. The boat has disappeared and left me to be swallowed by this overpowering mass. Despite the blackness, I can still make out the white foam churning around me. Salt water streams from my mouth, nostrils and eyes, and I retch again into the inky waves.

I feel a sudden surge against my sphincter and I undo my belt. I drop my shorts and seconds later feel the warm liquid swirl behind me as I relieve myself.

How bizarre, I think to myself, that you're worried about

crapping in your pants and want to make sure they're not stained! That your A-type personality and need for perfection is overriding even in these circumstances.

Suddenly, I hear the sound of a hyena barking into the African sky. I realise the sound is emanating from my own throat: I'm laughing uncontrollably, hysterically, at the hopeless absurdity of my situation.

I'm alone in the ocean.

'I'm going to die out here,' I say again to no-one in particular.

Yet I feel no fear, only an overwhelming sadness that I'm never going to see my beautiful wife and children again.

3.30AM TO 4.30AM
SECOND HOUR IN THE WATER

Night covers me, but the darkness is not impenetrable. Ambient light comes from an almost-full moon hidden behind heavy storm clouds. I can still make out the ghostly white crests of the waves as they continue to buffet my body and break like hooded cobras over my head.

Sea foam bubbles and fizzes around me. My pharynx feels grated raw from the salt water. I can see the outlines of my arms outstretched in the water, moving at right angles to my body in an aquatic crucifixion.

So this is how you're going to die?

It's more a statement to myself than a question.

Here in the middle of the ocean.

I never thought it would happen like this – which poses the next thought.

Well, how did you think you'd die?

I've done crazy things in my life – skydived, paraglided, leapt from rooftops – and I've often speculated that something dangerous and dramatic might keep me from old age. That my reckless ways might see to my demise. But I never imagined I'd die by flopping overboard in the middle of the Mentawai Strait.

Oddly, I don't feel fear at the certainty of my death – only resignation. There is no chance of surviving this, I find myself thinking. Why bother being afraid?

I take a moment to try to identify my emotions. Again, I find it strange that I don't feel panic, just a profound sadness. A sense of emptiness, hard to define. This is where I'm going to spend my last hours. This is where I'll be for the rest of my life: in the sea, trying to stay afloat until I can do it no more.

The rain has let up a little, falling now in flurries. The wind remains relentless, however, blowing in swirling gusts, whistling sharply, then whispering, from what seems like every point on the compass. It makes even the gentler drizzle hiss.

I slowly turn in a circle, treading water, to take in what I can. Waves rise up like mountain ranges and I'm being pushed from peaks down into deep troughs. Since I'm set so low in the water, I can't see beyond the height of the waves, but I can feel the ocean's expanse. I feel its press against my body, pushing the air from my lungs. But the water is warm, like a tepid bath.

This surprises me.

I look up to the sky. It's thick with cloud and above me the storm produces a spectacle: lightning in the distance lights up the horizon like a disco strobe.

Without warning, great rollers come from the gloom to dump me. I swallow what feels like a gallon of salt water and I cough and retch and spew it all out again. I have to concentrate to lift my chin above the water line.

I perform a quick check, patting down my T-shirt and cargo shorts under the water to make sure I'm still intact. I feel for my pulse in my left wrist. It's easy to locate because it's racing at machine-gun speed.

'This is bad, Brett.' I decide to talk out loud. 'Pure adrenaline is coursing through your body and when it stops, you're going to sink to the bottom.'

I imagine the cavernous depths beneath me; the dreadful secrets they hold. The ocean, while I've loved it since I was a child, is still unknown. Unknowable. It's alive with creatures that I might well encounter soon.

I've never felt this vulnerable before. Ever.

I'm taking in too much water. It has caused me to vomit as vehemently as I did off the side of the boat; wracking, stomach-heaving retches. What an unglamorous way to die, I think. People drown in their own vomit, but not like this!

My stomach lets go again – the detestable pizza still doing its wicked work. Once more I undo my belt and the top button of my shorts, dropping them mid-thigh before defecating in the water. I wash myself, pull up my pants and re-buckle my belt.

The ludicrousness of this act suddenly strikes me.

Who's going to care what your bum looks like when they find your body?

I vomit again.

I know that I have to focus, that I must think only practical thoughts. I pull myself to the present. I'm gasping so I decide to concentrate on my breathing. I try to keep watch for the big, thudding waves that come at me, scoop me up in great swells and drop me in their fall.

As a surfer, I've learnt to read the geometry of a wave. When a monster reaches me I now try to take a deep breath and swim through it.

Forget everything else, I tell myself. Adrenaline is driving me now; I have to bring my heart rate down.

I did first aid during my Scouts, school and army days, so I begin another set of structured counting – this time to calculate the pace of the blood pumping in my wrist: *one-thousand-and-one, one-thousand-and-two*. I get to *one-thousand-and-fifteen*, multiply it by four and estimate that my pulse is between 150 and 170.

I close my eyes and start a slow breathing technique that I learnt while training for the various sports events I've done over the years. As I scull my hands around and around in the warm water, I am amazed at how quickly I manage to get my heart rate under control. The wild pulsating slows.

Solitude is like a spell over me now. Being alone will truly test me, but I know that I cannot let that fear take over. Keep calm, I coach myself, you must stay alert and aware of everything around you.

I think of Skippy's GPS screen and know that I'm between 30 and 40 nautical miles from Padang, where we had set off. The entire crossing is 110 nautical miles, more than 200 kilometres, and I estimate that we were approximately a third of the way across when I went overboard.

It's mainly surf charters that make this crossing, but suddenly I remember that in the early hours local fishing boats come out from the mainland, surrounding islands and atolls into the shallower waters.

Look out for lights, I tell myself. Perhaps another boat could come this way.

But the chances of a boat seeing me adrift in the ocean in these conditions are slim, I realise. I also know that fishing boats are unlikely to venture this far out into the open ocean. I try to put the thought of another boat out of my mind.

My tongue is beginning to feel heavy and ungainly in my mouth. I am already dehydrated from the continuous vomiting and all the salt water I've been swallowing. A rasping dryness in my mouth announces the onset of thirst.

Generate saliva, I tell myself. I purse my lips and try to swirl my tongue around my mouth as if rinsing with mouthwash. An indolent lump, my tongue is beginning to swell and doesn't feel like it belongs there. It takes several minutes for my salivary glands to produce a little secretion of thick, chewy spit.

Alone, exposed, vulnerable in this vast ocean, I'm aware of the great test ahead. And I'm going to need help.

'You have to find something to hang on to.'

I say this aloud to the water around me. I long for my board, my trusty partner in the surf. I scan the area around me for something to launch my body onto, something that will help me stay afloat.

Of all things, I think of the many cheap flip-flops I've seen on the beaches of Indonesia – never matching pairs, never the same colour or size.

I plan and speculate. You could shove them in your shorts for buoyancy. Or look for a log or plastic packet that you can blow up and tie to your belt. I smile ruefully – another ludicrous thought.

I take comfort in the fact that the ocean around Indonesia is one of the filthiest I've ever seen. On a previous crossing we'd laughed when we'd seen an old fridge bobbing by. Imagine if the boys come back to find me in a floating fridge drinking Bintangs? Another absurd notion.

I tread water as I turn 360 degrees, tracing the surface of the sea for flotsam while focusing on my breathing. But the sea is angry and flings me around like a ragdoll – a log could move right past me and I wouldn't see it.

Besides, I need more than something physical to hang on to.

It must be around 3am. South Africa, I know, is six hours behind us, so it's around 9pm there. I think of Anita and the kids at home, still oblivious to the fact that I'll be lost to them.

Suddenly I am overcome with guilt. I'd promised to phone Anita before the crossing. She knows there's no phone signal over the ocean and that I wouldn't be in contact for another day or so. But in catching up with the guys and contemplating the coming storm, I hadn't contacted her before we'd left Padang. And the BBM I'd fired off at the last minute hadn't gone through. Why hadn't I just called as I'd promised?

There is still no fear or panic, just acceptance that I am going to die. I'm overwhelmed by my recriminations, though, and I start talking out loud to Anita.

'I'm so sorry, baby, that I didn't get to say goodbye. I'm sorry, my darling, so sorry to leave you like this.'

Apologies crash over me just as regularly as the waves. I beg forgiveness a thousand times. 'I'm leaving you with our two little kids. I'm sorry you're going to be on your own.'

My thoughts turn to a conversation I had with Anita before I left. It took place in the car when she dropped me at Cape Town International Airport. I'd checked in and come back out to sit with her for an hour or so to say my farewells.

'Baby, I handle all the finances in our family. We've written our wills and everything is taken care of, but if something ever happened to me you wouldn't know what to do.'

I don't know why I felt it important to have that conversation then. For years I've travelled extensively for business. I commuted weekly when we lived in London and have taken several all-guy leisure trips without Anita. I had never before thought to discuss our affairs like that. It was early Sunday morning, 7.30am, and after only three hours' sleep – following a huge party at her cousin Karmen's wedding in Stellenbosch – we were beyond tired.

Anita had groaned when I ventured into uncomfortable territory, but I pressed on.

'If something happens to me, you must immediately transfer money into your own account because banks freeze accounts until estates are resolved. You'll need to pay bills and school fees and…'

She cut me off. 'Don't talk like that,' she scolded. 'Nothing is going to happen to you!'

Still, I wrote down all our banking details, the log-in details and passwords, and I clearly remember saying as I handed her the piece of paper, 'Neets, we're being irresponsible. We have two young children. We can never know what life might throw at us and I don't want you without access to our funds in an emergency. You have to be aware of these things. We're going to go through these item by item.'

I pulled out my laptop and took my wife through our household's financial matters for about forty minutes. I gave her the details of our private banker, who had become a good friend, and told her about my two friends, Greg McKenzie and Steve van Coller, whom I'd chosen to handle my affairs if anything ever happened to me. 'Call Greg and Steve straight away,' I told her. 'They'll manage everything.'

Eventually, Anita turned to me. 'I don't want to listen to this talk any more,' she said. 'It's silly. You're going to be fine and I want to spend the last fifteen minutes with you without discussing all this.'

'Okay,' I replied, 'but when I come back we're going to sit down and I'm going to take you through all our financial affairs.'

Now, with the wind blowing ceaselessly and the wave-tossed sea curdling around me, I berate myself while reflecting on that exchange. It's typical for me to leave such an important conversation to the last minute. I take some comfort that my life insurance payout will leave Anita and my children looked after. Still, I pray she will remember everything I've told her.

'Please, baby, when you get this news, transfer the money.' I am talking out loud again. 'Please, please, please – because I'm not going to make it out of this. I'm not going to make it back.'

Neets, my beautiful wife.

I imagine cupping my hands and shouting to her across this canyon between us. Would she hear? Could she receive a spiritual voicemail? I emigrate back to her in my mind, to reconnect our special synchronicity.

We've always enjoyed an uncanny sync, the two of us. We feel that we often communicate on another level, finishing each other's sentences or saying what the other is thinking. It's a little spooky sometimes.

I remember Anita telling me once that if anything did ever happen to me she would never be able to be with anyone else.

'But you're young, only thirty-eight,' I say out loud to her now. 'You're going to have to find another man because Jamie and Zara need a dad. You have to have someone else in your life.'

Thinking of my nine-year-old Zara and Jamie, only six, makes me vomit again. Even though I'd sat with them in the early hours of Sunday morning before leaving for the airport, and I'd hugged them and chatted about my trip, I feel that I haven't said a good enough goodbye.

My daughter is my princess with whom I have the most incredible bond. She's an old soul, who's wonderfully wise way beyond her young years. My son is my quirky, humorous and zany little Mini-Me, who we nearly lost through a virus that attacked his heart when only two weeks old.

'Zara is going to be okay,' I say to Anita, 'but Jamie needs a dad.'

Then I speak out loud to both my kids, telling them how much I love them and that I will always be with them. The ache in my chest feels like a concrete weight within me, making me feel heavier in the water. It's also making it harder to breathe.

How sad and pathetic we are, I begin an internal diatribe. So often we undertake to do meaningful things with our families – rich, fulfilling things that we promise and plan, but we never get around to. We get caught up in the daily grind instead. I feel profound guilt at the pacts I've made and not kept. The walks on Table Mountain, time on the beach, the holidays I've promised – now all opportunities lost. What we had done together had been sporadic and, on reflection now, not nearly enough.

Regret is folding up my insides like origami.

I reflect on the talked-about family breakfasts and 'sitting together at dinner' intentions. That's why you gave up the rat race and your corporate career in London, I remind myself. You returned to Cape Town expressly for the lifestyle, but instead you've been completely immersed in your bloody business, Awnmaster.

Awnmaster Cape is an outdoor awning business that I bought from the Singletons three years ago. Things have gone awry and it has become a massive stress, sucking up much of my time, while bringing with it an abundant supply of ordinary, everyday unhappiness.

Now you're going to die and you've used it as an excuse not to do any of the things you committed to.

I think about the few times the four of us went rollerblading on the Sea Point promenade. And the single occasion I took Jamie to play soccer on the field in front of our house. Part of the reason we bought our house in Camps Bay was because of that field. I'd promised my son that every Sunday morning we'd go there to run, play rugby or kick a soccer ball.

'You're a typical little boy' – I can't seem to take in enough air, but still I speak out loud to my son – 'and I haven't played with you enough, my boy. I'm so sorry…' The thought of him makes me shake uncontrollably.

My grief and regret are suddenly overtaken by rage. From my quiet talking to Anita, Zara and Jamie, I feel a kind of fury. I pick a fight with God.

'This is not fair!' I shout to the swirling clouds above. 'Why are you letting this happen? How can you take me like this? I've only been married to Anita for ten years. She's my best friend, my soulmate. We still have plans…'

It builds up to a fury that I haven't felt for a long time.

'God, you're going to make me suffer, aren't you? I haven't been a good Christian, a good follower. I know that I only talk to you sporadically. Only when I need to say sorry for something I've done wrong, when I need forgiveness. Is this your punishment? Are you going to make me pay?'

Torrential rain begins to fall from a blackboard sky. The drops are enormous, stinging my face like needles. I tilt my head back as far as I can and open my mouth. The downpour pummels my eyes, my cheeks and my painful tongue, and the fresh water collects at the back of my throat.

It's an elixir.

I swallow in great gulps and move my tongue around my teeth and along the inside of my cheeks. The relief brings a calm that silences my angry lamentations.

But I still can't stop thinking about dying.

What happens when one drowns? Will it be painful? When will it come? And what will happen after?

I've often contemplated and questioned death. And, of course, I've thought about what's beyond. I was raised an Anglican, and though I've strayed from that formal Christian grounding, I've always considered myself spiritual in my own way.

You're going to find out pretty soon, Brett. You're going to find out what happens after.

There is no comfort in this thought.

I look up. The rain is still falling heavily onto my face. 'So God,' I shout into the night, 'if this is your plan, come! Come and get me!'

4.30AM TO 5.30AM
THIRD HOUR IN THE WATER

Time crawls by. Minutes feel even slower because so much hurtles through my head in the space of 60 seconds. My thoughts dart about; one is disrupted by the next, as if my mind is afraid to rest on a single subject.

The sound of the sea is deafening and it somehow sounds louder in the darkness. It teases and toys with me, like we're in a childish game of hide-and-seek.

For a time I feel strangely disconnected. My mind seems too wound up to allow feelings to enter, too muddled for solid thought. For now, I issue myself with a 'swim or die' ultimatum, so I take a conscious decision: to separate my tasks. I decide to concentrate on my strokes, on my breathing, on my counting.

I've always been a rubbish swimmer, and over the years my ocean swimming has been very limited. There were sea swims during the triathlons I did in my twenties, and at university my digs mates and I would go down to the beach early every morning to surf for an hour. If the surf was bad, we'd run on the beach, swim around the piers, shower and head off to work. Five days a week. But recently the longest I've been in the sea is about two hours, and that was with a surfboard to hold on to.

Now I have nothing.

Consciously focus on the mechanics of swimming, I tell myself. And, concurrently, prepare for your death.

I start to talk to my late father, which is strange as I hardly ever think of him these days. He had a full mental breakdown when I was seven and for the next thirty years I disliked him intensely.

That night comes back to me now, that Friday night when everything changed. When my world transformed. The picture is vivid and it produces a feeling that is intense and pure.

My parents had gone out for an evening at the movies. My grandmother, a piano teacher, had driven through to baby sit us and she was telling us a story, providing the sound effects on the piano. I was surprised but so pleased to see my parents return home early, but when Dad stormed past all of us to his room I knew something was wrong.

'Dad's not feeling well,' Mom told us distractedly.

I was sitting in the dining room. My sister Sandra was on the couch and Gregory, who was still little, was playing on the floor. I decided to check on my dad. When I couldn't find him in his bedroom, I walked through to my parents' bathroom calling his name. The scene replays like a movie in my mind.

I push back the sliding door when I hear the water running, but get no response. Gingerly, I pull back the shower curtain. Then I see it: a scarlet red on the walls, all over his torso, spreading around the floor of the shower and swirling towards the plughole. His life is leaving him, going down the drain.

I rush to my bedroom, too stunned to utter a sound. After that, there is a lot of activity that swamps me from behind and the image becomes blurred. We three children are corralled into a corner.

My father had attempted suicide by cutting his throat in the shower with a breadknife. He hadn't succeeded, and later he would follow it up with mad, weapon-wielding incidents which carried threats that took us all to the edge. I grew up that night, having faced things that children aren't equipped to deal with. Childhood left me right then.

Bipolar disorder is what they called it eventually. I'd witnessed the fall of my hero, a man who was highly intelligent but emotionally unstable. He could rise to extraordinary heights, but also plummet to great depths. It resulted in us living in fear as a family, moving through a more sensorial, unpredictable existence.

My father and I eluded one another after that. Although we had made our peace before he died, we never reached out. I never truly healed the resentments I'd harboured, and we'd allowed questions to haunt us both for far too long. Recollections of him still often open up a vortex of pain.

'Hey, Dad, I'm coming to meet you!' I shout out now. 'Are you upstairs or down?'

I scoff at the cruelty of the thought.

He was a good father before his breakdown. He was the sales manager of a hospitality supply company and travelled a lot. In those days, people went by road for business. He'd drive to what I considered exotic places around the country, and during school holidays I couldn't wait to join him on his road trips. I'd pack my little school suitcase and jump in the car. I remember once sharing a room with him at the Royal Hotel in Pietermaritzburg. After a long day driving we arrived and I unpacked my entire suitcase into the cupboard.

'But, Brett,' he'd laughed, 'we're leaving early tomorrow morning.'

'It's okay, Dad,' I replied, filled with the wonder of it all. 'I'll pack it again in the morning.'

I loved being with him.

He could be hard on me, too, I suppose. I got three hidings from him that I'll never forget. His face comes to me now, but the expressions change rapidly. Like an old 8mm film, frame by frame, showing the gamut of his emotions.

It brings thoughts of death again that come in eerie swirls. They colour my mind and rattle me somewhere deep inside.

The same questions return to haunt me. How does one drown? Will there be a white light? Will someone or something come to take me? I don't want to be alone…

I decide that talking to the dead might make encountering it easier.

So I speak to Rob de Beer, who died three days before we flew to Indonesia. It's weird to think that it was only a few days ago.

Rob, a particularly close friend of Banger's, had also matriculated with us all those years ago in Westville. Banger broke the news as we set out from Padang. The week prior, Rob, a marketer for one of South Africa's major consumer goods companies, had gone to Thailand on business. During a conference he'd sat beside a woman who'd coughed incessantly. He'd returned to Durban that Sunday, felt horrible on Monday, and on Tuesday a client told him he looked awful. A feverish Rob went to a doctor on Wednesday and was prescribed a course of antibiotics. On Thursday night, he returned to the doctor who immediately admitted him to Westville Hospital. On Friday he slipped into a coma before dying later that day. An otherwise healthy man, he'd picked up an unidentifiable lung infection and it had killed him – within a week.

One week. I remember being shocked by that.

For me, it's going to be a matter of hours.

We held a little wake for Rob on the boat as we departed from Padang. It left us mournful and more subdued than on previous trips. Losing a friend, while a reality in these middle years, is like a paper cut to the heart: seemingly invisible, but undeniably painful.

'Rob, where are you?' I shout out now. 'Can you hear me?

I'm going to drown. Tell me what happens from here. Will my body simply sink down? Where will I go?'

The depth of the ocean beneath me is a notion that constantly tugs at the edges of my mind. I've scuba-dived occasionally so I know the sensation of being in a body of deep water. I decide to swim down to gauge the depth.

I put my head under the water and open my eyes to look below. The salt water stings my eyes and it takes several seconds to become accustomed to the burning. I try to focus. It is so dark – a warm tar-like black. All I can make out are even darker shadows that gobble up everything beyond the stretch of my arm.

I decide against it.

I am in the deepest part of the ocean, unlit, enigmatic, with hundreds of metres of briny deep stretching beneath me. No wonder the ancient mariners called these depths 'fathoms'. The word turns over in my head… 'fathoms'.

This is another world, a place I don't belong.

And it's going to be my grave.

Does this questioning, this reconciling, happen to all people who have time to face their death? Is this like an extended death row? God's way of getting a man to face up to the things he's done?

My introspection is interrupted by the heavens opening for another downpour.

Again it rains very hard. The drops pound the top of my head like little lead bullets. They fire at me – *splat, splat* – and, as I try to shield my face, I wonder whether they could actually cause me injury. How can something that can save my life be so horribly cruel?

The surf continues to roar and I feel great swirls of current moving the waters around me.

Practicality takes over again. I decide to take off my T-shirt and tie it around my head. It'll cushion the hammering and if the weather clears by morning it will also protect my naked scalp from sunburn.

The sun. Am I really thinking about daylight, about what lies beyond these hours of darkness? Is there a glimmer of belief that I can make it to dawn?

I kick my legs and thrust my body up as far as I can out of the water to pull the T-shirt over my head. Wearing my T-shirt like a bandana is an old party trick I've used many times. I pull the arms behind my head and tie them in an Arab-style knot, so that the back of the T-shirt hangs down over my neck. Now that it's sodden and cumbersome with the weight of water, it takes me some time to flip the fabric over my scalp. I find it surprisingly effective in deflecting the missiles that smash down on me.

It also helps me focus.

I open my mouth again to take in fresh water. I can't tell if it is rain or sea water that continues to pound my face, but it's a cool balm to my swelling tongue. I refuse to think further about thirst. It's a negative thought, I tell myself, and I expel it from my mind.

Don't think. Just endure.

Instead I do my mouthwash action and instruct my glands to make saliva.

It's the strange time before daylight, the hour when suicide risks are told by Lifeline counsellors to push through until sunrise. It's as good a time as any to say goodbye to the people who've meant something in my life. It's a time to acknowledge them, to honour them, to make amends.

Memories from my early childhood in Westville begin to

crowd my mind. Playing in my parents' garden, building forts in the sand, riding bikes on the streets, our neighbourhood gang of mates pretending to be Robin Hood and his band of merry men. I always made sure I was Robin. That makes me smile.

I think of my mother. Shirley. She's been through so much and now this. How will she react? How will she deal with this loss? The loss of a child…

And my sister Sandra and brother Gregory. Will they be okay? I've always felt a responsibility towards them. Even in adulthood.

A monumental crushing pain solidifies in my chest at the thought of my mother and siblings. Once again, I feel as if I can't breathe.

Surely you should be crying, Brett? You know you're going to die.

The question bothers me. Saying goodbye to those you love should surely bring tears?

I do feel grief, but it's not self-pity. It's a broiling pain for my family, my wife, my children.

I imagine my funeral. White roses, Anita in black, Zara and Jamie looking lost. I picture my mother weeping, my brother giving the eulogy, my sister holding my nieces and nephews, and my friends in dark suits with melancholic faces.

It suddenly makes me recall an exercise I once undertook with Nick Christellis, the corporate life coach at the company where I'd been a director. He'd asked us to write our own obituary.

'How do you want to be remembered?' he'd asked. 'How do you think people would describe you?'

It had been a thought-provoking test at the time, if not a little disturbing.

I can be brash and loud, I know, full of cocky bravado. Most people think of me as a party animal. But there's a gap between that reputation and how I am deep down; it's also not how I want to be remembered. That obituary task had stayed with me, and for years afterwards I'd often quietly wonder how my behaviour would add to my epitaph.

Forget about what people *say* about you, Brett. I shake my head now. You should want them to know what happened to you.

It's starting to get lighter. I know that sunrise is around 4.45am. It's still drizzling and very overcast, but the darkness is beginning to give way to a lugubrious grey. The sun, when it does rise, won't be visible through the gloom, but I look around and at least I can now see several metres ahead. The sea is still choppy and tumultuous.

I've been in the water two or three hours, I calculate. My brain has churned, and I'm even a little surprised at how I've kept myself busy. Another curiosity occurs to me: I don't feel that tired.

My mind quickly changes gear again. No-one saw you fall over, Brett. Anita, the kids, Mom, Sandra and Greg, they're not going to know what happened. You've got to tell them.

I have a mad idea. I fumble as I take off my belt, treading water as I do, but I manage to carefully manoeuvre it out of the belt loops. It's my black golf belt that I'd worn to the wedding in Stellenbosch, an expensive Cutter & Buck leather one with a silver buckle that I'd grabbed in a hurry when I couldn't find any other. It had also been my last resort when packing as a way to hold up my slightly oversized shorts.

I've shaved my normally hairy chest for the first time as well, an old surfer practice. The other guys had teased me on previous trips when I'd been the only one painstakingly picking wax out of my chest hair. They'd tell me to shave, but I'd self-consciously joke: 'I don't know what I look like underneath this carpet. I haven't seen my body since I was nineteen.'

I run my right hand across my smooth chest. Scratch a message on it with the belt buckle, I decide. I start down near the waistband of my shorts and write upside down across my stomach. I separate the belt's metal clip from the buckle and draw it across my belly beginning with Anita's nickname, 'Neets'. I'm only on the first down-stroke and the pain is unbearable.

I grimace. This is going to be hard.

After the second stroke, I come to my senses. This is really stupid, I admonish myself. Tattooing a message will draw blood. Sharks can smell blood miles away and if they show up no-one will get to read your note anyway.

I change my mind. What, I think, belt in hand, can I do with this? It's just going to weigh me down. So I throw it away and watch as it sinks at speed and disappears beneath the steely waters.

As the sky lightens, my mind focuses and the torrid thoughts of the night begin to dissipate. I picture the guys on the boat. They'll be realising around now that I'm not there, I tell myself. In a worst-case scenario, they'll sail for another seven or eight hours, get to port, discover I'm missing, turn the boat around and take another seven to sail back. I know, without a shadow of a doubt, that my boys will come back to find me.

Best case: they'll reach me around lunchtime...

With two or three hours already behind me, I calculate that I need to stay afloat for another eleven hours – fourteen at the most. Fourteen hours.

The thought forms: I have to hang on.

It's a sudden transformation.

I stop thinking about dying. My thoughts are ungainly and lumbering, but slowly I begin to feel that there might be a chance. My heart begins to pound in my chest.

There's a stronger likelihood of seeing a boat in the day. There's a chance, even if it's a remote one, of being seen. I glance sideways at the grey shirt slumped across my shoulder where it slops and floats on the surface of the water.

'Wish I'd chosen a brighter T-shirt,' I say out loud.

I need to defecate again. This time, I don't take my pants off. With nothing left in my system, just salt water passes.

You've got to get swimming, I think. Immediately I know that it's going to be a titanic goal that will require supreme concentration, but I decide to set out with that intention rather than retreating into defeat.

By now I've turned around so many times, I'm completely disorientated. I want to swim in the direction in which the boat sailed, but I can't tell where that is any more. With no sun in this first light, just a heavy, leaden sky, I can't take a bearing.

It feels like it's drizzling now, but I can't tell if it's rain or spray coming off the sea. I don't even know which direction I'm facing. I absentmindedly watch a storm move across the horizon. It moves like a stage set, complete with its curtain of rain, across the sky. Distant thunder is like an orchestra.

With at least eleven hours stretching ahead of me, I have to conserve energy. I try to lie on my back but the waves, coming at me from every direction, toss me over. Water washes over my eyes and nose. I swallow litres of sea water that make me cough and retch all over again. Floating in these conditions, I realise, is not going to be an option, so I try to tread water.

This isn't possible either. Waves continue to hit me in

the face and break over my head. The skin on my face is beginning to feel tender to the touch and the smack of each wave is painful. I shout at the wall of water as it connects. My eyes sting from the salt; they burn under the eyelids. I desperately want to close them, but when I do I feel very disoriented. I hope my eyes last, I think.

The ocean feels like a torturer, an interrogator: blinding me, abusing me, pushing me to my limits. But its punishing watery slaps also keep me awake.

The only solution, yet again, is to propel myself through each wave. I swim towards each one and consciously take a breath to avoid swallowing water. My throat is thick and sore; it's painful every time salt water washes down.

Years of surfing have left me with some upper body strength, but my arms feel withered now, my shoulders yolked. How, I think, can you pull yourself through a wave without wasting energy?

Breaststroke will be tiring, so I opt for sculling with my hands and making big gentle kicks with my legs – a kick and a stroke, a kick and a stroke.

I'm not moving very fast, but I'm moving. It's slow but steady progress.

A sense of calm descends which I manage to translate into positive thoughts. A new ambition germinates. Maybe there's hope? Perhaps I can stay alive until my boat comes back? Hang on, I keep telling myself. Hang on. The boys will come back for you.

I decide to swim in what I hope is the direction the boat has taken. Even if you take eight hours to swim one kilometre, you'll be one kilometre closer to them when they return for you, I tell myself.

I feel more in control swimming this way. The water no

longer slaps my face, I'm managing to contain swallowing sea water and I think I'm moving in a good direction without overextending myself. After the previous three hours of rage and self-pity, this, I feel, is constructive.

Still, I'm frustrated that I haven't seen anything floating in this filthy ocean. Not a leaf, a log or a coconut. Nothing.

'God.' I look around me. 'You're doing nothing to help me. I'm going to tire soon. Please give me something to hang on to. A broken surfboard, a body board, something!'

I'm not sure why, but I suddenly think to pat down my shorts. I feel a hard cardboard rectangle in the fold of my right-hand pocket. I put my hand in and pull out a small purple cardboard folder. Slowly kicking my legs, I gently open it. My hands are trembling.

In it is a hotel room key, the credit card-style key from the hotel we'd stayed at in Jakarta. We'd left late and rushed out so quickly I'd forgotten to hand it in.

Damn, I know how annoying that is for hotels. I think of my time in the travel industry; it's a huge cost to them.

I'd prepaid for the room, but the hotel reception had printed a nil slip which is tucked into the folder. The little piece of paper is surprisingly dry and well preserved. Strange that it hasn't completely dissolved. I turn the black and silver card over in my fingers and am about to toss it away into the foam when a thought comes to me: if the sun comes out, I can use the silver on the card as a reflector to flash a signal to an oncoming boat. MacGyver style. I return the card to my pocket.

Out of the blue, I begin to feel really tired – suddenly my arms feel heavy and my legs stiff. I'm not swimming particularly hard, but it's sapping my energy.

Be realistic. You've been in the water for nearly four hours – you're going to get tired.

I start questioning whether I can last twelve hours. Suddenly I don't feel so sure.

You need to take charge, I coach myself. Run yourself like a business. So I decide to start a company in my mind.

I name my mouth 'Bob'; he will run operations. My left nostril is 'Emily', director of sales, and my right nostril is the marketing director, 'Hilary'. I'm the CEO. I decide that I'm going to have regular board meetings to assess my situation. We will discuss matters amongst ourselves, and if I get tired or despondent, between us we'll kick back into action.

I give a little snort. It feels stupid. Why are you doing this? I ask myself.

My mental reply is almost immediate: for structure, focus, something to keep working on. You need to feel in charge. Perhaps because I was usually the one in authority in my corporate environment, this makes me feel more in control, no matter how exhausted I feel.

Waves are no longer breaking over me, but around me the sea is seething. I can't feel its pull, but I know that I must be in a current.

I fumble in my pocket and edge out the purple folder with the hotel room key and credit card slip. I tear a tiny corner off the edge of the paper and put it into the water. It sweeps away from me at speed.

It's an epiphany.

That's why you're so tired! You've been swimming against the current.

For nearly four hours, I've been battling against a force far greater than I, a power that has been pushing against me.

The only thing to do is to turn around and go with it.

5.30AM TO 6.30AM
FOURTH HOUR IN THE WATER

I'm in the current, allowing it to carry me. Its momentum feels ancient. The relief is immediate. After ploughing for hours against the ocean's drag, I'm now working with it. Swimming, even staying afloat, feels instantly easier. Renewed ambition surges like an electric charge through my body.

I can now see where the current is going and I know from surf lore, folklore and all my knowledge of the sea that ocean currents eventually lead to land. I speculate whether this one sweeps down from Padang along the length of the Strait. Either way it will finally hit the mainland or one of the islands. The duel with the current also explains why the boat crossings take so long.

I keep the piece of paper in my sights for as long as I can, but it quickly becomes waterlogged. I put my face into the murky waters to watch it sink and slowly disappear. Every so often, I tear off a piece about the size of my thumbnail and use it to assess the current's direction.

I look back at the till slip, its one edge showing a tiny serration. I'll need to use it sparingly.

I don't want to think beyond midday or early afternoon, past the prayed-for rendezvous with the *Naga Laut*. I can't be certain how long it will take the boys to return, but I can hang on until then. Deep down I know it's going to be an all-out struggle.

The current will take you closer to them, I reassure myself.

The thought cheers me. Just as daylight is gathering in the east, purpose feels like a flame flickering within.

My company is working hard in my head, truncated voices jabbering away.

'How's production?'

'Marketing – all good?'

'Sales, set your targets?'

'No slacking now.'

I commune with Anita again for long periods, still frequently apologising.

'Talk to me, Neets.' I try to get into her head. 'If you're with me, if you talk to me, I can do this. I can get through it.'

I wonder whether she knows yet that I'm missing. When I get tired, I call out to her. 'Keep me focused, Anita. Push for me, fight for me. Keep me strong.'

Again, I think of my mother. But the image of her face that comes upsets me.

Again I start negotiating with God, doing what I know best: making pacts and promises. 'If you help me through this, I'll change my life, God. I'll be a better man.'

I hear my own voice reply, answering my own questions. I've always been good at bargaining.

I laugh out loud at the notion: a conversation with God. I've read the books and now I'm having my own conversation with him.

I think again of my church-going youth when my parents took us to services every week and enrolled us at Sunday school. I was an altar boy from Standard Four to Matric and I tried to play guitar in the church band. As a teenager, I even became a Sunday school teacher. I loved the social side of church, the youth groups we belonged to, the weekend camps we undertook.

The memory envelops me. It's a quiet comfort. In the dim dawn, I begin to sing a hymn to the heavens.

O Lord, my God, when I in awesome wonder . . .

I only remember the first two verses, but I yell them out over and over as I'm heaved about in the lumpy sea.

As if in answer to my prayer, the wind begins to die down and the rain reduces to a persistent heavy drizzle. The waves that have buffeted me for hours seem to grow weary and instead flop over me and then lift me up and over in great sweeping undulations.

Who have you been? I hear God ask me through my thoughts. *How have you been in your life?*

'Very far from perfect,' is my whimpering reply.

The truth is I had been a dog before I married Anita, and I felt horribly guilty about it. I still do.

Before our wedding I confessed all my conquests to her. I didn't want there to be any surprises, so I told her about every one of my seductions. I wanted her to be certain that she still wanted to marry me.

My philandering has been an area of personal reproach for me, a blight on my conscience, and over the last fifteen years I've wrestled with it in consultations with my life coach. The guilt raises its head now, an amorphous spectre.

I feel the need to confront this stuff again. To open up the place where I store my hidden shame. Curiously, an expression suddenly comes to mind: *Memento mori*. I remember being taught this at school. 'Remember you must die...'

Despite my initial hope, dark thoughts keep pulling me back to this inevitability.

'Well, God, if I'm going to die, shouldn't I confess? Shouldn't I seek forgiveness? Shouldn't I go out having cleansed my conscience – of these things and everything else I'm not proud of?'

This is emotional quicksand, I know.

Negative thinking.

Regret.

Self-loathing.

It's a strange response, this sudden desire to purge myself of my sins.

I know that I can be quite hard on myself. I am sometimes my harshest critic, but there are things about myself that bring on feelings of profound disappointment and emptiness.

'Why, God?' I ask now. 'Why do feelings of inadequacy cripple me in the heat of battle?'

I have explored much of this hypersensitivity, these feelings of guilt and self-consciousness in my life-coaching sessions. It still puzzles me that I suffer from a lack of self-worth that I can't explain, but it's a darkness within me that I've become used to.

I scull through the swells, my thoughts now in full flow.

I've made this admission to my wife, to my life coach and to a couple of my closest friends. And, as if in release, I disclose it now to the elements. My musings churn. Most people think life has gone easy on me. Those friends have said as much in solemn booze-induced chats in bars. On the surface, they see a successful executive; a man who has walked onto stages to host major events; a sportsman who has undertaken significant physical challenges for charity. They've never seen the scared side, the man behind the façade. It's a divide that has, for most of my adult life, been unsettling, even bewildering, for me.

I think back on my time as a director of RCI. On the face of it I was in professional cruise control, but in reality I wasn't. It was a time of very hard work that came at a painful price.

My staff would often find me at the offices at 7am. And I

would still be there at 11pm. They didn't know that this was because I was divorcing my first wife, that I was emotionally hung up and had nowhere else to go. That I was living out of my car in the company's garage.

Pathetic, I think to myself. Why am I like this? What do I need to prove?

I jolt myself from my inner torment and mentally change gear.

Why aren't you screaming for water or feeling hunger?

But just as immediately I rebuke myself for thinking about my physical state. Rather focus on things you do have control over, I tell myself: swimming and generating saliva.

I look up. It's still heavily overcast, but the dim light suggests the sun is up behind the substantial clouds. Dawn at last.

Almost immediately I need to pee.

My stomach feels bloated and there's an instant agonising pressure on my bladder. All the salt water I've swallowed, I speculate. I start to urinate, but the pain of peeing is torturous. It feels like a burning hot poker is being pushed up inside my urethra. I shriek and howl as the urine warms the already warm water around me. The pain seems to magnify and crescendo as I imagine the salt crystals ripping and shredding their way through my penis.

It's the longest pee of my life.

The agony keeps my thinking coherent. My senses are sharp and I feel quick on the draw again.

I look down at my hands. My fingers are pale and the flesh around my fingernails is beginning to puff up like little pork sausages. They look ugly, fragile, like animal specimens in formaldehyde. I recall the frogs in jars that had freaked me out in my Standard One science lessons. For the first time I wonder what will happen to my flesh. Will I start to disintegrate? Just dissolve?

If I start to bleed, it will be like the recess bell for sharks and barracudas.

'Swim carefully,' I keep repeating, 'don't do anything that could cause injury. Blood in the water could end this day in the worst way.'

6.30AM TO 7.30AM
FIFTH HOUR IN THE WATER

The storm in which I've been entangled for hours seems to have passed, but the ocean remains choppy and changeable and hellbent on making me work to stay afloat.

White water ripples along crests of enormous waves like knitting unravelling.

The sky is battleship grey with heavily laden clouds that only hint that the day has begun.

Although it is a blurred light, I can see some distance around me for the first time. There's no land, no vessel, nothing but open water in every direction. The sea yawns wide and featureless around me, but it's still convulsing in the aftermath of the storm. For a moment, I imagine it engulfing me, sucking me down.

I'm unnerved all over again.

I have to keep calm, I know. I have to breathe properly to stay alive.

'Just until the boat comes back,' I keep repeating.

The clean smell of the ocean is pungent in my nostrils as it descends through the drizzle and morning mist.

As with the night, it's going to be a day of heavy weather. I watch as big rainstorms fall from scudding clouds that move slowly in the distance. Sheets of water move in ghostly dances; their shadowy veils seem to stop eerily just above the water's surface. I watch them, track them and sometimes pray that the storm will come my way. I need the fresh water, but it also makes me anxious. If the storm whips up the waves again, my boat could miss me…

I run a company audit: 'Bob, how are you doing?'

'Emily, what are our time frames?'

'Hilary, have we calculated correctly?'

'What do you think the time is?'

'Sales, marketing, how are our projections?'

'Good show, guys, keep in good spirits. I want a report by midday.'

I sweep up the slope of a wave and along with it I feel my rolling emotions threatening to swallow me again. I know that I have to keep order; that chaos is gnawing at the edges of my mind.

Determined to stay cheery, I start singing again as a diversion. This time I go through the playlist I've created on my iPod.

As a child, I'd dreamed of being a singer and fancied that I could hold a tune. But my little-boy dreams had been crushed by my Class One teacher, Mrs Puesey. 'Archibald,' she'd said one day in choir practice, 'go and play the triangle.'

It didn't stop me. In high school, I learnt to play the guitar. Again my music teacher said, 'Brett, you can't sing. I can't teach you any more until you can.'

I was devastated.

As I start to sing now, an odd memory flashes. I recall listening to my iPod on the hour-long flight over from Jakarta to Padang. Only yesterday? Really?

I had my head tilted against the headrest, my eyes were closed, and with the music turned up I didn't realise I was singing out loud. Niall elbowed me in the ribs, laughing. When I looked around, the Indonesian passengers around us were frowning disapproval. My singing was that bad.

Of all the things to think about now...

I begin to sing the songs on my favourite playlist, a pumped-up compilation of rock that Banger had put together for me. I can only call to mind nineteen songs, but I start to sing them in chronological order, starting with Ram Jam's 'Black Betty'.

Out here there's no-one to criticise, no-one to complain.

No-one can hear me. No-one can hear.

No-one.

Next is 'Dancing in the Dark' by Springsteen, Bob Dylan's 'Like a Rolling Stone', Queen's 'Bohemian Rhapsody'. I can't remember all the titles or artists but the words of those songs are programmed into my hard drive. I remember them by heart. My memory's precise for this kind of detail.

The songs remind me of Benoit, the man we call Banger. Benoit owns a property company and is based in Mauritius. And since I'd looked after Africa and the Indian Ocean islands of Seychelles and Mauritius when I was in the travel industry, I went there often for business. During that period I flew to Mauritius eleven times.

It's how I earned Banger's nickname for me: 'Jetman'. I call him 'Bang Bang Makatini', recalling an iconic South African chocolate bar ad on TV. I like to put my own spin on names.

Banger and I enjoy a special friendship, one that has survived long separations. Even if we don't see or speak to one another for five years, we pick up as if we'd been together the day before. Our parties in Mauritius were often off the charts, but there were also quiet times that have stayed with me.

Banger is musically gifted. I often made him pull out his guitar when I visited and we'd sit on his patio and sing. The embodiment of my unfulfilled ambitions, he forgave me for being tone deaf.

I think now about the steel-string guitar he bought for his son while coming through Kuala Lumpur the day before. It's in his cabin on the *Naga Laut*, and last night at dinner I'd begged him to take it out to play. He'd been bashful and refused.

Cat Stevens and Rodriguez. I bellow out the lyrics as loud as I can. Sometimes I remember only a single verse, so I repeat it over and over again.

My mind is trying to construct meaning out of this randomness; my thoughts are faltering, uncertain. It comes to rest on my boys, my friends on the *Naga Laut* who must soon discover that I am no longer on board. I recall our time, just hours ago, in the café in Padang waiting to board the boat. The rousing mood, the excitable conversation, the laughter. Ten Green Bottles. I remember the photograph the waitress took of us all, posing behind the lager bottles that were lined up like sentries.

Ten green bottles, hanging on the wall,
Ten green bottles, hanging on the wall,
And if one green bottle should accidentally fall…

I've started singing it absent-mindedly, but the irony of the line hits home. It magnifies the ridiculousness of my situation. The hopelessness. The impossibility.

I look around me at the surrounding sea, at the sheer volume of it. In the early morning light, its steely grey merges into a distant darkness in every direction. It's haunting and mysterious. I turn full circle and watch, mesmerised, the shape and motion of the waves around me. They seem to take me up into an open sweep, then hunch their shoulders and drop me again. Flecks of water carry on the wind and sting my face. Those are traces of sea salt on my face, not salt from my tears.

You're still not crying…

It's bothering me.

An image of Anita laughing appears in my mind's eye and while it brings an agonising sweep of sorrow, there are no tears. As if to force the emotional release, I break into the Bee Gees' 'Words'. I'm a sucker for romantic songs.

The lyrics lift snapshots from my memory. Small, everyday, seemingly insignificant things. The way Anita makes coffee just the way I like it. How Zara does her hair. The sound effects Jamie makes when he's playing on my iPad and doesn't know I'm watching him.

I think again of my father and of how the words to Neil Young's 'Old Man' were like an anthem to him for me while I was in my teens. I'd learnt to play it on the guitar, and at the time I felt it spoke to me about my relationship with my dad. Part of me probably hankered for his friendship.

'Old man, look at my life. I'm a lot like you were.'

I sing the song a hundred times and search the sky. Can I understand him a little better now, now that I can identify with some of his demons?

'Hey, Bally,' I call out again to him. 'Are you here? Can you see me?'

I want him to give me a sign.

I rise and fall with the swells and try to float on my back. It's such a relief not to have whitecaps crashing down over my face. Floating means I can rest my limbs.

My thoughts continue to change. Like skittles smashed down and sliding in every direction.

A childhood image springs to mind: my mother is floating on her back in, what seemed to me, the monumental

Westville swimming pool. She's gliding serenely, in absolute control, like a crocodile on the surface. As a boy I'd try to copy her but each time my leaden legs would drag me down. I could never float, never get it right.

The same is happening now. The sea feels like liquid mercury and its gravity is overpowering. My legs are no counterweight for my head and I quickly sink. The water pulls me under, fills my mouth, nose and ears and I furiously kick myself back up to the surface, coughing.

I go back to treading water. Back to the small circles I make with my arms and legs.

Even though the water is warm, a cold sensation is creeping into my joints. My arms and legs feel thick and arthritic.

How long are you going to be able to keep this going? The thought flashes through my mind. All of a sudden I lose my sense of balance again and head back towards that dark place. Back to where I started.

I'm going to die out here.

My thoughts are ragged again.

I mean, for God's sake, Brett, be realistic! Who the hell is going to see you? There is no-one bloody well out here!

I'm drawn, inexorably, to the same repetitive thought: how will death come? I don't want to panic, to flail about, cry and scream and fight it when it does.

A knot forms in my throat.

'Please make it swift.' I beg God, nature, even my own body to grant me this.

Sing. Sing. Start singing again, I tell myself. I switch to a couple of verses of 'How Great Thou Art' and then repeatedly bark out 'The Lord's My Shepherd'.

Suddenly the face of a long-time business nemesis appears in my imagination.

Jesus, why now? Why here, of all places?

This is a man I'd disliked intensely for years, a festering thorn in my side.

My travel industry career had started when I'd been a client of the Johannesburg-based licensee of a worldwide company. I was persuaded to join the South African team by the then CEO Steve, a man who would become one of my closest friends. Those ten years were, from a business perspective, the best of my life. Steve and I made an astonishing team. He was an off-the-wall thinker who had a vision that took the business from being a relatively small organisation to a major player in the South African travel industry. We did radical, adventurous things and were often the guinea pigs for other divisions around the world. They'd watch what we did and then implement our strategies in their home territories.

Over time I became a director on the company's board and was awarded shares. But I also made an enemy who seemed to resent Steve's and my success and, in my opinion, hated us for it. Our enmity was mutual.

Eventually, he pulled what I felt was an unscrupulous putsch. He forced out Steve and made himself the CEO, and in the process set about arranging a company sell-out. I was devastated at the time, but also pragmatic; I wanted to build my career.

After a spell of protracted professional politics, the senior management team gathered together at the IT director's house one weekend. We spent a full Saturday thrashing out what to do. We decided to approach the company that was about to buy and offer up a vote of no confidence in the new CEO. When it came down to it, though, the vote wasn't unanimous. Three of the management team bailed in the heat.

I decided to resign. Immediately. I knew that I could no longer work with a man who'd tried to derail me at every turn. I called him straight away, got in my car and drove to his house to tell him.

I worked my month's notice and then hightailed it from the building. I was out of work for three months but then Steve offered me a job at a newly listed start-up travel company he had moved on to create.

But the world's a funny place, I've found; a year later the newly appointed global CEO of our original company asked me to join the international team to head up Europe, the Middle East, India and Africa. This division bought back the South African licence and I was able to ensure there was no place for the man who'd made my life so miserable. I just wanted him out of my life. He subsequently left South Africa, but despite his departure – despite the fact that I'd had the last say – I carried him as a nemesis inside my head for years, a festering cancerous growth. All that bitterness and resentment. It was an anger that had eaten me up for so long.

I don't want to die with this unresolved emotion, I decide now.

'God, help me let go of this. Help me forgive him.'

Almost immediately I feel a physical release, as if a heavy burden is lifted off my body.

Just like that. I even imagine myself more buoyant.

That wasn't so hard.

I'm amazed.

Why didn't you do that years ago?

For years I've fantasised about the scene of us meeting up again. I've replayed it many times in my head. I've imagined walking up, spitting forth some choice words and punching him straight in the mouth. It seems preposterous now.

Sculling in the water, the ocean still steaming and heaving, all sound seems to disappear and I'm filled with a strange composure.

'I've forgiven him, Neets,' I say out loud to my wife. 'Can you believe it?'

Mentally, it has exhausted me. I consider counting again but the task of organising my thoughts is suddenly daunting. I don't think I'm up to it any more.

The soundtrack of *The Big Blue* fills my head, complete with the dolphins chattering.

Am I going to go mad?

It's not a far-fetched fear.

The film had such a big impact on me when it was released in the late '80s. It brought home to me the duality of the sea: its dangerous, deadly side, but also that it can offer peace, a kind of redemption. Here, despite the turbulence of the waves and the wind, I feel a stoic resignation.

You're ready. You can die now.

I feel like I can accept it. It seems fitting that it will be in the sea.

The place you love.

I try to sink. I can consciously put a stop to this, I think. I can end it before it gets ugly.

I open my eyes to the grey, murky depths below.

A drilling pain thuds behind my eyeballs. They sting like hell.

You can't! You can't leave Anita, Zara and Jamie that way.

I remember the tragic tale of a friend of ours – it's as if someone has hit me from behind. I think about this woman and try to remember the story she shared with us. Her youngest son had left for Singapore after university to spend a gap year travelling around the East. From Singapore he'd boarded a plane for Nepal, which crashed, killing all aboard.

Distraught, the family travelled multiple times to Nepal to search for answers. They enlisted police and private detectives yet it took an interminable time for them to find parts of his body, which they were eventually able to bury. I couldn't stop thinking about the look in our friend's eyes whenever she talked of him. The hollow look of loss. She has never fully recovered. Who can ever recover from the loss of a child?

My special mother Shirls, I am so, so sorry.

I kick furiously and surge to the surface, the salt water corroding my eyes. I don't want my family to go through that. I don't want them to spend the rest of their lives wondering what happened to me.

Then a thought comes as a shock.

What if my life insurance doesn't pay out in the absence of a body? I recall reading about cases where it took at least seven years to determine if an accident was indeed just that.

There'll be questions around what might have happened, all sorts of theories. Some might speculate that I'd done this on purpose. Me, commit suicide? The absurdity of the thought is fuel for me. I'm adamant: my kids have to know what happened to their dad. My mother, my sister, my brother...

my wife – they cannot go through life not knowing how I died.

Don't go down this road. It's a mental slap. You have to stay alive until the boat comes back. You have to.

7.30AM TO 8.30AM
SIXTH HOUR IN THE WATER

I have chosen life. This means there's no room for self-pity. No more despair or remorse. No more vacillating, no more uncertainty. My goal is to stay alive until my boat comes back.

From this moment onwards, I tell myself, it must never enter my mind that this won't happen. It's a victory over fear.

I picture the guys on the boat mobilising into action. As soon as they realise I'm not on board, probably over coffee in the galley, they'll come back for me. They won't freak out and not know what to do. They'll be organised. JM, Ridgy, Banger, Tony, Snowman – they've been on surf trips before and know the local lie of the land – they'll know what to do.

I picture their individual faces.

'Weyne,' I say, remembering our conversation of the night before, 'I'm so sorry, buddy. This was your first surf trip, your fiftieth! It's the first time we've spent time with you in years and this has ruined everything. Fucking hell…'

I vow to apologise in person.

I scoff as it occurs to me that I nearly didn't come on this trip. Awnmaster has been such a stress to me, with so many problems, that I had thought it unwise to disappear in the middle of a crisis. I called JM and Tony a few days before to say I wasn't going to make the trip.

It was Anita who talked me back into going. 'You need to get away,' she said in bed one evening. 'The Mentawais are your soul place. You need to go, to be in that warm ocean. To have time with your "brothers".'

Ironic. I even manage a chuckle. I wanted to be in the

ocean, yes, but not like this. Had I stayed for Awnmaster I wouldn't be out here.

One hell for another.

My mind is galloping a mile a minute, processing, churning, as turbulent as the sea around me. I'm still being bounced around on the swells, and though no longer assaulted by onrushing waves, the wind whips up a sprawling spray that flies into my face, mists up my eyes and shoots up my nose. My throat feels as it if has a hole in it.

I keep counting – my breaths, my strokes. They're the metronome for my mind.

The bumpy waters ensure I still can't see more than ten metres in front of me. The misty drizzle is also making visibility poor – probably a good thing. I don't want to give my brain a chance to consider the physical things: the wild water, its green-grey immensity around me, the gaping grey sky above, the stiff sensation now beginning to numb my joints.

For a time I'm not even aware that I'm swimming. My brain is driving my body. I simply have to keep it going. I'm going to have to be resourceful.

Like in that movie.

It's another ridiculous, random train of thought. What's that movie with Tom Hanks? About the guy who gets washed up on a desert island? I can see his face by the end, all hairy, and his body, lean. Like me, he talked to himself too – and that bloody ball. I can't remember – did he go mad?

Crusoe?

Survivor?

He survived… I remember that much.

It takes several minutes to access the film title from the recesses of my memory.

Castaway!

I whoop to the sky, shout to the blustery clouds above as if I've just won the Lotto. The most minor things suddenly feel like great achievements.

'Why don't I have a Wilson, God? Or a raft?'

I think about *The Life of Pi*, a film recently released. I haven't seen it yet, but I know it's about a man who goes overboard when his ship sinks. Everyone is raving about it. He's on a raft with a tiger. What a story!

At least he wasn't alone.

I try to scan the waves as they fold over and around me. I'm looking for something to hang on to and it enrages me that I see nothing. Absolutely nothing. After a quick consultation with Bob, Hilary and Emily, I decide I need something else to occupy my thoughts.

I'll get my house in order. Literally. I think about the impending renovation to our house in Camps Bay. Everything is packed away in boxes.

There are books all over my house, but most are packed away in a sky rise of boxes in the garage. Bloody boxes. There are hundreds of them and, as the months have passed, it's driven me nuts that all our possessions are gathering dust entombed in there.

I think about those books; all the books I've bought and read in my life. How many I own. I've always wanted to have a library in my home. There was a library wall in the house in which I grew up, and by the time I was twelve I'd read my way through the entire thing.

I want a library for our new house. I want to unpack my books, arrange them alphabetically and read them all over again. I imagine myself going through the boxes now. I'm so anally retentive, I alphabetised them when I packed them away. I mentally unpack them now, sorting through them one by one in a slow, steady fashion, title by title – starting at A. I visualise the titles, remember the authors and catalogue them like some virtual librarian. I count each book as I go and match its title with a large sweeping breaststroke. I stop to tread water when my memory runs out of individual titles, but I continue to count the number of books in the boxes that I know are left over. I know how many there are in storage, because I've numbered each box. Finally I reconcile the total. It's just short of two thousand books.

An unexpected breaker comes from nowhere and cascades into my face. Better to keep swimming.

As I kick off again, I do some mental arithmetic. Two thousand books at an average of R200 a book, I calculate, as my arms pull through the rough waters, means I've spent around R400,000 on books.

That could have been very welcome in our renovation budget… You could have just gone down to the local library or downloaded them off Amazon. These are crazy thoughts; they seem so trivial. But my brain needs a new task.

The same goes for CDs. I must have three thousand discs and I've alphabetised them too. I picture my hand-written labels on the boxes and consider how I've archived some in music genres.

I go through the same exercise with the CDs. I count all those plastic squares stacked in precarious towers, put away in dark oblivion. What a fucking waste.

My frustration is silly and out of place, but the task occupies my mind and stops me from thinking of anything else. I'm determined not to allow my thoughts to go beyond what feels safe and manageable. I don't want them to creep past the end of my fingertips into that deep, unimaginable emptiness.

I refuse to think about time, about the monotonous hours that lie between the boat and myself. I refuse to let fear interfere.

Instead I make a decision. When you get back, you're going to download your music and throw away those CDs. And you're going to sell those bloody books.

THE NAGA LAUT
TUA PEJAT HARBOUR, NORTH SIPURA
9.16AM

'Who was the last one to see Brett?' JM is looking into the faces of each man standing in the galley. 'We have to backtrack and work out what time he could have gone over.'

The dining table has turned into an operations room and the men gather around it like generals planning an assault. Ridgy has been up to the bridge where he has tried to work out how the captain's navigational equipment works, but he finds it unreliable and inadequate.

Instead he asks Yanto for the boat's charts of the area and spreads them across the table. As a pilot and yacht master, he is confident he can calculate an area where Brett most likely fell in.

'Brett and I had a nightcap on the deck last night after you guys had all gone to bed.' Weyne's voice is strained as they discuss the events of the previous night. 'But the sea began to turn on its head and we went down at around midnight, I think. I went below. I thought Brett was right behind me.'

Weyne feels sick. Privately he's been plagued by guilt, assuming he was the last one to see Brett. He's been berating himself for not checking whether his friend had tripped on the stairs behind him or if he'd got to his cabin safely.

He feels a selfish relief when Banger announces that he was with Brett after that. 'We were so ill in our cabins, the two of us went up on deck for fresh air. I lay on the bench outside vomiting into a bucket. Brett was also very sick. He was hurling over the side of the boat.'

Weyne recognises the flash of guilt on Banger's face,

the automatic feeling of responsibility. It's an unspoken anguish.

Banger is uncertain of time. 'It could have been around 3 or 4am,' he shrugs. His face is pale. 'I don't know.'

'I saw him up there too.' Ridgy is the last to speak. 'I wasn't sick last night but I went up to the top deck to check on you guys. Brett was vomiting over the port beam. I asked him how he was and he said, "Not good, Boss. I haven't been this ill in a long time."'

'What was he wearing? Did he have anything on?' Niall is thinking practically.

'Shorts. I think he also put on a T-shirt.' Banger rubs his eyes and frowns.

'They were Bad Boy shorts.' JM remembers the brand; his business in Durban sells licenced surf gear to major retailers. He gave Brett those shorts as a gift.

'It's fucking cold out there now,' Banger nods towards the galley door.

'Yes, but thank God the water's warm.' Craig is thinking aloud. 'If this was Cape Town it'd be another story…'

The crossing from Padang to the islands' safe anchorage at Tua Pejat is pretty much a straight line. To calculate the approximate point on the chart, Ridgy lifts the paper, corners it and folds it to graduate the course. He calculates the time of departure out of Padang and the time of arrival at the islands.

'Halfway is round about here,' he says, putting a Bic pen point down in a square in the middle of the Strait. 'Two-thirty, when I saw him, would have been here-ish.' He marks a circle on the spot.

'It could've been later. It could've been around 4am,' Banger interjects.

'Well, 4am would have been about here.' Ridgy circles again. 'The 2.30am mark is the worst-case scenario. That's the furthest away he could be from us.'

He looks at the faces, drawn and solemn, staring at the chart in front of them. 'That means he's been in the water between five and seven hours already,' Snowman says sombrely.

'Yanto!' Ridgy calls the young man who has retreated into the passage. 'What's the current like here?'

'Current?' Yanto's face is a mask of constant tension.

'The captain should know,' Craig offers. 'He sails these waters every day. But now he's bloody well off the boat.'

'The current is two knots. Going south.' Yanto speaks softly.

Ridgy sucks on the end of the pen as he considers the drift of the current. He looks out the galley window at the grey skies and the rain trickling down the pane.

'We also have to consider the prevailing sea and the weather conditions…' Niall follows his train of thought.

Ridgy slowly outlines a square grid on the map. 'This is it. This is the window of our search.'

Still in a fogged and befuddled state and incredulous that their holiday lies in tatters, the men take a few moments. While they all live in different parts of South Africa and the world, they all surf. They all know the sea and its complexities. They love it for its power, its magnificence, its treasures, but they also know all too well its dangers, its reputation for peril. A relationship with the ocean, every surfer knows, is one of careful balance: it can be entirely captivating, but it also demands respect.

And now their friend is alone in its hazardous currents, hopefully swimming for his life.

JM breaks the silence. He voices what everyone is thinking. 'We have to tell Anita. And Brett's mother.'

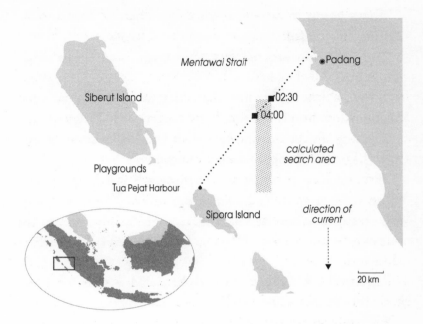

'Oh Jesus...' Tony runs his hands over his newly shaved head. Brett took a razor to it during the sundowners they had after they boarded the boat the night before. Their collective thoughts turn to Brett's family, his wife of ten years and their two children. They also know they have to break the news to Brett's mother Shirley and his siblings, Sandra and Greg.

'Actually, I don't know if we should tell Anita just yet,' JM adds quickly. 'Let's try and find him first.'

'I agree,' Niall said.

'No fucking way.' Ridgy is impatient and agitated. 'We need to tell her, no matter how hard it is. She's got to know that this has happened. We can't tell her in another three or four hours and have her ask "Why didn't you tell me?"'

'You're right,' JM quietly acknowledges. He doesn't want tempers to flare. The other men nod in agreement.

'That's going to be a difficult call…' Banger seems to be casting around for the right words.

'And what do we tell her? We don't even know what happened!' Niall says.

'So we tell her that. Just that. That we don't know what happened, but we think that Brett's overboard,' Ridgy replies.

'Hearing it over the phone is such an awful way of getting news like this, though. Someone should tell her face to face.'

'If we're going to tell Anita anything, we should get Louise to do it.' Craig, normally laconic, speaks up now. His wife is a strong woman, he tells them. She'd be straightforward but careful and gentle. 'We also live in Camps Bay, so she's close by.'

'Good. I'll ask Lulu to go with her,' Ridgy adds, thinking his wife would also be a stalwart in this situation.

'And while we still have cellphone signal, I'll put it on Facebook. We need to get the word out there. Tell everyone that Brett's overboard.' JM can feel the momentum picking up again.

'Well, don't do that until Anita knows. God forbid she finds out that way, before our wives tell her,' says Craig.

'Listen, it's still the small hours in South Africa. We're going to have to give it a couple of hours…'

It's heading for mid-morning now. The men wait for the captain but the turgid passing of time is agonising. They're desperate for the *Naga Laut* to leave the sheltered bay and head back out into the open sea.

While the South Africans have been making their bleak assessments and planning their rescue mission, the Indonesian crew have been readying the boat for the return sail. Disconsolate and defeated, they are plainly less hopeful of a recovery.

'Man can only last three hours in the sea,' Yanto comments

to Ridgy. He cites the longest time that he knows of someone surviving in these waters. The crew's unhappiness at going back out into the storm is evident.

The South Africans grow impatient. Seething that they're wasting time, their annoyance at the lack of actoion becomes more and more difficult to control. The situation is becoming volatile and eventually sharp words fly.

'We are going out there. And we're going to bring him back,' Ridgy, his self-control finally cracking, barks at Yanto.

'Where the fuck is the captain?' Banger asks.

'Where the fuck is the navy?' Weyne adds. 'We have a man overboard here and we're helpless. We're on our own!'

Downstairs in the galley, Craig Killeen puts the call through on the portable satellite phone to his wife Louise. It's 5.30am South African time. After multiple attempts and several dropped calls, he gets through.

'Babes,' he croaks, 'we have a big problem. We've lost Brett. He's not on the boat.'

'What? Where is he?' Louise's voice is still thick with sleep.

'We think he's gone overboard. We have no idea how or where, but we're going back out to look for him.'

'Oh shit! Oh God, are you sure? Oh shit!'

'I'm sorry to have to do this to you, baby, but you need to be the one to go and tell Anita.'

'Oh… Oh Jesus. Why me?'

Craig breaks down. By telling his wife, the news is out. Real. Fact. Up until this point they haven't shared it with anyone, but somehow this is verification.

'I can't believe this is happening,' he says, 'but Brett is missing.' He struggles for a few seconds to regather himself. 'But we're going back out there to find him. We *will* find him.'

'Oh God,' Louise repeats, as the weight of the responsibility just given her sinks in. 'You will find him, my darling. And he's going to be fine. I'll go. I'll go and tell Anita.'

Some of the others now use their cellphones to try to get in touch with their wives back home, but reception is poor and the calls keep disconnecting. There will be no signal out in the Strait, however; the only hope of communication will be the satellite phone and a radio with dodgy reception.

Tony has been in touch with Chantal Malherbe, the tour operator whose company arranged the Ten Green Bottles tour and many of the other charters Tony has been on before. Chantal runs the company from Hermanus, a seaside town about an hour and a half out of Cape Town, with her husband Gideon. She will play a pivotal communications role in the hours ahead.

Ridgy calls his wife Lulu in Rondebosch, Cape Town, and asks her to call Louise and accompany her to Anita and Brett's home in Camps Bay.

'We also need to find search and rescue numbers for this area, babe, and Australia too,' he points out, displaying the canny judgement he's known for.

It's still very early morning in South Africa but Lulu propels herself into action, locates the information, and sends through text messages with the emergency numbers.

JM calls his wife Tessa. He sent an earlier text giving news of their arrival at Tua Pejat, but this was before they'd realised Brett wasn't on board. It gave no presentiment then of the trouble ahead.

Things have changed.

'We realised this morning that he wasn't on board,' he tells Tessa emotionally, 'but we're going to find him.'

Tessa is distressed. 'Oh my God, love. Have you told Anita?'

'Louise is going to tell Anita, but you can't tell anyone else yet.'

As it happens, Tessa is going to meet Tony's wife Barbara for breakfast.

'Don't say anything,' JM cautions again. 'Don't put it out there before Anita knows. She'll get hold of Shirley, Sandra and Greg. We can't have information out there until Brett's family knows. Then we can consider putting it on Facebook.'

The conversation makes him shudder and he lets out a grimace.

'Also call my Mom and Pierre. Ask them to start prayer groups. Pierre's a journalist; tell him to get this out on bloody Reuters. Listen, love, we're going to lose comms soon. I don't know when we'll be able to speak again but I'll update you as soon as we get signal.'

Ridgy, Niall and Craig have persuaded Yanto that they can't wait for the captain any longer. The *Naga Laut* is turned around and the captain is called on his cellphone and notified. He can catch up to them in the tender.

The boat's engines grind back to life.

Nothing further is said amongst the men as they move quickly and quietly to the various points on the boat to take up their places for the search. Each is left with the enormous strain of his private thoughts.

'Four on the starboard, three on the portside.' Tony marshals the party. 'I'll join you up there – I first want to try get hold of the Australian coastguard.'

Ridgy also stays behind. As the man calculating logistics, he feels this responsibility keenly. He opens the paper on which he has written down the emergency numbers Lulu sent him.

Some of the men who'd brought rain jackets take them out

as they set off. The wind has picked up to a steady force and the rain is falling sideways.

It's strangely cold.

As Weyne passes through the galley, he catches sight of JM at the table. They're about to lose signal and JM has been typing into Facebook on his phone. Now he's staring up vacantly out of the window at the falling rain. Weyne sees tears rolling down the tall man's cheeks. He lays a hand on JM's shoulder for a moment and stands beside him. Neither says a word.

Then, after a few moments, JM says emphatically, 'He's swimming. I know he is. We just have to find him before his strength runs out.'

'We will,' Weyne replies softly. He leaves to make his way up to the starboard side to take up the watch with Tony, Snowman and Craig.

The men grab the rails of the upper deck to face the oncoming weather. On the bridge, Ridgy asks Yanto to steer slightly south. The wind produces a cross swell that sets the boat pitching and yawing as they leave the bay; the search party on board the *Naga Laut* is setting off into a wild and turbulent sea.

8.30AM TO 9.30AM
SEVENTH HOUR IN THE WATER

I need to keep track of time. I decide to measure more accurately how long I've been in the water so that I can calculate a timeline until the boat comes back. My thoughts are systematic, disciplined again. I start to count my strokes as I fight through the waves.

These are real deep-sea rollers. There must be another big storm brewing. I'm quite impressed by my suddenly more rational, pragmatic state of mind. The ponderous swells are interrupted every few seconds by sharper waves that shoot up unexpectedly. The wind blows incessantly, roaring like a cheering stadium crowd heard from a distance. It's drizzling again.

I'm doing around 22 strokes a minute. My arms are stretching forward in big, wide circles, but because my fingers are beginning to feel petrified, my palms are flatter now. I can't cup my hands like I did earlier.

I multiply my 22 strokes by 60 seconds: 1,320 strokes an hour.

It must be around 9am, though the lack of sun isn't helping my guesswork. I take it as a time-check to count the hours until midday and my boat's return.

Increasingly, slate-grey clouds gather in crowded clusters; they all seem to jostle for the front row. In these parts a storm can blow up quickly and without warning.

The ocean is still reeling in the wake of the night's ferocious storm and every minute or so I have to inhale and swim through a wave's looming curl. I move between enduring the burning in my lungs, with its accompanying slow-sucking breathlessness, to feeling more controlled and able to take in enough air.

71

I'm also aware that my tongue is swelling further, but again I consciously flick away that thought. I'm now programmed not to think of water or food.

Avoid negative thoughts and I can insulate myself from reality.

Instead I think about the 850 kilometres of cycling I've done over the last six weeks. 'Bob,' I talk to my imaginary staff, 'luckily we did the Cape Rouleur and your legs are still strong. You did that, so you can do this.'

The road cycle race, between 150 and 200 kilometres a day over three days, was gruelling, especially in the summer heat and wind. I hadn't trained properly for it. I'd taken out my bike at the beginning of January and for six weeks I rode around the streets of Camps Bay. They were more like Sunday cycles than training rides.

The race almost got the better of me – I felt broken afterwards. I managed to get past the physical pain, however, because the very next day I got back on my bike for a 100-kilometre charity ride from Franschhoek to Cape Town. And two days later I rode the Pick n Pay Cape Argus Cycle Tour, the world-famous 109-kilometre race around the Cape Peninsula.

Cycling, after surfing, has become a passion of mine. And, like surfing, it's meditative. When I'm on the bike, it's me, speed and the technicalities of the road.

I've had my scrapes. I remember my first accident now, another random offering of memory. I was seventeen and on a church sleepover weekend. I was part of a group running a table-tennis-thon to raise money for charity. Eight of us had to play table tennis continuously from 4pm on the Friday through to the end of the weekend.

During my break, I sneaked out with my bike. We weren't

allowed to leave the church but I left without telling anyone and set off to visit a girlfriend down the road.

While I was whizzing down a hill, a car came around a corner at speed. I heard screeching brakes and in a split second I realised the vehicle had connected with the back of my bike. I left the saddle and went over the handlebars. In the moment before I hit the tar I saw the faces of my mom, dad, brother and sister. I put my hands down to cushion the blow but still my face smashed into the road and my body followed. I skidded along, tearing off skin.

I got to my knees, stunned that I was still alive, and managed to make it onto my feet. Then I ran off into the bushes, terrified of the repercussions of leaving the table-tennis-thon. The driver chased me through two front gardens, caught me, put me back in his car and drove me home. Several stitches later, I was fine.

'So you see, Bob, you're strong. I don't want any complaints out of Production.'

The wind snatches my words away. My voice is strange and hoarse. I sound like my dad when his emphysema was at its worst.

I pride myself on being quite sporty. Even at fifty I'm fit and able to do the active things I love – surf, cycle, play touch rugby down on the beach. I've consistently relied on my body to pull me through physical challenges.

This time is going to be no different.

My brain is flitting across time – from past to present; it scratches sometimes at the future. Brain busy, keep it busy. Catapult your mind back and focus on your physical feats, I decide.

I recall the Four Peaks Challenge that I did in the UK in 2009. I was one of a team of four, three of whom were required to run up and down each of the highest mountains in Scotland, England, Ireland and Wales. We ran the last peak as a team, but as the designated driver I had barely slept in 56 hours.

We started at 4pm on a Friday. Three team members first sprinted up Ben Nevis in Scotland; that took about four hours. Afterwards I drove us overnight to get to the base of Helvellyn in the Lake District by 6am; the team took three-and-a-half hours to get up and down. We had to reach Mount Snowdon in Wales by 2pm, and the team took three hours to scale and descend. We then drove like hell for the Holyhead Ferry Terminal to take the overnight ferry to Ireland. It was a four-hour drive across the country to its highest peak, Carrantouhill, which we all ran. It took another four-and-a-half hours to get up and down.

That mountain almost killed me. The other runners were younger, and I was by far the weakest. I felt mind-blowing pain. I remember getting to what I thought was the summit and shouting to Rebecca, 'We've made it, we've made it!'

I'll never forget her face. 'Brett, we're not at the top,' she said. 'Look up there.'

I turned to see another 600 metres going straight up. My grimace echoed off the rocks and tears came to my eyes.

Rebecca hauled me up and we ended up winning the mixed-team category.

The Darwinian principle had applied: adapt or die.

And now the same is true again. Literally.

The small frisson of pride at these memories gives way to a more brooding and quiet questioning.

Why don't you just give up, Brett?

I know the answer.

It's something I've spent years working on in my life-coaching sessions. I have a huge fear of failure. It's a self-imposed sentence that has dominated my life. Ever since I was a little boy I would mentally flagellate myself for small failings, average weaknesses, minor transgressions. Call it a deep-seated insecurity, but for most of my life I've been driven by what others think. I've been afraid of people saying, 'He couldn't do it.'

It suddenly strikes me as strange: here I am, lost in a massive expanse of water and I'm not thinking about dying. Yet again I'm more afraid of what people might think of me than of simply surviving this.

It's a different fear.

Since turning fifty, I've become less self-judgemental but I think how, for years, my choices and decisions have been dominated by this maddening motivation. So many times I've acted out of stupidity. Out of pride.

Like the time I ran the Comrades.

The Comrades Marathon, described as 'the greatest human race', is a ludicrous 90-kilometre race between Durban and Pietermaritzburg in KwaZulu-Natal. It was first completed in 1921 when 34 men decided to run between the two cities to honour their comrades who had fallen in The Great War.

Now more than 15,000 runners from all over the world attempt the race annually, helping one another along the way in a spirit of camaraderie and good sportsmanship.

In South Africa, the race has ball-breaker status.

One year, a couple of months before the race, I was in my home-town bar in the Westville Hotel. 'Guys,' I'd teased a few mates, 'Comrades can't be that hard.'

Of course I knew it was one of the toughest runs in the world. But, full of bravado, I wanted to rev them up. By the end of the evening they'd bet a case of beer that I wouldn't be able to run the distance and survive. So juvenile.

I had just three months to train. Most runners take at least a year to prepare, and for some of the top runners it's their only race of the year.

During that time I became paranoid about not being able to finish. I was so terrified that I'd end up being the laughing stock that one Sunday, two weeks before the event, I left my mother's house in Westville to run part of the route.

After fifty kilometres, I thought, 'You might as well finish it.' I ran the last thirty or so kilometres pretending it was race day. I entered the stadium at the Cricket Oval in Pietermaritzburg and imagined that I was running to the finishing line, crowds cheering, flags waving, commentators yelling over the broadcast system.

Childish, I know. As I ran, the theme to *Chariots of Fire* played in my head and I cheered myself along. I was like a six-year-old.

My stopwatch read my time as a little shy of a silver medal.

I had no fear after that. I knew I could handle the distance and two weeks later I ran the race.

Those boys never did buy me my case of beer. And they certainly didn't believe I'd run the Comrades twice in two weeks.

'Don't get ahead of yourself, son.' Cantankerous Bob's voice disturbs my musing. I'm snapped back to my precarious circumstances.

A second later, an immobilising pain simultaneously crushes both my legs. It's like a thousand volts is ripping down the length of my body. My lower half turns to lead and I feel completely paralysed.

Cramp.

I sink like a stone.

THE BARRENJOEY
TUA PEJAT HARBOUR, NORTH SIPURA
10.12AM

'Pak Doris! Pak Doris!'

There's an edge and urgency to Anas's voice that's instantly troubling to Tony 'Doris' Eltherington, captain of the *Barrenjoey*. Doris is standing in the slightly raised wheelhouse of the 70-foot steel ketch watching three of his surf charter guests alight from the tender with two crew members. The men have braved the deplorable weather to go into Tua Pejat.

'This weather's fuckin' shit, mate,' Doris observed to his Western Australian guests earlier that morning when he'd dropped anchor in Dreamlands after their overnight motor into port. They'd arrived in overcast darkness and driving rain. 'Yer don't want to take yer dog out in this!'

Reaching for another Marlboro, he told them, 'There'll be no surf out there today. My crew needs to go into Tua Pejat to sign yer all out since we're leavin' the islands tomorrow, but I think yer should chill out here on the boat. Have breakfast, go snorkellin', if yer like. Hopefully the weather will subside and yer can get a surf later…'

Colin Chenu, Jeff Vidler and Pete Inglis, three of the nine guests, chose to go into the small, scruffy town for an hour; despite the interminable rain, they managed to do some local shopping and take photographs.

Later, they joined up with the crew, Aneraigo 'Anas' Laia and Aroziduhu 'Elvis' Waruwu, on the veranda of the harbour master's grimy office. The harbour master was leaning back on his chair against a paint-peeling wall the colour of rotten papaya, smoking a clove cheroot and strumming his guitar.

At the other end of the veranda two men were drinking coffee and playing dominoes. 'Not bad – the life of Indonesian public servants,' one of the Aussies joked.

They didn't understand the animated discussion in Bahasa that took place shortly afterwards, but whatever was said clearly upset Elvis and Anas, the two local men.

'Why did yer drive the tender at fuckin' five million miles an hour, Elvis?' Doris shouts down as his two crew members quickly make their way up to where he's standing. In the moment he is brusque, which is unusual for this expat captain who has a reputation for being fair and respectful to the locals.

Unlike some of the other captains, Doris is known for his decent wages, the comprehensive training he gives his crew – he's taught them to swim, surf and scuba-dive – and his deferential aphorism 'I'm a tourist in your country'. It has never been his style to operate with a heavy-handed 'colonial' attitude. It's why he's lasted in Indonesia and others haven't.

A rough, tough Queenslander, Doris Eltherington is a veteran sailor in these parts, known amongst the locals as a hard-living Bohemian, perhaps a trifle eccentric, and like most of us, occasionally irascible. But it's the way he handles boats and his knowledge of these waters that commands open respect. A laconic salty sea dog with a colourful reputation.

But there is also something else about him, a deep-down fragility or a hint of sadness that's hard to define. People often find it difficult to engage Doris in any lengthy conversation. It takes a while to break through.

Doris's voice, rough-hewn and raspy due to his larynx having been crushed in a motorcycle accident in Bali in 1999, and quite likely further enhanced by his sixty-a-day habit, has become his trademark. That and his original signature – his nickname Doris – given to him when he was a kid by Queensland locals who had teased him that his then mop of blond hair made him look like Doris Day.

Anas gets to Doris first. 'Emergency, Pak Doris!' the small man says breathlessly, using the local term of respect for an elder. Then he lets the first mate take over.

Elvis has known Doris for many years through his permanent employer, also a favoured Australian surf charter captain, John McGroder. He and Doris are firm friends.

'Tony!' Elvis's eyes are wide open and he is clearly upset as he comes into the wheelhouse. The use of the captain's real name is an indication that something serious has happened.

Although Doris speaks Bahasa, Elvis's English is better.

'Tony, a *bule* has gone overboard. The harbour master has just told us.'

Bule, literally 'albino' in Bahasa, is the locals' term to refer to white people.

'What?' Doris whips around. The news is a jolt. While death by drowning is fairly common in these parts, this is the first time in the seventeen years he's worked the Mentawais that a tourist has gone overboard. It rocks him.

'Yes, a *bule* has fallen off the *Naga Laut*. In the night.'

'A tourist has gone overboard? Off the *Naga Laut*?' Doris repeats the statement, a doleful expression spreading across his face. As the seconds pass, his unsettled demeanour turns to distress.

'Last night? Are yer sure?'

'Yeah, the harbour master told us. The crew of the *Naga Laut* just reported it.'

Doris begins to feel a walloping in his chest. His heart feels as if it's about to erupt into his throat. His next reaction is explosive, and is a little surprising to some of the Western Australians who have just started to come up on deck.

'Fuck! Shit!' Doris yells as he spins around the wheelhouse. 'But they're just over there.' He points to the *Naga Laut*, rocking dejectedly beneath a veil of rain about 500 metres away. It looks deserted, a ghost ship.

He flicks his cigarette into a half-cup of cold coffee and snatches up the radio.

'*Naga Laut, Naga Laut, Naga Laut*. This is *Barrenjoey, Barrenjoey*. Copy? Copy?'

Loud static hisses from the speaker above Doris's head.

'What the fuck are they doin' there?' he says to himself, staring at the vessel that seems abandoned. Doris knows the boat's owner, an Italian expat, but he's not sure who its current captain or crew are.

'*Naga Laut, Naga Laut*. It's *Barrenjoey*. It's Doris.'

'Oh, Pak Doris?' The voice that comes over the radio is barely audible. Outside, the rain begins to fall heavily again around the boat; water streams off the glass windshield. The *Naga Laut* is a smudge through the downpour.

'Who is that?' Doris barks into the receiver. His hands are shaking. He's angry.

'Yanto speaking.'

'What's goin' on, Yanto?' The question comes out in a low guttural drawl.

'Oh, ah, *bule* in the water, Pak Doris.' The anxiety in Yanto's voice is indisputable.

'Where? Where did it happen?' Doris shouts at the boat through the rivulets rushing down the glass.

A barrage of hysterical Bahasa explodes out of the receiver.

It's incomprehensible. Doris turns and without taking his eyes off the *Naga Laut* hands the receiver to Elvis.

'I'm losin' him. Can't understand a fuckin' thing he's sayin', mate. Speak to him in Indo – try to find out the lat and long where they think he fell off. We must find out where on the passage from Padang it happened.'

Elvis talks loudly and at speed into the receiver. Doris, fidgeting with his box of cigarettes, talks over him.

'Ask them why they're here. Why aren't they out there lookin' for the guy? Why the *fuck* are they still here? It's gettin' too late to set out – '

For the men watching, a kind of madness seems to be settling over Doris. He starts pacing through the wheelhouse as if something inside him has been let loose. He's growling to himself under his breath.

Elvis hangs up the receiver. 'He says the man was sick. Vomiting over the side. He's from South Africa. He go over at around 3am.'

'Did he give yer co-ords?' Doris takes three steps up to Elvis, who has already written down with a blunt pencil the *Naga Laut*'s assumed co-ordinates at the time of the incident. In the same movement, Doris takes the radio receiver again and puts a call through to the harbour master.

'It's Tony Eltherington. On the *Barrenjoey*. Yer need to go out for this guy!' He skips any kind of greeting or preamble to this stern injunction; instead he is shouting into the radio. The volume has been turned up to ten so that the conversation is crystal-clear.

The reply is somewhat disinterested and booms through the wheelhouse: 'Weather too bad.'

Doris is not in the mood for the calm negotiation that these situations normally require.

'Nah, nah, mate. He's still missin' at sea. Get SAR, the navy guys, the TNI.' SAR is Search and Rescue; TNI the Indonesian army. 'Your boat is out here, there's also a SurfAid boat anchored here. We need speedboats. They all have double motors – we could go out a lot quicker on those.'

'Too much storm. Weather too bad.'

The irritable reply puts an end to the conversation. A loud click signals that the radio has been turned off. It underscores the insuperable problems with Indonesian officialdom that Doris has come to know only too well.

He turns to look at the island of Sipura in silence, his jaw clenched, his eyes narrowed. He knows that there will be no official response to this incident. There rarely is unless it's a major disaster – a volcano or a tsunami – and even then it's often disorganised and deficient. In such emergencies, it's regularly left to the charities and surf charter boats to help co-ordinate and offer assistance in rescue and recovery operations. In a place where thousands or hundreds of thousands of people die in devastating natural disasters, why would the island's government worry about one man?

Doris is like one of the archipelago's volcanoes. Rumbling internally, he seems about to erupt. He's accustomed to the host of official excuses or the unspoken way of getting things done, the frequently undisguised medium of exchange: bribery. Its presence hangs over everything.

He looks down at the handwritten co-ordinates for several minutes before he closes his eyes.

At this moment, four of the guests come up to the wheelhouse. They step just inside the doorway to get in out of the rain.

'Has a man really gone overboard?' asks Lyall Davieson. He is a slight man, a little older than the others, with a sweep of sun-bleached hair that's now rain-stuck against his forehead. 'He was seasick and vomiting over the side in the middle of the night?'

'Yeah,' Doris speaks softly now, brooding. The others can see that he's not in a good frame of mind.

'Gee, that's awful,' says Simon Carlin. Simon has known Doris from his early surfing days on the Gold Coast; he can tell that the news has profoundly affected the skipper. 'That's never happened before over here.'

'Nah.' Doris seems transported to some kind of other world, unable to imagine a way back. 'He fell off the *Naga Laut* at around three in the mornin'.'

Doris nods towards the other boat which he now sees is leaving the bay. It's just visible through a mantilla of worsening weather, as it makes its way towards the horizon. 'They're going east,' he observes wonderingly, 'back to Padang. Surely they must've realised that the current will have dragged him way off that bearin'?'

'Jesus Christ,' Simon exhales.

All the men stand silently as they look out at the departing boat; then they look down, not knowing what to think or what to say.

Outside, a new squall is moving in. The sky is heavy with low cloud and the wind is picking up once again. The *Barrenjoey*'s rigging is clanging against the aluminium mast like change ringing in a belfry.

'*Naga Laut, Naga Laut, Naga Laut. Barrenjoey.* Do yer copy?'

The radio static is an amplification of the humming rain outside. There is no reply to Doris's call. He repeats it and when again he gets no response, he says to no-one in particular: 'Out of range.' He stares blankly out at the sea.

'They're not goin' to go lookin' for this guy. No-one's goin' to go look for him.' Doris seems to be in a funk, talking to himself.

After a momentary pause, Colin Chenu, a Perth solicitor asks, 'What are you going to do?'

Intuitively, he knows Doris is not about to be defeated by the lack of action. Nudging his misted-up glasses along the bridge of his nose, he senses an announcement.

'Well, I don't know what yer guys are doin' – ' Doris is suddenly assertive, decisive, in charge. It's as if his seafarer's soul has been rebooted. He gathers up his glasses, puts on his cap and then starts shouting orders. 'Elvis! Load up that fuel tank on the speedboat. I want food, life jackets, blankets, water, sat phone, everything. That guy's alive. And we gotta go get him.'

9.30AM TO 10.30AM
EIGHTH HOUR IN THE WATER

The cramp consumes me.

Water fills my mouth, my throat, my ears. I feel its relentless pressure around my head and against my chest. I open my eyes under water. The green-grey water around me merges seamlessly with a deeper black that makes it impossible to see beyond five metres. I focus on shining wave caps eddying about in front of my face, like silver flakes in a child's Christmas snow-bowl.

I'm going to drown. It's a panicky thought as I look up to the under-surface of the sea, being whipped this way and that by the merciless wind above. It's very dark beneath me.

I can't move my legs – they are completely numb – but my arms swing forward in an automatic, instinctive action. With my hips as the fulcrum, I grab my toes and pull them towards my body, stretching out my hamstrings. My limbs feel alien, like I'm using them for the very first time.

I've cramped before in the ocean while surfing, but I've always managed to hang on to my board while working through the withering agony.

I'm a few feet below the surface and my lungs want to explode. I need air. I need to take a breath. I pull my legs back together and like an ungainly mermaid, I manage to propel myself back to the top in a single manoeuvre.

I breach inelegantly and splutter and cough as I slap my open hands onto the surface. The fizzing salt water that I retch whirls around my chin. My lungs are on fire and my throat feels stripped of flesh.

I gasp for air, but it feels thin and inadequate, as if I'm at 8,000 metres. In the Death Zone. Every breath is a torment, but I draw as many slow, steady intakes as I can, hacking as each one catches the back of my throat.

The cramping brings on tremors of mental uncertainty. I think again about the odds of being found. I've sailed this crossing four times before – I know how vast the Mentawai Strait is: around 200 kilometres wide and more than 1,000 kilometres long; that's over 200,000 square kilometres of ocean. Am I imagining that it feels more dense around me now?

I glance up to the sky, all the time trying to keep my head above the relentless waves. I search for a break in the clouds, something to offer more light. Instead the gloom closes in and it starts to rain again. Another storm begins.

A plane or helicopter will never see you, Brett.

Pessimism is partnering my lethargy.

They'll never find you. With these waves breaking and in these conditions, the chances of seeing your little head are zero.

The raindrops against my face begin to blur all view, so I close my eyes. I hear a strange sound, like children whispering, as the rainfall gets heavier. My feelings are as fluid and shifting as the water around me and the pull of despair is again at work. Despair. Such a debilitating emotion.

I must excise these thoughts from my mind.

There's nothing you can do to change any of this, I scold myself, opening my eyes. You can't make your head bigger. You can't put a flare on top of it. You must ignore the things you can't change.

It's a weird sense of disassociation, but I don't want my body to start believing that it's going to stop working, that it's going to give up. To console myself, I quickly start to sing again. Three songs are on a subliminal mental loop: 'Words' by the Bee Gees, and 'Daniel' and 'Candle in the Wind' by

Elton John. I start to yell them out as loud as I can, over and over, but every few seconds my voice cracks and splinters. I turn to telling jokes from my long and colourful repertoire.

That will keep your spirits up, I scoff. I sound like my father.

I tell one joke after another and instantly my mind changes gear.

Since I was a child, I've been able to multitask. To this day, I can compose a letter, talk to someone and listen to a conversation all at the same time. But now my brain is doing more than multitasking. It feels as if it's a nest of termites, teeming. I visualise a computer screen on the fritz, number sequences scrolling furiously from top to bottom, windows opening and closing at a ridiculous speed. I can't seem to slow it down.

I start going through the contact list on my mobile phone. I think about the device, lifeless, useless, in my bag back on the *Naga Laut*. There are more than 5,000 names and numbers stored in that phone – they're not all friends; most are acquaintances I've garnered over 25 years primarily through work.

I do the maths. I was CEO of a company with 3,500 employees in nineteen offices around the world; we had more than a thousand clients who all had management teams with whom I had active business dealings. I nurtured those relationships over decades.

I mentally go through some of the names, alphabetically, on my phone as a way to pass time. I stop at the names of close friends: the boys on the boat, my other close friends – Chris Joseph, Dylan Pooley, Gary Knowles, Pete Jones, Steve Griessel, Ute Latzke – people who mean so much to me but are scattered across the globe.

I work hard at my friendships. I make a point of contacting

those who are dear to me on their birthdays – either with a phone call or an email. Many don't even know when my birthday is, but birthdays are special for me. They have been since I was a child.

I carefully consider the people I care about, my family and friends whom I count as blessings. It makes me feel strangely dreamy.

With the rain streaming down my face, right now I am not convinced that I'm going to see them again. I say goodbye to each of them; I start to say things I've wanted to say but might have held back. I make peace with my adversaries, and release long-held anxieties and angst. I forgive myself for things that I'm not proud of.

If this is a way of easing towards death, I think, you've had a good opportunity to reflect on things. It hasn't been mad or hysterical; it's been a weirdly slow experience, a steady process. I decide that it's a better ending than people who die suddenly.

Anita.

Is she waking up now? Has she heard? How will she tell the kids? I hear her laugh in my head. I'm determined that the sound is heartening instead of upsetting. I know that if anxiety gets the better of me, it could open the floodgates.

I continuously beg Anita to talk to me.

'Are the guys on their way, Neets? Will they find me? When I get tired, you have to tell me to keep going. You have to make me carry on.'

FISKAAL ROAD
CAMPS BAY, CAPE TOWN
WEDNESDAY 17 APRIL 2013
6.13AM

Her face appears suddenly and unexpectedly out of the rain through the front-door cottage-pane windows. Louise Killeen has had to climb over the garden wall because the pedestrian gate is padlocked. The overcoat thrown over a tracksuit and a scarf pulled around her neck are both soaking wet. Her blonde hair is pulled back into a loose bun, but strands are stuck to her forehead and rain is dripping from her chin. Her face is ghostly under the weak light in the alcove.

She taps urgently on the glass with her index finger. The doorbell must have stopped working again in the driving rain. It's a few minutes after six, still dark, and the weather on this autumn morning is a spectacular display of the peninsula's fearsome reputation. This is the Cape of Storms, after all.

Even through the dripping glass, Anita registers her friend's look in an instant. Something is very wrong. It is the hopeless look people have when they've come to comfort the bereaved.

She takes a millisecond to consider Louise's missed call registered on her cellphone; she'd seen it at 6am just before waking the children. She'd gone to her bedside to check whether Brett had responded to her text of the previous night, but there was still only the BBM tick indicating that the message had been sent. It hadn't been read.

With no landline at home, Anita never switches off her phone, especially when her husband travels.

She'd thought it odd that Louise was trying to reach her so

early and made a mental note to return her call on the school run. She'd decided first to go downstairs to make tea and start breakfast.

The urgent tapping on the front door glass strikes a chill. It's an ephemeral moment, but it's full of foreboding.

Anita has already started trembling although she hardly realises it.

'You are freaking me out, Lou.' Anita opens the door, pulling her pyjamas closer around her. Then, almost without hesitation: 'Where is the boat?'

'It's not the boat,' Louise says breathlessly, a cluster of emotions crowding her face.

'It's Brett. I'm so sorry, Anita, but he's fallen overboard. They don't know where. They don't know when. They think he's been missing at sea for about seven, maybe eight hours now.'

Louise says it all quickly, determined to get it out in the open. Then she swallows hard.

For Anita, everything seems to slow down. She feels a physical force, like a blow across the face. It's as if she has left her body and is watching events from the corner of the room. She can't breathe and hears herself gasp, but it's a strange animal sound that comes from her belly.

'No! No, no, no.' Her head is swirling. Is she fainting? Her shoulder hits the wall and she slides to the floor. Air. She can't seem to inhale. 'No. This can't be.' She's shaking her head and her hands have gone to her mouth, then to her throat. It feels as if it's closing up.

'There must be some mistake. It's not Brett. They've got the wrong man.' A thought flashes through her mind and she throws an accusatory glance at Louise. Why Brett? Why him? Why not your husband? She doesn't voice it, though. It is a fleeting thought, quickly replaced by a remote hope, that out of everyone else on board that boat Brett is the only one who could survive something like this.

She sits crumpled, her legs at unnatural angles.

Louise pushes open the front door and bends down to gather up her friend. She has no words of comfort. Her sombre expression, matched with her silence, add to Anita's steadily increasing awareness that this is not a dream. Panic suddenly rising, Anita feels the quick sting of tears.

'What do I do, Lou? What do I do?'

Nine-year-old Zara comes around the wall from the kitchen. Her expression is strange – somewhere between confusion and knowing. She's still wearing the pink bunny rabbit onesie she sleeps in. Her blonde hair, normally tied back, hangs loose around her shoulders.

'Mommy, what's wrong?'

Louise and Anita glance at one another. Anita gets to her feet, pushes her glasses back on her nose and takes a deep breath. She pulls her dishevelled ponytail tighter at the back, an act of composure.

In that moment, she decides to lie to her daughter.

'We can't get in touch with the boat. Dad and the guys are doing the crossing in Indonesia, but we can't make contact. Some of the other moms are going to come here today and we're going to try reach them on the satellite phone.'

Anita is fiercely blinking back tears. It's her personal rule: she never allows the children to see her upset. She cannot tell her children that their father is lost.

'Go get dressed, darling,' she tells her daughter. 'Get ready for school.'

'I don't think they need to go to school today,' Louise says gently.

Anita looks at her imploringly. Uncertainty and bewilderment paralyse her for a moment, then she recovers. 'Take Jamie and go and watch TV.'

Zara gives her mother a long quizzical look. Then the little girl turns slowly and walks to the stairs where her brother is descending.

'Come,' she says, taking his hand. Unquestioningly, he follows her.

Lettie Marondera arrives just then at the open door. The housekeeper has worked for the family for three years. She shakes the rain from her coat.

'What's happened?' she asks, immediately alerted to Anita's pale face, quivering lip and shaking hands as she stands in the passage. Anita bows her head to her chest and Letti moves forward. Intuitively, she abandons her questions and puts her arms around her employer in a comforting embrace. It's a poignant, private moment. The younger woman recognises this kind of pain.

Louise walks through the dining room to the sliding doors. Despite the early hour, she needs a cigarette. She turns on the lights at the wall as she goes. The globe in the outside patio light flickers momentarily before it blows. She hears the low hiss of air and then a soft pop before the light is snuffed. Her eyes slowly adjust, making out the grey shapes outside.

It's the shadow time before daylight, an indecisive half-light. The morning feels suffocating as the rain continues to fall from a cavernous sky.

Louise's phone starts to ring after the first drag. It's Lulu Ridgway, who is turning into the driveway. Louise raises her hand to wave in recognition, hangs up and then shields her eyes as she squints into the headlights. Stripes of rain flash in their beam. Louise pulls her scarf over her hair and rushes past the empty pool to open the gate beside the garage for Mark's wife.

Lulu has been up since 4am. Her husband's call from the *Naga Laut* roused her from an already interrupted night. She'd been tending her two croupy young sons, both of whom had slept on mattresses beside her bed.

'I need you to get up,' Mark told her. 'Go to the computer and Google 'search and rescue in Indonesia'. I can't talk long. Brett's missing and we think he's fallen off the boat.'

She was devastated at the news but awake and alert in an instant. She could tell from her husband's tone that it was a parlous situation. She also knew he'd be feeling impotent and frustrated – it was always difficult for Mark to not be entirely in control.

For the next two hours, Lulu sat in her pyjamas in her home office, poring over websites that could give some clue as to whom to call. Frantically, she scoured Indonesian sites for an official coastguard, navy, any organisation that could launch a rescue initiative.

Instead she found stories of local boats sinking in those waters, people lost, entire families drowned. She was stunned by the lack of land and sea rescue infrastructure. If boatloads of people were abandoned to their fate, what chance did one man have?

Slowly the *Naga Laut*'s isolation and the magnitude of their situation had come home to Lulu. She fully grasped the hollowness her husband was feeling.

She texted Mark all the numbers she could find – local ones in Padang she tried to ring herself, but as the calls went unanswered she was left with a rapidly growing sense of unease. She also sent Mark what she thought might be their saving grace: emergency numbers in Australia.

Now Lulu rushes, head down, shoulders hunched against the rain, to embrace Louise.

'Where is she?' Their faces are soon wet in the downpour.

'Inside. She's in shock.' Louise takes her arm as they huddle together and half run back to the covered patio.

Anita is standing in the kitchen. It's as if a phantom fist is squeezing her heart inside her chest. She talks to Lettie but has a sense of her own fragility. Like a pond skater, wobbly and uncertain, on the surface of the water.

'Please feed the kids, Lets.' They are both weeping. 'Give them some toast or something and keep them in the TV room. I need to start doing things, something... something useful to find Brett.'

Anita glances at the cartoons darting on the screen in the other room. Their hysterical hilarity makes the moment all the more surreal.

Lulu finds Anita standing at the door, arms suspended at her sides, her face strangely contorted. She weeps quietly as they embrace. 'How am I going to find him, Lu?' Anita whispers.

'They're going back. They're looking,' Lulu says, herself crying. 'We're going to have to be strong.'

Outside, Louise ends a call on her cellphone and walks in from the dripping darkness. 'Anita, get out your laptop.' She speaks quickly, but her tone is authoritative. 'Chantal Malherbe from the company that handled the charter booking just phoned. She got my number from Craig. She's trying to send you an email about launching a rescue.' Louise wipes raindrops from her face. 'We have to find Brett's travel documents, find out if he has travel insurance. Do you know his ID number? Is there any record of his insurances in the house?'

Anita stares at her blankly. She's floundering. Brett travels so often, she doesn't always keep track of his comings and goings. She knows he's in Indonesia, of course, she took him to the airport, but she isn't certain of where exactly in the Mentawais the guys are. She doesn't know Brett's flight number, the name of the boat they've chartered or anything of the events leading up to this.

It's this swinging between careful organisation and her credulous dealings with the world that frustrates but endears her to her husband. For Brett, Anita's mixture of togetherness and dreamy naivety is a charming cocktail. But now, in the face of this adversity, she's swamped by guilt.

'I haven't a clue. I don't know anything.'

Despite the fear seeping through her limbs, Anita takes a breath and mentally regroups. Over the next few minutes, she becomes calm, even a little detached. It's somehow admirable to Lulu and Louise. Although cushioned from the details, Anita feels certain of one thing: her husband is not dead. She can feel it.

'Before that I must phone my mom. And Shirley and… oh God, I need to tell Greg and Sandra …' It's as if Anita has just looked down and realised that she's on a perilous ledge. She feels pinned down by the responsibility and it fills her with dread. How is she going to communicate this news with her emotions at such an imprecise stage?

She pushes back a wisp of her coal-black hair and turns, as if sleepwalking, to go upstairs. She needs to be alone to make these calls.

As she enters their bedroom, Anita immediately glances to Brett's side of the bed; she looks over to his personal effects on the bedside table. Also there is her wristwatch; it stopped unexpectedly in the night, Beside it is her phone, with her unanswered message to her husband.

Her mind flicks back to the night before. She had taken the children to have dinner in Constantia on the other side of the mountain, at the home of her younger sister Helene. It was a chance for Zara and Jamie to spend more time with their grandparents, who were staying with Helene, her husband Andrew and their children after the weekend family wedding in Stellenbosch. But Jamie had eaten a biscuit with traces of peanuts in it, and since he had an allergy to nuts he'd been violently ill in the car all the way home. Anita had seen Zara to bed and taken Jamie through to her own bed to monitor his breathing. Glancing down to check the time, she found that her watch had stopped. The hands immovable on 10pm. Irritated that she hadn't heard from Brett, she took off her watch and decided to send him another message.

'Why haven't you phoned or sent me a text? You promised! Jamie has eaten something with traces of peanuts. He vomited the whole way home. I've put him in bed with me. It's going to be a looooooooooong night…'

Her throat tightens now at the prophetic nature of that text. She closes her eyes as she makes her way towards the balcony, turning on the outside light as she slides the door open. Outside in the semi-darkness, the weather seems to be laying siege to the house. It's a storm from some appalling nightmare. Despite the swirling rain, Anita swipes the screen on her phone and in that moment decides to call her sister first. Hands shaking but immune to the cold, she dials Helene's number and gets her voicemail. Then she tries her mother. The phone connects but there is no greeting, no lead up conversation.

'Mommy, Brett's fallen off the boat,' she says into the device and hangs up.

Anita decides to phone Gary Knowles, one of Brett's closest friends, who lives in Australia and works for another travel industry colleague, John Spence. Spence owns hotels in Bali and Indonesia. 'They'll have contacts, networks. They'll know what to do,' she mutters. Gary's phone is also on voicemail.

She then tries Chris Joseph, a South African friend of Brett's based in Singapore. Since he and Brett met at a major golfing event at Erinvale in 1996, Brett has been like a brother to CJ; affections run deep. She finds CJ in the transit lounge at Jakarta airport.

'*What* did you say?' CJ is stunned.

'He's lost… overboard, CJ.' Anita is feeling frantic again, but she desperately tries to control the hysteria that's building in her voice. 'I need eyes and ears over there. I need aeroplanes in the sky. I need you to organise things on that side, whatever it takes…'

She breaks down and for a few moments is unable to speak. 'Help me bring him home, CJ,' she finally sobs.

'Let me make some calls, Anita. Find out what's going on.' CJ sounds breathless on the other end. 'I'll call you back.'

Anita swallows hard and blinks. She has plucked up the courage at last to make the hardest call of all. She dials her mother-in-law's number. Shirley Archibald is about to leave for her usual early Wednesday morning church prayer group and is already at her front door, a cake for a friend's birthday balanced on one hand, when her landline rings.

'Mom, I have bad news. Brett's missing.' The news is delivered in a remarkably calm fashion. 'We don't know anything. I'll stay in touch.'

Anita's equanimity persists as her call to her sister-in-law, Sandra, goes unanswered, and continues when she reaches Brett's younger brother, Greg, who is en route to the Drakensberg for a holiday with his family. They are breakfasting at a roadside Wimpy. 'The details are unclear,' she tells Greg. 'I'll call you when I know more.' Her response to their shocked reaction is almost a lack of reaction. She seems inured, as if a shadow has come over her.

Later, Anita will hardly remember making any of these calls.

Shutting out the pounding from above, Anita closes the sliding door and picks up her laptop from her bed. She needs to read the email from Chantal Malherbe. She returns downstairs and flips open the computer on the dining-room table. 'MAN OVERBOARD IN THE MENTAWAIS' reads the subject line. The sentences begin to blur and Anita cannot read through the tears of fear and confusion that inevitably come.

'She's sent the boat's details, the satellite number, the owner's contacts...' Lulu reads over her shoulder. 'They're the same numbers Mark sent me on SMS.'

'You need to see what documents you can find, honey,' Louise says tenderly.

Anita's anguish is unmistakable, but she controls the outburst.

'Apparently, Brett organised his own travel arrangements to get to Indonesia,' Lulu continues. 'He didn't go through Chantal. That information must be in his office upstairs. Search his computer. There must be records on there. Also, she's going to email you a document authorising a search. You need to sign it.'

Anita turns back to the stairs and heads up to Brett's office.

Lulu closes her eyes, distilling the moment. It's a visceral sensation, delivered by a single phrase: 'fallen off the boat'. She rubs her upper arms – it's cold inside – and slowly turns to follow Anita.

There are papers everywhere in Brett's office.

It's not like him. To leave everything so disorganised. It's a tangential thought that fleets through Anita's mind. She leaves Lulu sifting through papers on the desk and walks back across the passage into their bedroom again.

She looks for Brett's travel pouch on his side of the bed. He normally leaves a copy of his itinerary in the drawer of his side table. Instead she discovers a wad of papers stapled together on the floor. She slowly bends to pick it up, already knowing what it is: copies of their last wills and testament.

'We are not looking at this today,' Anita says aloud. It's a bad omen dispelled by ignoring it. She opens the drawer and places the papers face down inside.

She doesn't mention the wills to anyone.

Outside the day is finally dawning, cold and uncertain. Louise stands and watches the gusts of rain against the lounge room windows; the wind is hammering against the eaves. The chaos outside matches her dismay within.

The Killeens and Archibalds have only recently reconnected after some years and Louise feels that she doesn't know Anita that well yet. She wonders how she will manage the crisis, tries to decide what she will say.

This day, she knows, will change everything.

10.30AM TO 11.30AM
NINTH HOUR IN THE WATER

A conversation I had with my life coach in January comes back to me. I'd been at a friend's long weekend wedding in Knysna on the Garden Route with Anita and the kids, but personal doubts and insecurities kept my internal compass spinning. I just couldn't relax.

For two hours I sat in my car on a Skype call to her.

'I've achieved my goals,' I told her, 'but I still feel in turmoil. It's messing with my head. I've made enough money to not have to work again, we have no debt, my kids' education is taken care of and our retirement is sorted. We've returned to Cape Town and have a very comfortable life, but I still haven't found my purpose.'

Many questions. No answers. A mid-life crisis?

We started working on a plan to find the engine that would drive the rest of my life. But now there isn't going to be the 'rest of my life'. I'm going to die without figuring any of it out. Perhaps I'll get some message, some epiphany, here and now?

Slowly, methodically, I wind everything back.

The first acknowledgement is the easiest: I've been ruled by money throughout my life. The more I've made, the more afraid I've become of losing it. When would enough be enough? Fear and avarice have imprisoned me.

In my early years we grew up with money. We lived very comfortably in Westville with a big house, staff, everything we could have asked for. Each year, we holidayed in wonderful destinations and we stayed in some posh hotels. But when my father had his breakdown and lost his job, it all vanished. Poof. He lost everything and my mom had to return to work.

100

For years, I couldn't move past the idea that my dad had let us down.

I have a vivid memory of my mother crying in the headmaster's office, begging for more time to pay the school fees. My brother and I sat there with her that day, witness to her humiliation. It haunts me still.

I vowed then that I'd never put my own family through that indignity. I would never owe money or suffer financial insecurity. Money became my yardstick, a measure of my manliness, my torch in the darkness. I followed it relentlessly. It seems easy now, so obvious to accept how meaningless and irrelevant it all is.

'Stupid, so goddamned bloody stupid.' I slap the water around me.

I can also be petty, pedantic and controlling. I'm an A-type personality, ultra-organised, a control freak. My shirts are colour-coded in my wardrobe. As are my jeans.

When we moved back to South Africa, Anita had wanted to take furniture out of storage to put into our house. She'd wanted to make it liveable, happy, a home. But with the renovation looming, I kept her from doing it.

'What's the point? It's going to be demolished soon.'

So for two years we'd lived in a stark, cold shell. The curtains remained packed away. I wouldn't let Jamie paint his wall some crazy colour. We hadn't even unpacked the dishwasher. What was wrong with just unpacking the dishwasher, for Christ's sake? We'd washed dishes by hand for two years and hated it – all because I needed to keep everything in neat little boxes.

'I promise, Anita, I promise I'll never say "Wait" again. When I come home, we'll put up those pictures.'

These mundanities are suddenly very upsetting to me. It's small stuff, but it feels as if it matters very much. The sea is still horribly choppy and the slow kicks I'm making to tread water are gradually sapping my strength, but I'm so cross with myself that I hardly notice.

You worry about all the wrong things, Brett.

I shake my head. Contentment has always been just around the corner, just out of reach.

You've always thought 'only if' or 'when I've done that...'

I've known it, but haven't listened: fulfilment doesn't come from the zeros on your bank statement or what car you drive. The superficiality, the vanity of our consumerist world is so pointless, utterly ridiculous.

Anita, Zara, Jamie, if I survive this, I'm going to be different.

I consider how wild and reckless I was prior to having Anita and the kids in my life. It was a time of such unbridled self-indulgence. You have your family to live for now. The thought is like a pulsating strobe through my brain.

I lost my religion in that world of high-flying and even higher expectations. But I turn to God now.

'Do you want me to go to church?' I shout. 'Because I'm not going to.'

I'm not into incense, cold pews and decaying hymnals. The ocean is my church.

I stop shouting, my thoughts still swirling.

Another storm has blown up and I hear the thrum of the rain on the sea and the wind whooshing past me in great rushes of air. Despite the ache creeping into my ankles and my knees, I feel reinforced all over again by my confession.

The boat is coming back for me, I'm suddenly sure of it. I feel galvanised and certain that I can make it until they reach me.

I can do it. I can survive.

THE BARRENJOEY
TUA PEJAT HARBOUR
12.16PM

'Do you want a hand?' Simon, Colin and Jeff gather around Doris at the stern of the *Barrenjoey*, where the 23-foot tinny, the *Bynda Laut*, with its twin 175 engines, is tethered.

It's past noon but the sky is so dark it's impossible to work out the time of day. The falling rain is softer now.

'We'd like to come out with you, if you're up for it.' Simon speaks quietly.

Doris is turning a hand-held GPS in his hands, checking that it's in working order. Elvis has finished provisioning the boat and is pulling a tarp across the small deck. He glances at Doris, uncertain of the coming reaction.

The assistance is a peace offering.

'The guy's been missing at sea for at least nine hours,' someone else said. 'He's gone.'

The callous comment seemed to push Doris beyond his limit. His reaction was one of fury.

'Fuckin' hell!' he bellowed. 'We've got to try find this guy. If it were me, I'd want someone lookin'! It could so easily have happened to any one of ya...'

Pacing around the boat like a caged lion, Doris cursed under his breath. He felt his decision to go out in search as an intolerable weight.

'Wilson!' he shouted to one of the deckhands. 'Get the rubber dinghy. Yer can drive these guys round to Icelands if they want to surf...'

The last sentence was spat out.

'Even if we find a body, I'd still want to be able to give it to his family,' he snapped as he'd walked away.

His guests knew then that the situation had changed dramatically, that Doris's decision to look for the missing man had become a personal quest.

'Come, if yer like,' Doris now replies to Simon's offer, avoiding direct eye contact, 'but I have to go up and make a call first.'

Some say that Tony Eltherington ran away. From a surf career of exceptional potential, from his family obligations, from himself. He left his home country Australia for Indonesia, first to Bali and then to the most remote place he could find, the Mentawais, where the ocean's call and the hunt for the perfect wave was the antidote to his fear of failure in an achievement-orientated society.

He started to make a life for himself on his own terms in one of the most isolated corners of the world.

Tony Raymond Eltherington was different from the outset. Destined, perhaps, to walk his own road.

He arrived a little unexpectedly when his mother, while visiting his grandmother in Brisbane in August 1956, went into labour and was rushed to the Royal Brisbane Hospital. Mother and last-born son returned to his butcher father, two sisters and a brother, who lived on the water behind the barrelling right-hand break at Burleigh Heads further south on Australia's Gold Coast. In those days it was considered one of the best waves in the country.

Tony's first few years were a heady mix of running barefoot in white-hot sand, long days of sun and learning a very skilled life in and on cerulean seas. From the age of four, the beautiful blond boy was already at the helm of his uncle's boat, falling in love with his life-long mistress, the ocean.

Even at that early age, he was looking to escape to her. When he was six or seven, the neighbours of Southport called Tony's parents in a panic, telling them they could see their son over the broadwater, sailing solo out beyond the bar. The seaway was considered treacherous in those days, before it was contained with rockfill some years later.

'I knew exactly what I was doin',' Tony protested when he got a hiding for his audacious afternoon caper. 'The tide was comin' in and I was just tackin' against it. Besides, I had my life jacket on…'

Scoldings didn't stop him. The young tearaway was often running off, either sailing alone, fishing or taking canoes or surfboards to the long, languid creeks around his home that ran down to the ocean.

'He's going to get lost,' his uncle would grumble. 'We'd better take the sail off that thing to stop him from scarping off like that.'

'But I like it out there,' Tony would say, defending himself to his mother. 'It's a beautiful green colour, there are dolphins and I can be by myself.'

Tony's mom would tear her hair out when her Huck Finn still hadn't come home long after dark; his siblings would go out in search just before Tony would saunter in with his catch of the day, squid or creatures he had discovered in the waterways around his home. His grandmother started calling him 'the vagabond', a nickname that must have subconsciously stuck because it would presage the rest of his life.

It was his eldest sister, Denise, who introduced Tony to surfing. At seven, he was standing on a 10-foot balsa surfboard on the estuaries around his home and paddling down those shark-infested watercourses to the ocean. And it was there, in front of the Southport life-saving club, that Denise taught him to ride the sea. Sometimes, she would pile all the kids, cousins and neighbours, plus 'the two old tanks [surfboards]' into the car and drive up and down the coast, in search of the best breaks between Tweed Heads and Burleigh. It was the only escape from their high-wattage household, where their abusive father fought his demons with the help of a bottle.

The Eltheringtons were far from well off, but with sandwiches and some of her father's sausages for a beach barbecue, Denise showed Tony a happy, free life; a different world.

'That's how it was. There was no TV. Only mosquitoes, mud crabs and beer. And the ocean.'

And so the boy began to live by the ocean's ebbs and flows.

Tony was a 'goofy footer' – he surfed with his right foot forward – which made him different from most other surfers. From an early age, he was able to develop an especially refined style that made him even more special.

At eleven, he was surfing alongside, and holding his own against, much older boys, some of whom would go on to become big names in Australian and international surfing: Michael Peterson, Peter Drouyn, Paul Neilsen, Keith Paull, Wayne Deane, Dick van Straalen and Wayne 'Rabbit' Bartholomew.

They were a hard-core crew, the best surfers who dominated the country's best break. And they protected their spot. Surfing is a tribal sport, and very localised, and the hierarchy of talent is topped by enforcers of the rules. The much younger Tony had earned kudos and respect in this line-up.

It was a small community in which everyone knew

everyone, and the Eltheringtons, proud of their Irish roots, were making a name for themselves. Not only because of young Tony's wild ways, but also because they'd developed a curious reputation: for saving people.

Tony's mother, Dawn, was known to take in and foster unwanted special needs babies who had been abandoned by their parents. But it was around 1963, when she rescued a little girl from drowning in a local creek, that she made local headlines.

The neighbourhood children had all learnt to paddle their surfboards in a pool of deep water in the creek, but it was considered a dangerous spot. Often there was news of someone not resurfacing from it.

That year, a young girl had gone down and those attempting a rescue had given up. But Dawn refused to accept that the child was gone; she plugged on and kept diving. Eventually, she pulled the little girl up out of the creek and Tony watched in some disgust as the child puked in his mother's mouth while being resuscitated. Bringing her back to life made his mother a hero in the town, but his father was not keen on the public acclaim.

Then, around 1969, Tony's older brother, Kim – nicknamed Bowie – saved a man and a woman from drowning in the surf at Main Beach over the Christmas holidays. The boy noticed that the couple was in trouble behind the breakers; he dropped his surfboard and swam out to them, bringing them in one at a time. He was fourteen.

For his heroic effort, Bowie got a medal from the Governor of Queensland, a watch and a crate of Coca-Cola.

With their homegrown steel and determination, the Eltheringtons practically carved out the Aussie 'can do' attitude. But back at home, the relationship between Tony's parents had become radioactive. The constant state of tension in the family house on the waterway came to an end in a bitter divorce and resulted in his mother's sudden departure for Surfers Paradise, further up the Gold Coast. Tony was shattered by the ordeal and dropped out of the Southport state school. 'Didn't last long there.'

He was ten years old.

For two years, Bowie, who was eighteen months older than Tony, raised him. The boys moved between family members, and they would continue to look in on their father, still a violent alcoholic. 'We had our issues over the years, but I still loved him the day he died.'

Throughout, the women in Tony's life remained steadfast – his grandmother ('my angel'), who lived until she was 103, his mother and sisters Denise and Kerry. But angry, shaken and deeply distracted by the disintegration of his family, Tony would take solace in the sea, sailing up and down the coast and perfecting his backhand tube-riding.

He was a loner, a solitary figure on the beaches at Burleigh Heads, a boy with a wounded heart. Often lost in introspection, he had difficulty expressing himself and so chose reticence. Even as a child, this gave him an aura of mystery and evanescence. The story of the boy, with his love of the ocean and his talents on its crests, started to take on the romance of a wild fable.

With the ocean shaping his life, Tony, at age eleven, started to use his understanding of its dynamics to shape surfboards. It would birth an uncommonly proficient talent that he would perfect with time, and which became his lifelong trade. It would also deliver a devoted following.

One day, young Tony walked into the shop of the famous Neilsen brothers, Paul and Rick, who would go on to own thirty of their iconic surf stores around Australia (and then lose them all). Rick was known then as the best board-shaper on the Gold Coast. With money from his paper round, Tony asked for a board. His paltry offering wasn't enough to cover the set price so he agreed to work it off by taking on the job of ding-repair boy.

He started an apprenticeship under his mentors Richard Harvey and Dick van Straalen. It was a unique kind of schooling under the grandmasters of surfing: they taught him 'not to lock his brain into the conventional', but to 'keep it open'. Using his understanding of the sea from sailing, of watching how a boat or a dolphin glides through water, he began to stumble on new ways of making and shaping boards. He also knew to experiment on his own boards, not on others', and so progressively learnt from his mistakes.

It's said that his boards were fashioned from old longboards using his mother's kitchen utensils. The results, at five dollars a board, became highly prized after a few short years and eventually earned a badge of distinction. They became known as 'Gold Coast Gold'.

At that time, *The Doris Day Show* was a massively popular international television hit. With Tony's sun-bleached blond locks, film-star good looks and coy smile, Paul Neilsen couldn't resist the bait and he playfully christened him 'Doris'. The nickname would be riveted to him from then on – Doris Eltherington.

At twelve, Doris surfed for the first time competitively. It was at the Duranbah Beach club contest in New South Wales on a board of his own making. Since he was under age, Doris surfed against fifteen-year-olds, and when he unexpectedly won the competition, the organisers were reluctant to give the trophy to a kid. He was given a leftover case of Coke instead, a stock prize back then, it seems.

Doris went on to win a fair few contests on Australia's east coast in the early '70s. He placed third in the national schoolboy championships behind Wayne Bartholomew (who would go on to become World Champ) and Bruce Raymond (who would head up Quiksilver). At sixteen, he was picked as part of the Queensland team to compete in Australian Titles in Western Australia. When he couldn't scrape together the money to fly there, he hitchhiked the more than 2,000 miles across the continent. He lived with the Aborigines on the Nullabor Plain and slept in his board bag on the side of the road during the cold desert nights.

The surf was enormous at Margaret River and Doris was overwhelmed. He couldn't feel the spirit of surfing at the event and the purist in him was disappointed with the aggressive, combative mood. He lost his first heat and hitchhiked home.

Doris didn't like competition. Despite his talent and hunger to test his nerve against a worthy challenge, his heart wasn't in it. He hated the megaphones, the prizes, the dog-eat-dog philosophy. Winning wasn't important to him and left him feeling depressed and empty.

For him, surfing was selfish. It was his obsession, a drug. But it was also his cleansing, a release, a meditation. 'It helps with life's problems. It's better than any psychologist.'

He didn't want to have to think about how he was going to surf. And he couldn't conceive of getting paid to do it. 'Once yer up and ridin' and yer get that first wave, you'll never turn yer back on the ocean again. You keep lookin' for that hit. All my life I've wondered, "What wave is around that corner?"'

Doris's life was on the water. He felt more at home out

there than anywhere else. And so the dreamer became the drifter. When he was seventeen, he built a Ferro-cement yacht with his brother on a friend's spare lot. In between surf contests – he won the Queensland state title two years in a row – he would sail it alone for days, wrestling with his internal conflicts.

He found drugs and alcohol – 'It was the '70s'. Despite the termination of his formal schooling, he had always been an avid reader and he embarked on a path of extraordinary self-education that would continue throughout his lifetime. Stopping school by no means stunted his intellectual ambition.

Those close to him noticed how he would swing between gentler, more pensive moods and angry introspection that would leave him anxious and restless. His hunger for adventure would be fuelled by pioneer surfers' tempting tales of a new place to surf, one with gloriously clean, virgin lefts, the size and beauty of which simply had to be seen to be believed. The stories came with two attractions for the teenager: geographical remoteness and the whisper of an exotic locale.

The 'new place' was Indonesia.

Doris became quietly obsessed with getting there to experience it for himself.

He scraped together his savings and at nineteen found himself deliriously surfing in Bali's Uluwatu and Padang Padang. In doing so, he created a name for himself – not so much as a competitor, but as an artist whose style was something beautiful to behold. He'd also discovered his soul place, somewhere that seemed to fill the loneliness within. Whilst over the next few years he would also make his way to the famous surf spots in Hawaii – to North Shore, Sunset

Beach and Pipeline – it would always be Indonesia that had his heart.

Doris was a real contender in Australian surfing, but he walked away from it all at the age of twenty-three after a single event that changed everything for him. He was surfing the quarter-finals of the 1979 Bells Beach Surf Classic in the Australian state of Victoria when he defeated his idol, Wayne Lynch. 'It was a random day and pretty irrelevant to him, but I had looked up to him my whole life.'

Like Alexander the Great, who wept after his greatest battle because there were no more worlds to conquer, Doris felt a profound emptiness in the victory. In shock, he picked up his board and left immediately. He drove the thousand miles home alone.

The experience had a deep effect on Doris. He disappeared from the surfing scene, leaving people wondering and whispering. He took to his back yard where he built himself a steel yacht, a 36-foot cutter sailboat, which he would sail alone to the Barrier Reef and beyond to New Caledonia, Vanuatu and New Guinea.

He married his childhood girlfriend, Lesley, a beautiful model whom he'd known since he was sixteen, but it was a troubled marriage. They would have a daughter, Taryn, in 1983, but a settled home life could never help him quiet the monster within.

In fact Doris could barely endure domestic everyday life. The ocean called him constantly and while he shaped his increasingly sought-after boards on shore, he would always find ways to escape, either sailing solo voyages or finding work only the ocean could offer.

When his marriage to Lesley broke down completely, Doris met Suzanne, with whom he would later have two children,

Jarrah and Madeline. They married and opened a surf shop on the Gold Coast. The money he made over those five years was average. The custom boards he moulded were not.

Some were more traditional, made from styrofoam and epoxy, others eccentric: he fashioned wooden boards like the originals, with vacuum-packed timber and no fibreglass in them. Once, he even made a board from plastic roof covers.

'To make someone a board, I first have to sum them up – surf with them to read their technique. Most people talk it up first, but then I watch to see how they really surf. I always add little bits in there that they can't see; a trick or two that I know will help them. If you make a guy the best board he's ever ridden, you've got him pretty much for life.'

While Doris gave a sedentary existence his best shot, he felt like a fly in treacle. The raw power of the ocean would always call and he would have to answer the call to harness its bounty. The family lived on a river within walking distance of the main beach, his yacht anchored out front.

'Suzanne would sit me down for a "we have to talk" discussion. I'd sit and look at her, but I'd also look right past her. I knew the swell was big, and that the surf was breaking up river. I'd let her talk but I'd also watch that boat. The moment it turned just a little, I knew that the tide had too, and that the surf was on. I had that place so dialled. I'd jump up and say, "I've gotta go."'

And he had to go. Doris felt imprisoned on land. Eventually, when he could bear it no longer, he decided to sell his shop, bundle up his family, including Taryn, and sail off to East Java for a life on the sea. Indonesia had won him.

But a peripatetic existence is not for everyone. After six months Suzanne had been beaten by the rudimentary life offered in a third-world country. Deciding that the children needed a roof over their heads and a proper education, she left one night without telling Doris and returned to Australia.

Doris didn't go after them.

Now, three decades later, Doris is a man who knows these waters as well as anyone. The winds and the waves; the vagaries of the currents. He's a good man to have on your side if you're lost in the ocean.

11.30AM TO 12.30PM
TENTH HOUR IN THE WATER

The sky is the colour of ash. It has cleared somewhat and appears lighter. Since I started counting at around 9am, I figure it must be around noon now.

Halfway through the day, I think. The boat won't be far away now.

Then a squall comes up out of nowhere. It creeps up on me – a bank of solid dark granite. I only notice it a few minutes before it hits.

'Where in hell did you come from?' I shout as grey sheets of rain descend. I hear thunder rolling, but it still seems some distance away. The wind has whipped up the sea again and I'm being thrown about through the swells. One particularly deep trough pitches me on my side and salt water again swamps my eyes and ears, streams through my nostrils and tears through my throat. Noiseless lightning flickers above me like flash photography.

The instant storm unsettles me. Oh no, this is not good. This is not good. It stokes up my lingering anxiety once again. If this storm lasts too long my boat won't see me.

At the same time I know that I need to get some rainwater on my tongue. My saliva is a thick, grey, glue-like paste and my tongue feels five sizes too big inside my mouth. I can't remember when last I swallowed comfortably, painlessly.

The elements and my body have conspired to bring me back to present reality. While negotiating the upsurges of water and what feels like sideways rain, I'm struck by a second round of debilitating cramps. Pain fires up the back of my legs, shoots through my hamstrings and calves and causes my feet to curl up like birds' claws.

115

I yell out in agony.

Leaning forward in the water, I grab my toes and try to stretch out my legs as I've done before. The spasm is excruciating and travels like a spark up my body. Again, I sink down into the water.

I'm going to start cramping up so badly, I'm not going to be able to swim any longer, I think. It's going to be horrible – I'll die in pain, unable to pull myself above the waterline.

Miraculously, the cramps release and I resurface, slowly pointing and flexing my feet. But the cramping has left me enervated. I'm too tired to feel sadness, too exhausted to feel anger.

And still, the ocean around me is relentless. It doesn't give me a second's rest.

I've been going for around ten hours now, I calculate. It's the most solid stretch of activity I've ever done. My Comrades run took eight hours; the cycle races between six and eight. This is uncharted territory.

Almost instantly all positive thoughts abandon me and I begin to feel overwhelmed by my helplessness again. I feel incredibly alone.

I look around. The wave heights are rising yet again, and for the most part I can't see over them. When I do get glimpses beyond, steel-grey water stretches to the horizon.

I look down at my chest and arms beneath the water's surface. My skin is changing colour. It's chalky and has started to wrinkle like crêpe paper. I splay my fingers; they're swollen and shrivelled and my wedding ring is beginning to get lost in folds of what looks like old decaying flesh.

'Dead man's hands,' I say aloud. It reminds me of when my schoolfriend Greg McKenzie and I, eighteen and innocent of these things, found a dead body washed up on the beach at Chaka's Rock on the north coast of KwaZulu-Natal. The sight of a man's body that had been in water for some time horrified and upset us.

My body will look like that.

Fatigue and the monotony of my own thoughts are taking their toll. Suddenly, the ocean feels as if it is closing in.

I'm held captive by these walls of water. And by my solitude.

I feel overcome.

THE NAGA LAUT
12.27PM

The rain beats down on the ocean, falling with a hushing sound in sheets that move over the boat like a stage curtain between scenes. The *Naga Laut*'s bow dips and rises through the swells that are now increasing in size as the boat carves its way back out to sea.

Tony Singleton, sitting cross-legged on the top deck, looks back over his shoulder at the receding islands. The shoreline has almost vanished, disappeared as if never seen. A grey smudge is all that remains on the horizon. The wind is high and unusually cold, bringing opaque walls from ahead.

The men of the *Naga Laut* are setting off into the unknown, not daring to think how this day will end.

There's a pain in Tony's chest, a swelling physical pain that sometimes feels as if it will come up and cut off his air supply. Rainwater running down the nape of his neck is a new, strange sensation and he thinks back momentarily to last night's head-shaving episode. He can hear Brett's mischievous teasing and he swallows to try to ease the constriction in this throat.

No-one speaks. The eight have taken up their watch around the boat, crouching, jackets or towels hooded over their heads, staring out at the churning ocean. Today, of all days, the weather is against them.

Not Arch, Tony is thinking to himself. Not Arch.

Tears well up in his eyes. He can't stop thinking back to the safety briefing that surf-charter organiser Gideon Malherbe gave him and JM on their first trip way back in 2002.

'Fall overboard on the crossing at night and you're a goner,' Gideon had warned. He'd spelt out the dangers then and insisted they make use of their life jackets; painstakingly he went through the rules, making sure they were aware of the risk of all maritime misadventures.

'Forget about that for now, it's not going to help the situation,' someone said when it was raised during the search of the boat.

But now Gideon's words echo in Tony's head: 'You're a goner...'

The mental seesaw will last much of the day for Tony. He'll fight the feelings of overwhelming helplessness and pessimism, the dips of imagining the worst; instead, he will talk himself into believing that Brett is out there, somewhere in that great grey heaving mass, and that they will find him.

He looks down at the pair of Celestron binoculars in his lap. He bought them in Singapore on his first surf charter ten years ago; they've come with him on every trip since. These will be his eyes today in this appalling visibility. These will find Brett.

'We're coming for you,' Tony whispers to his friend under his breath, 'we're coming.'

JM, also on the starboard side, is quietly assessing his muddle of emotions. He feels marginally better now that he has started putting the word out. It makes him feel less alone. Less helpless.

He waited as long as he could for Louise Killeen to reach Anita back in Cape Town, and then as the boat pulled out of Tua Pejat harbour he quickly typed up the first world bulletin of what had happened on Facebook.

Brett Archibald, a man from Camps Bay, has fallen overboard in the dark, in the middle of the Mentawai Straits.

119

He fed it out as stark fact, but added a desperate plea for prayers that Brett would be found – a cry in the cyber wilderness.

He copied the same message onto WhatsApp and sent it to his wife Tessa and to his brother Pierre, the latter a Reuters reporter and a widely connected international surfer. Surfers, he'd reasoned, should know about this. One of their kin was lost and perhaps with the tangled global social networks and the quirky communities that technology has spawned, the word would be out there to alert other surfers, even other boats in the area.

JM also sent a message to Gigs Cilliers, a friend and radio personality who gives the surf reports for a local South African radio broadcaster. He'll send text updates when he can, he tells Tessa, and asks her to upload them onto Facebook.

'We have to get this wider attention,' JM commented to Banger as he typed into his cellphone. 'We need much more support in our search.'

During the course of this day, the live updates will go viral; the news about a man lost in the ocean off Indonesia will spread rapidly around the world. Media in far-flung places will get hold of it and soon Brett's story will be headline news in many countries.

But JM is not thinking about that now. He pulls his cap down low over his eyes to keep out the rain and he scans the water in silence. The initial adrenaline of searching the boat for Brett and readying the *Naga Laut* for a return crossing has dissipated. Shock has given way to a residual feeling of anxiety and a surreal detachment.

He looks at the clouds hanging low over the boat and feels the wind cutting across his face. The fitful sea, which has the boat bumping and lurching through it, stretches on endlessly. With nothing in sight but the white furrows of the wave tops, JM is struck by a profound sense of isolation.

The only constant is the rushing of the ocean.

'Where in hell's name did you go over, Brett?'

He stares at the choppy swell. He has a flashback to his high school Scouting days with Brett; to a weekend survival course they'd done as sixteen-year-olds. They'd camped together but it was Brett who was always the leader: always in charge, always capable, always resourceful. JM recalls the one-mile swim they did that weekend and Brett's fierce competitive streak.

He'll be swimming, JM tells himself.

He also reminds himself that Brett was a conscript in the apartheid government's defence force. He underwent survival training on his officers' course. It will have triggered his brain into *vasbyt* – pure survival mode. JM's confidence is building. As long as he's not hurt, he can do this. We just have to find him before his strength runs out.

His strength.

JM has surfed with Brett and knows all about his friend's brawn in the waves. But he also knows that Brett caught his flight after only two hours' sleep; he's spent 54 hours travelling, wilted for hours in the stinking heat of Padang, and eaten a dodgy meal from a not-so-clean village. He also vomited for a couple of hours last night. The others who were sick were decimated by it. How long could Brett last, exhausted, dehydrated and with no fuel in his system?

Ridgy wants to pace the captain's cabin, but it's too small and he needs to appear calm and collected. The captain returns to the *Naga Laut* in the tender. It has bounced through the volatile sea and he alights just as Ridgy and Yanto are poring over the ocean chart yet again. After a brief discussion with Yanto, the skipper stalks off to the wheelhouse.

'What happened?' Banger puts his head into the cabin.

'He reported it!' is Yanto's peremptory reply. 'They have to tell immigration because you are foreign.'

'Will they send the coastguard?'

Banger's next question is met with a shallow shrug and Yanto turns away.

While the storm rages outside, another is raging inside Ridgy's head. He's frustrated at the lack of decisive action.

'What's the boat's radio frequency?' he keeps asking curtly. The international distress frequency is 1215 and he wants to broadcast a Mayday. But Yanto and the skipper look at him blankly, leaning forward every now and again to turn the knob on the radio. They're like actors who don't know their lines.

Static screeches through the small room.

Ridgy hates this kind of inefficiency. He grits his teeth. This is going to take clear-headed thinking, quick decision-making and calm.

'Tell the captain we must sail this line, a little south of what we did last night from Padang,' he explains firmly. 'That should take into account possible drift with the current, right?'

Yanto nods mutely, then he and the skipper talk in low tones.

'I'll be here to make sure we keep on track.'

The strain on the crew and the discord it has caused are obvious.

The satellite phone rings and Yanto automatically hands it to Ridgy. It's the Australian coastguard in Darwin returning his call.

'If the captain has told their port authority and it's in Indo waters, we can't do anything, mate,' the man's voice is professional but his tone seems to indicate that he understands the misery this message might impart.

'You can't help us?' Ridgy is stunned. 'But this is an emergency…'

'We can operate in those waters but only if we get an official request from the Indonesian authorities. We'd need to wait for that…'

Ridgy knows that Lulu has been trying to reach someone, anyone, in Jakarta and Padang. There's been no word from her.

'Okay, thank you. We'd like to stay in touch, if that's okay?'

'Sure, mate. We'll monitor things too. Good luck.'

Ridgy goes out onto the deck and stares from the stern out at the lumpy sea. He's quietly confident that the 2.30am spot he's circled, the time he last saw Brett, is good. He's less certain of the proposed 4am one. 'If we continue on this line, there is a chance, an outside chance, that we'll see him,' he tells himself.

The sea is shifting and moving in a motion that seems curiously fast and slow at the same time. It makes him dizzy. He fixes a line of sight that can't be more than 150 metres ahead and repeatedly imagines things floating in the dips and troughs. Blinking and focusing his concentration, he looks again.

There's nothing but a seething sea.

Ridgy thinks about the book he's reading. Laura Hillenbrand's *Unbroken* is the true story of Olympic runner Louis Zamparini's ordeals after surviving a plane crash in the Pacific during World War II. It's an extraordinary tale of endurance.

If that guy could survive, Brett, so can you, Ridgy says to his friend in his head.

He reflects on his sometimes prickly relationship with Brett. Their playful rivalry and mutual challenging has existed since school, but it has never gone beyond just that. He takes a deep breath as he contemplates the traverse ahead.

They've passed a point of no return. Ridgy makes a mental promise that they will pursue this with dogged determination. He's convinced of Brett's incredibly strong will. And the luck that always seems to befall him.

'If there's one guy who can get out of shit, Brett, it's you.' This time he murmurs the words out loud.

12.30PM TO 1.30PM
ELEVENTH HOUR IN THE WATER

I feel dreadfully cold. Despite the warmth of the water, my body temperature is dropping and I'm getting colder and colder. I've started to shiver. My teeth are chattering; they're catching the sides of my ever-swelling tongue and I can taste a faint metallic swirl of blood. My lips are swollen and dry, like coconut husks.

My concern about the cramps is slowly ratcheting up into anxiety.

If they keep coming thick and fast, you won't be able to control them. They *will* drown you.

I imagine my entire body cramping up: my legs, then my arms and shoulders, then my hands. Will I simply seize up? Will my body fail me after all this, after making it this far?

Again I contemplate how it will happen. Death by drowning. Will I sink beneath the surface? And then? I think about breathing in water. Would that be it? Water instead of air in my lungs. Black out. White light. Dead?

The rain begins to soften and after several minutes, it stops completely. The rain clouds overhead move off and it looks surprisingly bright. It might even clear up, I think to myself.

You've got to see something now, I tell myself, but waves are still breaking around me and I can't see very far in any direction. A boat. A boat must be crossing the Strait around this time. Or perhaps you'll see land…

But there's nothing. Just water.

Then, out of the corner of my eye, I think I see something. What's that? It's peripheral, something fleeting, and then it's

125

gone. I turn in a circle. My exhausted arms pull my frame around as fast as they can. I'm desperate to catch sight of it again.

A coconut? A tree trunk?

I start to swim desperately towards whatever it is that I think I've seen. I stop and look frantically around, but the waves are too high. I can't see beyond their summits.

Is that it again? I can't get a sense of scale – is it a box floating there or could it be a boat in the distance? I swirl around and around. Only sea.

I'm confused and highly agitated. For the first time, it feels as if my emotions are going to bubble up out of control. Are my eyes playing tricks on me? Am I beginning to hallucinate, lose all sense of reality and perspective?

Again I think I see something a few metres ahead and to my left. I stop, focus for several seconds and once more embark on a frenzied swim in that direction. Distress rises from my stomach; it's a very powerful sensation, moving from my belly through my chest and into my throat. My sightings are so frequent that I realise they can't be real. I'm clutching at straws, growing anxious.

A descent into madness starts with seeing things that aren't there...

My legs ache from exhaustion. The weight of my limbs makes me feel clumsy and ungainly. My lungs feel scalded. Deep down, I don't know how much longer I can go on. An undercurrent of desperation seeps into every sinew. I have to stop it before it turns into full-blown hysteria. That kind of fear is not easily overcome.

Calm yourself down. I slowly counsel myself, trying to sound measured, trying to dial back to being logical. You're desperate to find something to hold on to, but it's not going to happen. Don't get excited by these visions. There's nothing there. The ocean is playing tricks on you.

I take out the hotel key folder from my pocket and tear off another thumbnail of paper from the till slip. Half is left. The paper floats for a minute, white against the sea foam, and is swiftly sucked away before me.

You're still moving in the right direction, I placate myself. You're still going with the current. Remember, currents are lifelines. That has to count for something.

THE BARRENJOEY
TUA PEJAT HARBOUR
12.48PM

Doris is in the wheelhouse when Pete Inglis comes through the door.

'Have you figured out where he could be, skipper?' Pete asks politely. It's another attempt at ameliorating the strained chemistry on board. Pete senses that the waters through which Doris have sailed run deep. He's doing his best to bring calm to the situation.

Doris is a hostage to his past. People had disappointed him and he, in turn, had disappointed others so he'd chosen to forge his own path in Indonesia, the only place where he believed he could lay to rest his personal ghosts. He sought to be *sindiri* – the Bahasa word for 'alone' or 'set apart' – solo on the sea.

'Because it's peaceful. You've got space. There's no-one annoying ya,' he would explain.

From the minute he experienced the exquisite thrill of surfing, he'd also been deeply driven by the search for new waves. He was bored by the money and braggadocio that characterised competitive surfing, and instead sought out remote pockets and isolated places where on a certain day, with the right wind and swell direction, he could experience a ride like no other. It's an impulse he still pursues with resolute dedication.

This fascination overtook his closest relationships, proving sufficiently powerful that when his wife and children left Bali in 1999, he remained.

In response, he went on a bender of monstrous proportions. It lasted four years.

Some believed back then that Doris Eltherington had a death wish. Death was certainly something with which he flirted.

One day in 2001 while others were walking out of the water at Padang Padang beach, Doris was determined to take on a dying swell. A rogue wave smashed him down in a wipeout of such force that his board slammed onto his right femur and broke it clean in half.

'My leg was still attached to my leash and was bangin' me in the back of my head,' he told Matt George for an article in *The Surfer's Journal*. 'I thought it was someone else. One more wave and I would've been a goner.'

Pulled from the waves by fellow surfers, he was evacuated to hospital. It took ten excruciating hours before an epidural was stuck into his back to dull the pain. The result was a titanium right leg held together by fifteen pins and a scar that runs the length of the limb. He was lucky, doctors told him. Had it been a compound break, he would have died.

Then, a year later, there was a wipeout of another kind. It was just after the 2002 terrorist bombing in a Bali bar. (Doris had left Kuta, the tourist area where the device was detonated in a backpack, just twenty minutes before the blast.) He was inconsolable. He'd known some of the 202 people killed, many of them Australians. A further 240 people had been horribly injured. Grief-stricken Doris raced his motorcycle down a steep hill during flood-filled monsoon weather. His brakes failed on the soft-mud road and he careened towards a cliff edge with a fatal drop. Hitting a tree face-first saved him. But only just.

The accident caused severe head injuries. It left him with a smashed lower jaw, a crushed larynx and a slit throat. Denpasar hospital doctors called his daughter Taryn on the

Gold Coast that night to warn her that they didn't think he was going to make it. Displaying his customary doggedness, Doris clawed his way back, but the recovery was long and agonising. 'You don't have nine lives, Doris,' his friends told him. 'You have nineteen!'

Taryn begged her father to return to Australia after the incident so that she could look after him, but Doris wouldn't leave his beloved Indonesia. 'It's a place where everyone smiles,' he told her. It was less crowded, cleaner and more consistent than any other surf haunts, he declared, not to mention cheap and, oh yes, very beautiful. 'Besides, I like the Indos. They're resilient. They've been beaten up by the Dutch, the Japanese and English for 400 years; they've endured earthquakes, volcanoes and tsunamis and they've lived through uprisings, coups, bombings and financial melt-downs. And they're pretty cheerful on it! I've been through a lot of that with 'em. This is my home.'

The motorcycle accident was a turning point, however. Doris realised his life was out of control; he knew the demons were close to defeating him. It was time to clean up his act – if not for himself, then for his children with whom he also had some damage to repair. He disregarded his naysayers. 'If someone told me, "You'll never achieve that", it was like my personal start gun. I went, "Oh really?" I'm not one to give up. Failin' is not on.'

Doris stopped drinking and started working on salvage operations from Bali's Benoa harbour, but most importantly he reached out to his estranged family. His children rushed at the opportunity to reform the bond with their father, while his extended family patiently listened as he attempted a deeply personal goal: to communicate and explain the deepest, darkest parts of himself.

Then one day in 2004, Martin Daly, while on business in Bali, ran into an energetic Doris. Knowing he was talking to one of the best seamen he'd ever met, Daly decided to overlook Doris's disreputable behaviour and ignore the warnings that were whispered to him behind hands. Daly offered Doris a job captaining one of the charter boats on his burgeoning surf charter business in the Mentawais. Doris clung to the offer like a life raft.

For eight years he sailed the Mentawais for Daly. His employer soon found that not only had he found one of the best sailors around, but Doris was also a highly principled individual. Unpredictable and unorthodox sometimes, he was also clever, arch and witty. He lived with a heap of regrets, but he'd emerged with a kind of peace and understanding.

For his part, Doris worked hard to rid himself of the stigma and quietly nurtured a new plan: to own his own charter some day. He also learnt how to become a father again and, over the years, a grandfather. He suppressed his worst fear – being confined in claustrophobic, crowded airplanes – and took every opportunity to fly back to Australia to reconnect with his kids.

But if Indonesia was home, the Mentawais had his heart. Doris fell deeply in love with the glorious seascapes, the island life, even with its hardships, and the people, and he returned to his original crush: the sea. So when the 2004 Boxing Day tsunami demolished this part of the world, he was profoundly affected. Over weeks and months, he worked tirelessly with Daly's surf charter fleet and other surf charter boats to rescue survivors and offer emergency aid throughout the traumatised archipelago.

Some say Doris didn't sleep for days.

By 2012 Doris had saved enough to buy his own boat. The *Rajah Elang*, a 65-foot surf charter vessel, was his floating palace and a chance to fulfil a fantasy: to run his own business in the Mentawais. Apart from the charters, the aid operations were central to Doris – small redemptive acts that helped him clear his conscience of all that had happened before.

Locals came to know him as unconventional but solid, and when they came up to him on the streets of Padang to take his hand in thanks and praise, he would simply smile modestly. Inside, he'd carry their approval around with him as totems.

True to family tradition, Doris had, it seemed, also cultivated a reputation for rescue.

Now, the two captains, Doris and Pete, bend over the ocean charts that the former has spread across the wooden wheel, and for some minutes the silence deepens. Two captains, a single intention.

'If the *Naga Laut* got into Tua Pejat at around 5am, and he went over two hours or so before that, he must be somewhere around here,' Doris says at last and he puts three weathered fingers over two squares of the chart.

'With a little bit of drift, he could be a little further east,' says Pete. 'Round about here, do you think? How far out is that?'

'About 25 or 30 miles. I'm goin' to take the tinny out to there,' Doris's forefinger falls heavily on the creased paper, 'to check what we can see in this filthy weather.'

Doris moves immediately to his radio and Pete takes the opportunity to duck out.

'Suley, Suley, this is *Barrenjoey*. Do yer copy?'

The voice that comes through the speaker is familiar. Reliable, solid, assertive. Doris has recently been working with Steven Sewell, also a charter captain from Western Australia, on a 127-day run in the Strait of Malacca. Their boats worked in tandem along gridlines for an oil-prospecting project.

'Suley! Mate, I'm in the shit here. The *Naga Laut* has lost a *bule* overboard.'

'Jesus Christ, when?'

'Not sure, but they think it was around 3am. A South African.'

'That's quite a while ago. Whaddya reckon?'

'I think he's swimmin'. The weather's up to shit, but there's been no sun…'

'Where's the *Naga Laut* now?'

'I have no idea. I saw them sail out of here about two hours ago.'

The men discuss the known facts and Doris confirms that he's been in touch with other boats in the area. He has to mobilise a search, he knows that now, and so he has called in the cavalry, the small network of charter boats who rely on one another in emergencies. He has contacted John McGroder, owner of the *Barrenjoey*, who is now on his family catamaran, the *Amandla*, with his wife Belinda and two sons, Fynn and Duke. He has also called Martin Daly, owner of many surf charters and Doris's one-time employer. Martin is about to fly out of Perth.

'I tell yer, Suley, this guy's alive. Belinda McGroder's been in touch with Chantal Malherbe – she organised the *Naga Laut* trip from South Africa. He's about 51 but he's fit – he's a cyclist or somethin'. He'll be swimmin' – I know it.'

'It's pretty shitty conditions, mate, but there's only one way to find out,' Sewell offers. 'Call me later. Let me know if you find him.'

1.30PM TO 2.30PM
TWELFTH HOUR IN THE WATER

My thoughts are becoming dangerous to me now. I feverishly search the sea and sky around me for distractions. The clouds above look battered.

I have to take charge of the looming feelings of frenzy or my mind could turn figment into fact. If that happens, I'll crack up. Shriek and howl, panic and flail.

I feel as if I'm in a game of Tetris, the cubes suddenly falling faster and faster, interlocking and intersecting.

I deliberately draw my attention to the back of my T-shirt which floats sometimes heavy and inconvenient around the top of my shoulders and at other times slaps against the back of my neck. It's sticking, like a cold, heavy second skin. It's causing some discomfort. Every now and again, I imagine the shirt coming to life, the fabric wrapping around my throat and choking the rest of the air out of me.

The weight of the waterlogged cotton pulls my head back every time I go through a wave. The constant tugging is tiring and makes my neck feel awkward and uncomfortable.

Psychologically it's also a constraint. I'm certain that it's pulling me backwards, keeping me from making progress.

I tied the shirt over my head to protect my scalp in last night's rainstorm, but also because I was afraid of getting sunburned. But the sun has abandoned today. A thin and miserable rain is falling again.

At last I decide to get rid of my T-shirt. It's a burden. The decision is quick, precise, definite. I hurriedly untie the knot at the back of my head, my legs working harder since I don't have my arms to support me, and I gather as much strength into my right arm as I can muster. I throw the T-shirt several metres ahead of me and watch as the current drags it off.

I feel an instant surge of regret.

'Was that the wisest thing to do?' I ask out loud.

Part of me wants to swim quickly after it, but that will take energy and I have precious little of that left.

'It's a hindrance,' I remind myself.

I laugh nervously. That old Tom Hanks in *Castaway* – he freaked out when he lost his ball. I know how he felt. That T-shirt has become a friend and now I too am letting it go.

Losing it.

Little by little.

THE NAGA LAUT
1.06PM

'Tony, what happened?'

It's Anita's voice on the satellite phone. The line is crackling and breaking up; he can barely hear her. They might as well be on the moon.

'Was Brett drinking? Who was the last person with him? How did he fall overboard?' Her last question is almost a shout.

Tony moves to the stern of the *Naga Laut* for some privacy. Snowman was the first to answer a call from Brett's wife a few minutes before. The line dropped just as he faced a barrage of her questions. Rocked by the frightened, aggressive tone, he mutely handed the phone to Tony.

'Oh Jesus, Anita, this is so fucking unbelievable. We don't know when he fell over. We only realised it at around eight this morning. But I can tell you that he wasn't drunk – we'd had a few yesterday, but we'd sobered up. Honestly. Five of the guys got food poisoning. Brett was vomiting all night.'

'He didn't call me like he said he would.' Her child-like petulance is overshadowed by what Tony can hear is a hollow despair. He can tell that she's crying too.

'He and Banger were vomiting badly off the side of the boat, Anita. Ridgy saw him up there at around 2.30am, but we were in a wild storm. He must've slipped…'

'Oh my God…' There is a period of silence. Then, 'Tony, please find him. You must…'

The line drops again. Brett's friend since junior school hangs his head in his hands and weeps quietly. His beeping phone diverts his attention. His is the only device receiving text messages, but with only a bar of signal the contact is intermittent.

He'd sent an SMS with news of this hellish predicament to their trip organiser, Chantal, and then before they left Tua Pejat he called her on the satellite phone.

Chantal has never had to deal with such unprecedented misfortune. Initially flustered by the crisis, she quickly pulled herself together. She and her husband Gideon have turned their home office into a hub of instruction between the *Naga Laut* and the ring of potential rescuers. A good friend and former world kneeboard champion, Gigs Cilliers, who knows Brett well, has driven up to Hermanus to help them. Chantal is liaising with her friends Belinda and John McGroder, who run their yacht the *Barrenjoey* as a surf charter in the Mentawais, with Anita in Camps Bay, with Tony and the men on the *Naga Laut* and anyone else out there she can reach.

Having lived in the Mentawais, Chantal and Gideon know the islands well. They also have experience of how Indonesian officialdom works and know they're going to have to rely heavily on the locals. They put out call after call to others they know in the area. They are the *Naga Laut*'s lifeline.

'Have contacted Aussie couple John and Belinda McGroder, friends who live in the islands and know many people. They're contacting other boats,' Chantal's text reads. Tony feels dizzy and queasy. This still feels like a nightmare to him.

The eight men stand in the wind and rain on the open decks of the *Naga Laut* and lose all sense of time. They swap sides now and again but stare silently into the grey swells. They scan through the spray that comes up off the ocean in great swirls. There is nothing else to do but keep watch and confront their thoughts. Despite the silence, there is a feeling of team solidarity on the boat, a comradeship that will bolster them through this day.

Craig pulls his windbreaker around him. He's surprised at how cold it is now, especially since the air was so thick and soupy when they flew in yesterday. Was it only yesterday? He recalls the events of the day before.

Padang's suffocating heat and humidity came as a shock, but Tony assured them that the ocean breezes would cool them once they got onto the boat.

They'd all been sweating profusely when Yanto collected them from the overcrowded airport in Padang. It was close to midday, the hottest time.

They were shattered. Ridgy and Craig had flown from Cape Town to Dubai, where they'd met up with Niall, who'd come in separately from Johannesburg. The three friends had spent their five-hour transit in Dubai with the tenth man intended on the trip Ed Pickles, who lived there. Over a beer, they discussed Ed's awaited pathology results from a suspected melanoma biopsy.

Could that have been the first sign that this trip was jinxed? Wiping his glasses on a towel, Craig considers all the other things that have gone wrong.

They'd travelled on to Jakarta for an overnight layover, but the journey had been unsettled. The humidity, out-of-time body clocks and a clout of jet lag meant that they'd all only caught a couple of hours' sleep.

That night Tony had left his awning and shade-port company, JM his surf gear franchise, and Weyne his retail shop outfitters. They had arrived from Durban's King Shaka Airport. The seven men had rendezvoused for the first time the next morning over a hurried airport hotel breakfast. Then they had made their way, wrapped surfboards at all angles, to catch the hour-long flight to Padang.

Somehow Brett went missing in the airport building. As

they made their way to check-in, he was nowhere to be seen.

'Bloody hell,' Ridgy cursed. 'He got on the bus for the other terminal!'

The first rule of travel – all stick together – had already been broken.

They called Brett on his cellphone and summoned him to rejoin the group. General cursing and ragging followed. For 45 minutes they milled about, checking their boards for any damage before they finally approached the check-in counter.

'This is not your flight, sir,' one of the ground staff told Niall. 'You need to be at Terminal 1…'

'You bunch of muppets,' Brett mocked. 'You need to listen to the chap who has more air miles than all of you put together!'

The race for the shuttle and the human scrum to make the flight left them sweating, dishevelled and stressed all over again. Brett had been right and he wasn't easily going to let them forget it.

But as the plane lifted off for Padang, so did their spirits. The months of anticipation had the men feeling like boys on a field trip again. Even the disappointment of Ed staying behind couldn't dampen the mood. Neither could Padang's third-world chaos. Cyclists, madmen on mopeds and dilapidated kamikaze cars hooted through traffic and screamed across crowded streets. Smothered by languid and sometimes foul-smelling vapours, the men were rescued by Yanto's air-conditioning.

Indonesians, Craig knew, are uniformly courteous and friendly. He'd taken a break from his healthcare marketing company a few years before and spent three months travelling through the East with Louise and his two sons.

Slight people with jet-black hair, chestnut-brown skins and soft eyes, they were all wide smiles and cheerful waves. Their good-naturedness made up for their limited English and the country's sauna-like conditions and offensive smells.

Instead of taking them to the harbour at Teluk Bayur, from where the boat had departed on previous charters, Yanto announced that the *Naga Laut* was berthed in the town's river estuary.

'We leave from the Batang Kuranji tonight.' Yanto talked over his shoulder as he dodged potholes in the road as big as shell craters. 'One problem. We have to wait for tide to rise before we go.'

'And when is high tide?' JM asked.

'About 9 o'clock tonight.' A moped almost connected with his wing mirror, but Yanto hardly noticed.

'Why aren't we going from the harbour?' Tony asked.

'Special surf guide deal. With me, the boat can go from river and we don't have to drive so far to harbour.'

'We've just travelled for 40 hours and had three plane changes to get this far. What are we going to do for nine hours in this shithole?' Ridgy's tone was still amiable, despite his words.

It was a unanimous thought, though, as the shuttle drove past the lopsided shantytowns and crumbling colonial buildings left by the Dutch who'd once come to Indonesia for its pepper and tin. The precarious constructions seemed to Craig to fight for space with the palm trees that stood out of the undergrowth like cockatoos' crests.

'I take you to restaurant near the river and we wait for other guests there too,' Yanto said.

'As long as they have ice cold beer!' Brett shouted loudly from the back of the car. 'Let's get this party started!'

Everyone laughed. 'Yee-haa!' someone cheered.

Yanto dropped them off at a street-side open-air bar, near a building that bore a rather ominous name: The Plan B Hotel. They thought the name hilarious.

The restaurant lived up to their low expectations. An enormous Heineken advert hung from a ceiling grid of acid yellow, orange and green squares that hovered over the bar like a garish '80s dance floor that had been suspended upside down. Indonesian pop music fought its way through roars of static over the restaurant's speakers.

The men chose a table under columned arches, painted alternately in sulphuric mustard and orange, to wait for Banger's arrival from Mauritius and for Snowman to come in from Australia's Gold Coast.

Yanto waved goodbye cheerfully as he launched himself back into the morass of buzzing scooters and diesel-belching buses to take the surfboards and baggage to the boat.

Grunting fans affixed to a sidewall above provided scant relief from the oppressive heat and humidity. Overhead was an incongruous arc of corrugated-iron roofing, an example of the arbitrary building styles that littered the town. Everyone immediately ordered Bintangs. The red star on the label stood out like a bullet between the eyes.

Over the hours of waiting, nostalgia reconnected them. The nine friends shared endless updates about their lives. They talked about surfing, their travels, their wives and kids. GoPros and iPads were pulled out to document their reunion.

'Weyne, buddy, Thursday's your fiftieth. We wish you the best barrel on that day!' Brett shouted across the room.

'Amen to that,' Weyne laughed.

The *Naga Laut* crew meanwhile was completing the final

preparations for the overnight crossing. Because of the late departure, there wouldn't be dinner on the boat, so by late afternoon the group ordered a meal. Most chose a gloopy looking nasi goreng from the grimy, well-fingered menus. JM was the only one who opted for a steamed rice dish with beef and chilli.

At the end of it all, the linoleum-covered table had a regiment of empty Bintangs standing to attention. 'This is the Ten Green Bottles Tour,' Banger quipped as the waitress took a photograph. They all laughed, enjoying the bond of identity the nickname gave. 'Only with Eddie not here, we're nine, I suppose,' Banger corrected himself.

'I can't sit here any more,' Snowman finally declared. 'Let's rather wait on the boat. We can settle in, unpack our boards, get the fins on.'

They all agreed.

It was a short drive to the river where the boat was moored. By now the sun was casting long shadows across the unkempt streets. Zip bags slung over their shoulders, the men disembarked from the van and made their way through the still merciless heat. The stench of sewerage was masked by the sweet smell of woodsmoke from the street vendors.

They found the *Naga Laut* sitting low in the polluted, green-grey water of the river. On the opposite bank, raw concrete boxes masqueraded as buildings between the old brick villas that had once belonged to Dutch merchants. They looked like bomb shelters.

Wooden houses, many on stilts, hunkered beneath battered roofs of tiles or rusty corrugated-iron. Wooden vessels, old barges and small motor launches lolled about in the scummy water that snaked out towards an equally dirty sea.

As the South Africans made their way down the rickety

wooden gangway to the boat, they received a solicitous welcome from the crew.

'Hi, I'm Banger.' The big man thrust his hand like a bear's paw towards the slight Indonesian crewman in boardshorts on the lower deck.

'Jaipur,' the man responded warmly. 'Engineer for boat.'

'*Jou moer*,' Brett teased, laughing uproariously as he came up behind Banger. They all laughed at Brett's play on the usually rude South African colloquialism.

'Hi. Brett – but you can call me Archie.'

One by one, the men introduced themselves to the other four coyly smiling Indonesian crew members. It was a gauche introduction, as the locals had little command of English. 'Skippy', Brett ordained the captain as he shook his hand. Jaipur had introduced his son and deckhand, Anton, and the chef, a grown man with the antithetical-sounding name of 'Boi'. Yanto was the interpreter.

As they boarded, there was another potentially calamitous incident.

Snowman ducked into the *Naga Laut*'s dark interior and was unable to adjust his eyes to the light change. Wanting to avoid a row of high-set cupboards, he didn't see the open hatch that led down to the lower cabins. He pitched forward and promptly fell down the six-step ladder.

'Jesus Christ!' Tony shouted as he ran in from behind. 'Snowman, are you okay?'

Snowman had had a major back operation two years before.

After a short silence there was a groan and a slightly shaken 'I'm okay' from below.

'Jesus, can you imagine?' Niall commented to Ridgy as they made their way down to the cabin. 'Snowman breaking a leg on the first day of our holiday?'

With their boards unpacked, the bags neatly folded under the seats and the men settled in their cabins, they all returned to the top deck to wait for darkness and the rising tide.

Someone plugged an iPod into the boat's sound system. With the soundtrack to their younger days – U2, Pink Floyd, Queen, Rodriguez – playing in the background, the clamminess of the afternoon gave way to a cool, calm evening and the magnificent spectacle of an Indonesian sunset.

Somewhere on the bank, children were flying kites that spread out against the splendour of the orange sky. The men jokingly argued about their altitude.

The night came in soft and warm. Every now and again, they felt a puff of gentle wind on their faces. It gave no hint of the vicious storm that was coming behind it.

Lulu Ridgway is at the driver's door of her car, about to head out for an emergency cigarette run, when Anita's family pulls up.

Loni and Paula Nicolopulos and their daughter Helene, Anita's younger sister by two and a half years, have driven around Table Mountain in silence from Helene's home in Constantia Hills.

The morning is still heavy and dark grey, as if reluctant to get going. The rain has let up to a drizzle when they arrive at the Archibalds' old two-storey Camps Bay house. Brett and Anita bought the property, with its sweeping views across the bay and over the Atlantic, in 2011, shortly after their return from the United Kingdom. They've drawn up plans to demolish the dark, creaking 1960s structure, but the paperwork for their new home is awaiting city council approval. Anita resents the house's dark passages, old fittings and gloomy paintwork. It feels more cold and oppressive in winter somehow, and today it has the air of a funeral parlour.

Lulu closes the car door and walks over to hug Paula and Loni, who seem oblivious to the gentle rain. There is no need for words. They embrace with closed eyes and slowly shake their heads, their shoulders already hunched over from the burden of the news.

Inside, the family comes together in a group embrace at the foot of the stairs. They stand for a few seconds in silence, but the air is punctuated with heavy pulses of their cumulative grief. Louise watches from a few feet away, her head slightly bowed, a witness to a reverential moment.

146

If anyone thinks that a search for Brett is futile, they don't express it. Instead Paula says softly, 'They will find him.'

Anita begins to sob once more. With emotion etched on his face, Loni doesn't trust himself to speak. He simply puts his arms around his eldest daughter.

'Dad.' Anita weeps uncontrollably, betrayed again by her emotions. The angle of her head against his shoulder is already a small signal of her exhaustion.

Louise, Lulu and Anita have spent the last hour trying to shake off the bewilderment that enshrouds the house and to switch instead into operational mode. Louise has Brett's travel pouch. His green travel insurance card and relevant paperwork are spread out before her on the dining-room table.

Lulu, all calm rationality, has Googled a map of the Mentawai Strait and has printed it out. It's the nucleus of a spreading web of papers that, like a police investigation wall, is an attempt at solving this riddle. The map portrays the search area as a relatively small section of a vast region. It makes them feel better.

A laptop is also open on the table and mobile phones are hooked up to their chargers – electrical drips for the lifelines they have become.

'Where are Zara and Jamie?'

Helene, the children's aunt, is a psychologist and drama therapist; she is also known for her practicality and prudence. Her voice now breaks the emotional intensity. No-one answers – they all know the children are going to require kid-glove handling.

Letti points to the closed door of the TV room.

'We haven't told them,' Anita manages to mumble.

Loni and Helene nod in unison. The three of them go into

the TV room and as Helene gently closes the door behind them, the others hear the forced cheer in her voice: 'Hi, guys.'

How this day has been shaken, disrupted from its ordinary course.

At 8am Helene had come out of a yoga class to missed calls and voice messages from her mother and her husband Andrew. The message 'Brett has fallen off the boat' was, she thought, another of Brett's pranks. Helene is close to her brother-in-law and knows and understands him as a perpetual maverick.

'This is a joke, right?' she'd announced as she walked through her Constantia front door. The sight of her mother made her realise immediately that her optimism was grossly misplaced.

To her, the facts still seemed far-fetched. 'It's impossible,' she clucked impatiently to her parents. 'We've only got half the story. Anita's never good at giving information in an emergency. He's fallen off, but got back on. He's hit his head or something. It can't be that serious.'

A follow-up call was like a judge delivering a shock verdict.

Loni and Paula were due to return to Johannesburg today. Now their flights have been quickly cancelled, handbags grabbed. The extended family is coming together in this crisis. Calls are made to cousin Karmen and Luke, the bridal couple from the weekend's celebrations in Stellenbosch. They leave their honeymoon hotel within minutes to come through to Camps Bay, the joy of their own occasion quickly overshadowed.

Anita's aunt, Zenda Stravino, was also at the wedding. She hurriedly leaves a meditation session in a Stellenbosch spa where she and her husband Joe are spending a few days. When Joe notifies her of the call from her sister Paula, with whom she has a close bond, she braves the foul weather to drive the hour to Cape Town despite not knowing the way.

After the initial shock the house in Fiskaal Road is infused with melancholy, but despite the dramatic intensity small pockets quickly form. Louise has been on a long call with the travel insurance company. She has been redirected to an executive in Singapore.

'Mobilising a search depends on in which country Mr Archibald has gone missing,' she's told. 'We'll need to call you back.'

She relays the message to everyone standing around her just as Loni and Helene emerge from the TV room. They all stare at one another in shocked bemusement.

There are nuances of feeling no-one can define. They all seem aware that information will come through today that will deepen its emotional register. It's going to require courage.

'You have to start thinking about money,' Louise ventures gently, taking Anita's hand. 'Have you got enough in your bank account? What if we need to release money for a search plane? Have you got access to funds?' Bank accounts are frozen in the event of a death, she considers privately.

Anita looks back at her mutely. She closes her eyes, suddenly remembering her conversation with Brett in the car at the airport. She wraps her arms around her belly as if afflicted by a physical pain.

I've lost the paper he wrote on, she thinks to herself. I can't remember the passwords. I can't remember who to call, how to move the money...

She hears a loud rushing in her ears, panic rising again. She silently prays that when she opens her eyes this horrid dream will be over.

The rain, heavy again and hammering against the large lounge window, brings her back to reality. The deluge is solid and mournful, a fitting accompaniment to the uncertainty in her head and fear in her heart.

Letti moves quietly towards her employer; she bends down and gently fits Anita's bare feet into a pair of socks and oversized black fluffy slippers. Without saying a word, she puts Anita's arms into her nightgown, the way she dresses the children.

Anita gets up and walks noiselessly towards her father, a man with whom she has always been close. At first his expression is inscrutable, but Anita knows the signs.

He has never been very good at hiding his emotions. She looks up at him; his eyes look set to overflow.

'What do I do, Dad?' Anita asks, her tone fragile.

'Nothing. Not yet. Don't do anything about the money just yet.'

For Loni this would be an acknowledgement of his worst fears – that Brett is dead – and he simply can't face that now. He looks at his daughter, searching for something to say but failing to find it.

'I want to phone the boat.' Anita turns away. She wants to talk to somebody, anybody who can give her answers. Louise walks up to her with a cellphone and dials the satellite phone number. Snowman answers and Louise hands the phone to Anita. Her fear and frustration bubble up in a clumsy, faltering anger.

'Where is my husband? Was he wearing a life jacket? What are you doing to find him?'

After a minute, the line drops and she redials. This time, it's Tony who answers and Anita breaks down as soon as she hears his voice.

'Tony,' she whimpers, 'what happened?'

She makes her way to the wooden garden set on the patio and sits in the chair, her head in her hand, for a fragmentary conversation. The call lasts minutes before it drops again, but Anita manages to whisper into the mouthpiece, 'Please, Tony, please find him.'

Inside Louise is on the phone to Brett's friend CJ, giving him the *Naga Laut*'s satellite phone number and the boat's co-ordinates. Still in the Jakarta airport, CJ has cancelled his travel arrangements back to Singapore and is now only a short flight away from Padang. He's considering what he can do from there in the circumstances.

'I'll call again later,' he tells Louise.

'Anita.' Helene is suddenly decisive. She puts her arm around her sister's shoulders. 'The kids must go to school. They can't sit around here all day. It's confusing and upsetting and we can't keep worrying about them all day, terrified that they'll ask questions.'

Anita takes the palms from her face and holds them out in acquiescence. Her thoughts vacillate from minute to minute. She nods, relieved to be overruled.

'We must keep their routine,' Helene continues phlegmatically, 'make things seem as normal as we can. Come, Dad.' Like her father, she needs to busy herself to escape emotion. 'You and I can take them. Letti, please help me get them dressed.'

In the sudden flurry of activity, Anita moves slowly into the lounge where she takes an old framed photograph of Brett off the mantelpiece. It was taken in the days when he had hair; the blond mop dips down to his eyelashes. He is laughing in the picture. She can almost hear that laugh.

'Brett.' Tears flood her cheeks. The others huddle around

the dining table, talking in low tones. 'Don't die. *Don't.*' Her thoughts are like shrieks in her head, but she whispers the words softly. 'I know you aren't dead. You're still out there. I know it. You have to come home.'

She moves quietly, photo frame in one hand, the printout of the Google map in the other, and places them on the small tray on the table in the entrance hall. Her slippered feet shuffle to the kitchen where a box of white candles from Karmen's wedding has been left beside the coffee machine. She takes three candles and returns to the tray.

'Do everything in threes.' The advice of her mother's artist friend, Pamela Prendini, is echoing in her head. Pamela is a deeply spiritual woman whom Anita has consulted at turning points in her life. Paula called her friend early this morning with the news and almost immediately Pamela sent Anita a text. She gave a simple instruction: 'Anita, call your husband with your mind, the way you call your cat. Call him and he will hear you.'

Anita organises the tray into a small homemade altar. She places the photograph of Brett's smiling face over the Google map, positioning it in the centre of the Straits, the speculated location of his going overboard. She then lights the candles in a triangle around it.

She closes her eyes and begins to pray, first the Our Father. Then she asks God to send a legion of angels to surround her husband. As tears roll down her cheeks, she begs the Virgin Mary to hold Brett like only a mother can hold a child. She calls on St Anthony, the patron saint of lost articles and missing persons, and asks that he be the eyes and ears of all those looking for Brett. And finally she prays to St Expedite for quick resolution. Time, she knows, is running out.

The wicks alight, Anita stands back, staring into the eyes behind the glass.

This altar will be the repository for her curious concoction of faith and fortune-telling. It will be a place of prayer, but also where she believes some strange divination might intercede. Either way, it's the place she'll come to be close to Brett, to talk to him. She closes her eyes and says, 'Come home to me, Brett.'

She imagines that she can hear him calling her name.

THE NAGA LAUT
1.38PM

Tony passes his binoculars around. One of the crew has found the pair belonging to the boat, but they are weak, misted and useless.

The men rub their eyes periodically after staring for hours into the intense glare reflecting off the clouds and surface of the sea. Their cheeks are tight and a little burned from the wind. Salt is beginning to form tiny crystals on their eyebrows.

'We'll need to see you, Brett. Seeing you in the water is your only chance.' Niall looks through the thin rain that is now blurring his view.

Visibility has been reduced to almost nil and the low groan of the engine straining through the surf is competing with gusting winds. Although he is tired, Niall concentrates his mind.

Then: 'What's that?'

Instantly he straightens up.

He can swear he sees something, but whatever it may be is quickly swallowed by a swell.

'Wait. Stop. What *is* that?' he exclaims, standing up and hanging onto the rail. 'Over there!'

Banger is beside him in a single step. Tony and Craig rush across with the binoculars, while the others all stand up or move quickly to the starboard side. They all crane their necks over the railing. A frisson runs around the boat.

'There. Did you see it? It's quite far away – about 150 metres.' Niall points to port as the boat continues on its line. His heart is beating furiously.

Yanto and the captain come out from behind the wheel. It's as if they've stopped breathing.

'I see it,' Tony says after half a minute scouring through the binoculars.

His tone is the giveaway.

'It's not him. It's an old buoy, not a man's head. It's a block of orange foam.'

The men return to their lookouts, their heads sunken on their chests.

'Sorry, guys, it really looked like a head from far.' Niall feels hollow, guilty at the false alarm.

'Not your fault,' Banger mumbles as he carefully steps his way around the bow window. 'It's the only bloody thing we've seen all day.'

Lunch is made and served, but no-one eats. Later, it's removed, untouched.

Information is slowly coming in via the satellite phone. Chantal tells Ridgy that the coastguard will be leaving from Padang, but the information is vague and sketchy. A follow-up phone call comes from CJ who, still sitting in Jakarta's airport, confirms that he and Gary Knowles are trying to assemble an air rescue team. Helicopters will soon be on stand-by and they plan to get rescue planes to come down from Singapore, he says.

It will take a Boeing an hour to get from Singapore to Jakarta then another hour to get to Padang, thinks Ridgy, who flies fixed-wing planes, helicopters and microlights. Smaller planes would take even longer. When the hell do they think they'll get here?

JM is quiet on the bow. He's thinking about Brett's antics on the boat the night before.

'Come on, Tony, you can't deny it, my buddy, you're bald!'

Brett had been ragging Tony relentlessly in the twilight. 'Why try keep that marsh scrub that you call hair? Time to shave it off. Here, right now!'

'Don't be silly, Arch,' Tony laughed, using the nickname he'd had for his friend since their school days.

'I'm serious. I shave mine. You'll be so much cooler.'

'Brett, it doesn't worry me. Barbara would shave my head for me if she wanted me to look cooler.'

'No, Tony.' Brett had that twinkle in his eye; he wasn't about to let this go. 'It's time. I've shaved my chest for the first time on this trip. It's time for change, Tony, time to shave your head. I'm getting my razor.'

First Brett cut a mad Mohican while the others cheered him on, catching it on film and in photographs. When he finally rubbed Tony's polished dome, he laughed: 'Now we have matching hairstyles.'

'My pip is going to roast like a chestnut,' Tony giggled, grabbing one of the crew's motor scooter helmets. 'I'm going to have to wear this for ten days.'

'Might need that for those big lefts, hey, Tone?' Banger teased.

As darkness crept in, the Bintangs gave way to a round of gin and tonic.

'Medicinal,' Niall announced, 'to keep away the mosquitoes!'

Not long afterwards, Yanto called them to a light dinner in the galley. 'Tide high. We can set out,' he told them as they gathered around the ten-seater table. Three manky-looking takeaway pizzas bought from a local eatery had been deposited at either end.

'Big storm tonight. Sea will get rough. Crossing gonna be bumpy.'

'That means we'll have good waves in the morning.' JM was unfazed.

Ridgy pulled a piece of pizza from one of the rounds. 'Will this old plonker hold up?' he said.

'It's solid, this boat,' Tony replied, a little more seriously. 'It'll be fine.'

'Two years ago we crossed through a storm. Remember, Tony, Brett, remember that hectic night?' JM recalled an incident that had rattled them at the time.

'Shit, yes! When Mark Nash almost went overboard?' Brett said.

Brett, using his usual theatrics, then recounted how their surf buddy had come close to falling over the railing as the boat had pitched from side to side in the storm, re-enacting how he and JM had caught Nash just in time. 'Shit, yeah. The decks can get really slippery.'

'You didn't put seasick tablets on your To Bring list, Tony,' Craig commented. The boat had already started to roll through the ocean's undulations.

'Why, you gonna need them?'

'I'll be fine, thanks. Although I'm not so sure about this.' Craig looked suspiciously at the calzone-style pizza on the table in front of him. 'You think the mince on here is *meant* to look a bit black?'

'It's fine. If you're hungry enough!' said Brett, chuckling, before taking an enormous bite.

2.30PM TO 3.30PM
THIRTEENTH HOUR IN THE WATER

Everything begins to blur. The light has a quality that I've never seen before and the drizzle falling on my face seems salty, as if the sea water is recycling itself.

My eyes are aching, stinging from the salt. They're swelling up, slowly closing. My face feels puffy and distorted and my legs have gone numb. I'm freezing cold.

Through the slit in my eyelids, I watch an enormous black cloud envelop others into a menacing storm in the distance. It approaches steadily from the horizon. Lightning flashes in dramatic flourishes, darting across the sky.

'You see! It was bloody stupid to lose the shirt. That's another monster storm and it's going to punish you,' I admonish myself out loud.

Some god of the sky is marshalling his troops, sending an army into a terrific tempest battle. I spend what feels like an hour watching the advance, hoping the storm will pass. It's probably a fraction of that time.

Don't let that come my way, I pray.

I think I'm keeping track of it; I check on it all the time. Then, unexpectedly, it's right overhead. A high wind comes from nowhere and whips up the waves. I'm punch drunk.

'No, God, no, God! Please don't put me through another one of these.'

I lift my head; my only focus is to get liquid into my body. Enormous drops fall from the heavens; they look like great silver coins raining down. I try to count the drops that land on my tongue. Now really fat and uncomfortable against my palate, my tongue is painful to move around my mouth.

The water will help. The water must help.

The storm, when its might hits, doesn't last long. It moves straight over me, disinterested in taking me as the spoils.

Fortunate, I decide, since the rain pelts my now bare head.

The dark clouds disappear, as if an ominous presence has moved past, its shadow going with it. A paler sky remains and the rain that's falling feels lighter, but the wind continues to buffet the ocean surrounding me. Oncoming waves seem determined to slap me about.

Then, through a momentary break in the water, I see it. About 300 metres away, through a shroud of rain: my deliverance. A boat. Unmistakable. Undeniable.

This is no trick of the eye or game of my mind. No mirage. It's our boat. It's the *Naga Laut*.

THE NAGA LAUT
2.37PM

The boat is pitching hard up and down. It's also rolling left to right in the swell. The Indonesian crew shouts excitedly at one another in Bahasa. Jaipur comes up from the engine room shaking his head. A minute later the engines wind right down.

'What the hell is going on? Why are we stopping?' Ridgy bellows.

'Boat top heavy. Engine room flooding.' Yanto's expression is inscrutable. 'From big sea. We need to fix.'

The boat slowly turns into the swell and the captain cuts the engines entirely. Ridgy knows that the crew is unhappy sailing in this weather. He recalls the fragile look on the captain's face in the wheelhouse during last night's crossing.

'What's he saying?' He notes the uneasy glances and muttered conversation between Anton the deckhand and the captain. He asks Yanto to translate.

Yanto is reluctant to reply, but after a moment he does: 'It's lots of hours. We think Mr Brett drowned. His body will go down, down, down. Come up after eight hours.'

It's been longer than eight hours, Ridgy thinks to himself. Probably more like ten or eleven. 'He's not drowned!' he snaps back impatiently. 'He's still out there. We must get back to looking.'

He turns and goes back to the stern where the other men have gathered while the boat is stationary.

'They think he's dead,' Ridgy tells them, adding some invective.

'They don't know Brett.' JM's voice is soft and thin, but he manages a half smile of encouragement.

160

Snowman voices the collective frustration. 'Well, what's going on?' he demands. 'I don't see planes in the sky or the coastguard out here looking.'

'Yes, well, they're on their way, apparently,' Tony replies.

'Have we done enough? Have we done everything we can to get a rescue thing going?' Craig has worried about this for the last couple of hours. 'I know nothing about this stuff, but *is* there anything more we can do? We only have the satellite phone. Who else can we phone? We'd have the NSRI out if this was back home…'

The National Sea Rescue Institute in South Africa is a well-organised volunteer service that executes countless water rescues all year round. Boats are ready to go along the length of the national coastline in minutes. The men on the Naga Laut are becoming increasingly sceptical of the existence of an Indonesian equivalent.

'They've said the coastguard's on their way. We have to believe them,' Tony shrugs.

'So it's hurry up and wait,' Snowman mutters as he turns away.

Diesel fumes hang in the air for a second and are then carried off on the brisk breeze. The heavy rain has moved off, the clouds have lifted a little and visibility is marginally better, but it's still a capricious sea. The silenced engines leave a yawning ten-minute gap for Jaipur to rush back below deck where he clears the blocked outlet in the bilge pump.

As the engines grunt back to life, the men return to their lookouts. For the next hour, not a word is said. The mood on the boat is as unstable as the weather. They feel cut off, abandoned, their uncertainty surrounding them like mysterious ether.

The boat powers along reluctantly at four or five knots. Then, once again, conditions change. Unexpectedly, the sky turns heavy and sombre and low cloud envelops the boat like a funeral shroud. The light is diffused and refracted; it seems to change shape and form, like in a dream.

Metamorphosing.

The men's eyes start to play tricks on them. What is that shadow? Is that a waving arm? They're wary of shouting out and risking having the boat turn around unnecessarily in the dangerous conditions, only to be met with another crushing disappointment. They curse this visual trickery.

A curtain of rain starts to fall heavily around the boat, blurring the surface of the water. It's accompanied by a fierce wind that antagonises the waves yet again.

The men cover their heads and shoulders like medieval monks. Their misery is confusing, even to themselves. It deepens as they enter 'the zone', the area on Ridgy's map where he speculates Brett went over.

'This is it!' Ridgy yells over the wind.

The ocean is inconceivably big when a man is lost in it. Craig's thoughts have him transfixed at the bow. He takes off his sunglasses; he can't see through the rain.

'I can't believe this.' Weyne moves quietly to stand beside Niall. 'We're completely on our own out here. Why can't they call up a satellite image, isolate this part of the ocean and zoom in to find him?'

It's an ironic comment. He knows from his ocean jet-skiing that even on a good day, one can be ten metres from a man in the water and not see him in the swell. After a short silence, he asks softly, 'Do you think he can make it?'

'Hey, it's Brett,' Niall shrugs.

'I've been thinking about how I'd cope if it was me.'

'I think we all have.' Niall stares, eyes unfocused, out at the ocean.

Weyne takes off his glasses for the umpteenth time and uses his T-shirt to wipe the rain off them. It's the middle of the afternoon, but time is measured here in the changing colour of the water. As the day has deepened, it has morphed from grey-green to inky black to an amniotic milky hue.

'What's that? What's that?'

Ridgy's shouts shatter the malaise. He is already moving over the top deck towards Banger, who has Tony's binoculars strung around his neck.

'I saw something out over there.'

3.30PM TO 4.30PM
FOURTEENTH HOUR IN THE WATER

I have to be sure this isn't another vision. I can make out the shape of our boat through the rainy haze, ethereal, indistinct in the distance. I watch it for several minutes and as it gets bigger and bigger, the three decks and the starboard blue signage provide the evidence I need.

The *Naga Laut*. The boys have come back. They've come back for me.

Relief floods over me. It's immense. My entire body feels warm again and the realisation that I'm no longer alone, that I'm within the boat's reach, is almost too much to bear.

I find myself trembling and the anxiety that has been building up over the last hours is instantly released. I feel it leave my body and imagine it spreading out in the water around me.

You've done it! I give a wild cheer, as loud as I can. My heart feels about to burst with elation. They've come back! It's all coming together. You'll be drinking beers tonight and surfing tomorrow. All of this will have been a bad dream. Everything's going to be okay.

It begins to rain harder again. I stop swimming and continue to tread water as I watch the boat approaching – they're heading straight for me. I'm high-fiving and back-slapping each of the guys in my mind. The emotion is tightening my throat.

I decide to gauge their course. Focus on where they're heading and swim for them, I instruct myself.

They continue straight towards me.

Think, Brett, think! You have to make sure they see you.

I take the hotel room card key from my pocket, but there

is no sun. I know it's useless trying to signal them with it, so I return it to my shorts.

Suddenly the boat stops. I calculate that it's about 150 to 200 metres away from me. 'Why are they stopping?' I shout out loud. 'They must have seen me! They must have…'

I start screaming, hollering as loud as my voice can carry.

'I'm here! Here, guys!'

A minute later, the boat turns broadside. I can just make out Niall, his frame smaller beside Banger, a giant of a man. They are standing on the starboard side with towels over their heads and shoulders. Rain is falling steadily again. It's cold up there. I can see that.

I scan the boat. Ridgy is in the stern shouting, gesticulating wildly.

They've seen me.

Although I can't see their faces, their body shapes are distinctive, strongly familiar, comforting. Where are JM and the others, I wonder?

Every few seconds, I wipe water from my eyes trying to better my vision. Everything has a hazy halo, blurry through the relentless downpour.

'Niall! Banger! I'm here. Here!' I shout it repeatedly but my voice is lost on the wind.

Then I see Niall's head fall to his chest and Banger fold his arms. And I know.

I know they haven't seen me.

I'm in a frenzy. 'No, God, no. No, no, no!'

I put my head down and swim like a crazed man towards the boat. I swim freestyle as hard as I can for what feels like ten minutes, then look up and realise I've made no headway. It can't take me this long to swim to them.

I stop. It's as if I haven't moved at all.

The current is between us and I'm caught in its powerful maw. It's pulling me sideways. I'm like a bird trapped behind a window indoors: I can see my way out, but the barrier is impenetrable.

'This is not possible!' I scream, raging. 'I can't get across there. I can't get to them.'

Again, I put my head down and give it everything I have. I swim as if deranged.

Each time I come up for air, I lift my head, shouting, waving, splashing water into the air. Please, God, they must see me. They're going to put the tender in the water – they're going to come for me.

The wind is howling around me now and the rain pelts down. It's raining sideways, away from me; it must be hitting the boat headlong.

And then they power up.

I hear it before I see the two billows of black smoke that cough out of the back of the boat. They start to move. Slowly they turn left and start sailing away.

I cannot believe it.

'Oh Jesus, no, no!' I bellow. 'Come back, Niall. Banger, come back.'

Stunned, I watch the boat sail away. I've survived this long and they've missed me.

My body sinks. It's all I can do to keep my face above the water line.

Despair hits with full force. As strong as the knowledge had been that death was inevitable when I first fell overboard, this is a thousand times more powerful, more certain. I know that I cannot carry on.

I start shivering uncontrollably. I'm cold, but I'm also in shock.

'How could you have done this to me, God?'

The injustice is overwhelming. I feel beyond exhausted. My body is utterly debilitated, as if someone has pulled the plug.

'Is this how you're going to let it happen? Allow them to come back for me. Let them get this close and then have them sail away. Why?'

It's as if the ocean is falling away beneath me. I feel utterly alone; a sense of cutting desolation. Yet still, I can't cry.

'Why?'

Tears too have abandoned me.

My limbs are hanging lifeless, barely keeping me up.

'Why didn't you let me drown earlier? Why torture me?'

Hope has been so coolly given and then so cruelly taken away. Anger overcomes me. I swear at the heavens, shouting, 'What kind of God are you? Are you punishing me? Making me suffer?'

I feel like I've crossed a line. The last hour suddenly seems unreal, as if I've dreamt it. The impossibility of my circumstances descends again like a great weight and I feel as though I'm hanging by a thread.

So close. And now my chance, my only chance, my last chance of rescue, is gone.

Still I don't cry.

THE NAGA LAUT
3.40PM

'What's that? What's that?'

Ridgy's shouts have set the men on edge again. They move in unison to the portside of the boat where they follow his finger pointing out into the swirling grey, several boat lengths ahead.

'Pass me the binos!'

Banger complies. Someone calls for the captain to stop the boat as Ridgy tries to focus through the rain into the surging sea. The engines cough as they slow and the *Naga Laut* lurches clumsily in the swell.

'There! There's definitely something...'

No-one else says a word. There's so much riding on this moment, on this day, but the men have already suffered one false alarm; they have started hardening themselves to the cruelty of hope.

The engines cut out suddenly.

'I can see it too.' But Snowman is less animated than Ridgy.

'Me too,' says Craig. 'It could be him but...'

Most of the men can now make out the object in the water and, as the powerless *Naga Laut* approaches, its pale lifelessness becomes increasingly apparent. A shared thought crystalises among them: if it is Brett, we're too late.

The moment envelops the boat.

Finally, Ridgy locates the object in the binoculars. 'It's not him. Just some junk or something.'

The men's collective relief is barely felt in the wind-driven rain. In the course of the longest minute they've been tossed from extreme hope to extreme despair and now – what? The familiar emptiness in the pit of their stomachs returns.

Craig and Weyne keep watching the piece of flotsam as it rises and falls into and out of view, now a mere stone's throw off the port bow; they can see clearly that it's a piece of polystyrene. 'Jesus, I though it was the top of his head,' says Weyne.

JM, Tony and Snowman move out of the rain back to their portside positions, while Ridgy, sodden like the others, trudges to the bridge to resume his search. Banger and Niall retire silently to starboard, where they stare in resignation out to sea. As the boat, buffeted by the wind and sea, starts a gentle turn to port, the rain powers directly into their faces, reducing their visibility almost to nothing.

Inside the bridge the captain and Yanto, both flustered, engage in a spirited exchange, evidently working out their next move. Barely a minute passes before Ridgy calls to the crew on the bridge. 'Yanto! I think I've seen something else! Tell the captain we need to turn back and search the area.'

This time the men don't respond as before. They automatically glance over to Ridgy, but this time they don't move, their natural self defences not allowing it.

'Captain say we can't go there,' says Yanto. He has a rumpled look as he turns to JM and Tony. 'He say we go to mainland.'

'We have to check it out,' says Ridgy, gesticulating out to starboard.

Yanto shakes his head. 'Not safe there. More storm coming. Boat not good.'

'This is the search area,' says Craig. 'Why are we leaving?'

'We can't go there,' Yanto is almost shouting now. 'Boat will sink.'

The men look at one another, uncomfortable with the unfolding unpleasantries. A couple of them look away, as if to block out the scene.

'We need to go to mainland to refuel.'

'Isn't there an island closer to us where we can do that?' Snowman's voice is desperate. Strained.

'No. Refuel on mainland.'

They can see the conflict roiling within Yanto. He's trying to accommodate his guests but he also knows that he needs to respect the authority of his captain. He seems uncertain how to proceed.

'Well, he's not prepared to stick around here and he's the captain.' Snowman is admirably restrained. 'It's his call.'

'This is fucking *unbelievable*,' JM shoots back. But he too realises that an argument is pointless. A mutiny would be ridiculous. And this is no time for rebellion.

'We can't risk all of our lives on a broken boat.' Snowman's eyes hide nothing as he expresses their wrenching dilemma: whether to abandon or continue.

'We go to mainland. Refuel. Set out again early. Yes, 3am and come back.' Yanto's face is pale and solemn. The consultation is over.

'I saw something, I'm sure of it,' says Ridgy to no-one, the wind whipping his words out to sea.

The men stand hunched in silence as the diesel engines start up and the *Naga Laut* begins the slow journey back to the mainland.

FISKAAL ROAD
CAMPS BAY
10.23AM

A purgatorial air fills the house in Fiskaal Road but, oddly, there's an equal sense of activity, clarity, even order. Its occupants are automatons wound up for action.

The coming and going of friends, relations and acquaintances escalates as the news spreads rapidly through Cape Town and beyond. For most of the morning, the house is a train station.

Loni and Helene are the first to leave. They head out on the rain-soaked roads with the children and drive across the city, now bristling with traffic beneath Table Mountain. Today the great looming presence feels strangely malevolent, hidden behind a cloak of cloud.

They drop Zara at St Cyprians School in the City Bowl and then skirt around Devil's Peak to take Jamie to Bishops Pre-Preparatory in Rondebosch. For now, the children must be protected from the terrible truth.

Helene tells their teachers what has happened and asks that the children be carefully monitored. 'If they want to come home early or if they start asking questions, please call me.' She tries to appear impassive.

On their return they buy bread and milk from the local convenience store. On every other day this is a mundane daily duty, but today it's astonishingly dispiriting. Everything is out of alignment, even the ordinary.

It's going to be a day of waiting, of wondering. Longing. Pleading. Praying.

Father and daughter return to find the lounge set up like a military operations room. Cellphones are ringing constantly; people scurry back and forth answering them. An array of laptops has mushroomed on the dining-room table. They illuminate the room, glowing with sites detailing the Mentawais, maps of the area, local weather patterns, sea conditions, wave heights.

The newlyweds, Anita's cousin Karmen and Luke, have arrived. The two are experienced sailors and have spent years sailing in international waterways; they even met on a yacht. With everything so uncertain, so unstable, they've cancelled their honeymoon flight.

Anita's family is close and Karmen has also called her cousins in Johannesburg, Claudia, Giulia, Luigi and Paolo. Luigi and Paolo both fly helicopters and have aviation contacts all over the world. They want to help with an air search. On hearing the news they immediately started to make calls, their contacts coiling across the globe.

From the small KwaZulu-Natal town of Harrismith, Brett's brother Greg and sister-in-law Joanne have decided that the Archibalds need to be together until they get further news. They instruct their eldest son Terence, who had stayed behind in Johannesburg to play a rugby match, to collect Brett's sister Sandra and drive with her and his girlfriend to join them at a friend's holiday home in the Drakensberg. Joanne and her mother Irene decide to take one of their cars and drive down to Westville to collect Brett's mother Shirley, while Greg, his father-in-law Mike, younger son Nicholas and the youngest, Megan, continue on to the house in the Champagne Valley.

After receiving Anita's call earlier this morning, Shirley has descended into deep shock. On hanging up the call she simply sunk to the floor, moaning quietly. Only two days ago Brett had called her from Cape Town International

Airport. 'Brett, you're a middle-aged man now,' she'd scolded him about the surf charter. 'It's time you stopped doing these ridiculous things.'

Trembling, she made several attempts to dial Sandra's number. When she managed to get through, Sandra, who recently injured her shoulder in a fall, was just about to leave for work. 'No!' Sandra howled, causing her son Neil, who has been taking care of his mother, to leap out of bed. In the kitchen, without even asking the news, her housekeeper immediately mixed sugar water.

'I know, S.'

Gregory used his sister's initial, their term of affection, when he took her call minutes later in Harrismith. 'Anita's just called me too.' Greg's heart quickly filled with dread and, overcome with emotion, he was unable to converse for long. 'Wait, we have to decide what to do,' he told her.

Now sitting in the back of Terence's car, her bad arm in a sling, Sandra is desperate for a cigarette. She stopped smoking just two months ago. She sits in anxious silence, weeping every now and again and obsessively reading and re-reading Anita's email updates as they light up her phone.

'Sandra, pull yourself together,' Terence tells his aunt finally. 'Brett's an Archibald. He's going to make it.'

In Camps Bay, Anita's friend Gaby Grieveson is beside her. Gaby and her husband Wayne met Brett when they worked together in the past. Wayne has a particularly close bond with his former boss and for years the couple has been enfolded in the Archibalds' inner circle.

Gaby keeps trying to call her husband's cell number, but it goes repeatedly to voicemail. Now a manager at Apple South Africa, Wayne's been at early morning swimming training at the local pool before starting his normally jam-packed day. He eventually turns on his phone to find fourteen missed calls from his wife.

Some of Anita's other intimate friends have heard the news through early dawn phone calls and lightning-fast social-network communication. The labyrinth of friendship stretches across South Africa and on to many of the world's major cities, where the news has fizzed and popped like a raw electrical current, traversing at speed, defying time differences.

Katya Laspatzis and Kirsten Horn are two friends who have dropped everything and come to Fiskaal Road. Gaby had received the news as a text message from a friend in Johannesburg who'd seen JM's post on Facebook. Katya, whose son is Jamie Archibald's self-ordained bodyguard on the playground, knew something was wrong when Anita failed to put through her daily call that morning. Instead Anita's text that Jamie wouldn't be going to school led her to intuit something was awry.

Kirsten arrived shortly before her husband, Dudley. Dudley has been crying openly. 'You're not helping,' Kirsten complains when she finds him weeping in the kitchen. 'Go home and look after the kids.' Dudley heads up the road to one of Brett's neighbours to commiserate with him.

Outside the morning is rugged with great grey clouds still battering across the sky and fast-moving squalls coming in-shore. They sweep up with an unstoppable power, marshalled over the many miles from the deep Southern Ocean.

Inside Anita is fielding endless calls: friends with questions, acquaintances with offers of help. Zenda Stravino's husband Joe, Andre Crawford-Brunt, Brett's good friend in London, and another close friend in Cape Town, Ray Cadiz, have all either called or emailed Anita offering to cover all search and rescue costs.

Although no-one says as much, those around her know that she's facing scepticism. They sense the tone of the calls, already laced with condolence.

But Anita stands resolute. Her refrain stays the same: 'It's not his time.'

The two moods divide the house, each wrestling for ascendency.

Could they be deceiving themselves with their optimism, a mood implicit with comments like 'He's alive' or 'He can do this'? Or should they face the dark undercurrent – the more likely reality that is sometimes betrayed in a gesture or an expression? It hovers on the periphery, like a ghost in the corner.

Anita calls the *Naga Laut*'s satellite phone repeatedly, needing to feel closer to where her husband has been lost at sea. 'Brett is MacGyver,' she tells Mark Ridgway. 'He can get through this.'

Lulu comes in from the covered patio where she has again been on the phone to Chantal Malherbe, the tour organiser. As the go-between with the *Naga Laut*, Lulu has also assumed this communication. Otherwise she and Louise have retreated somewhat.

The conversation in the room is around the information gathered by phone and computer. Groups stand in knots and huddles, processing it, speculating, hypothesising.

'It's good if it's raining. He can get fresh water,' says Karmen, conjuring the most benign conditions.

'The current goes south.' Luke looks up from his laptop. 'He'll surely hit an island.'

'That's what Chantal said,' Lulu nods, walking up to the

table. 'She also said there's a lot of rubbish in that sea, he'll find something – a piece of driftwood – something to hold on to. To keep him afloat.'

'The current will take him to land,' Luke continues. 'Most of those islands are uninhabited, but he'll be able to last on land…'

'Knowing Brett, he's on an island sipping a cocktail with an umbrella in it.'

The comment comes from Anita's father Loni, who's sitting on the sofa across the room. Until now he's been stern-faced, silent, a shadow of himself. It's the first thing he's said this morning. Everyone looks across at him, as if they've just remembered he's there. Most manage weak smiles.

Automatically, they turn their gaze to Anita who, still in her nightgown and slippers, is seated at the dining table. The coffee in front of her has gone cold, the milky film on top breaking up and moving apart like miniature tectonic plates. Her brow is creased, a deep scar. She looks exhausted. She wipes her red nose with a crumpled tissue before she shifts her glasses back up the bridge. Despite all the people around her, she's experiencing this all as a profoundly isolating experience.

'Also there's no real threat in the water,' Luke offers again. 'Most of the sharks have been fished out and if there are any they'd be reef sharks which tend to stay in-shore.'

Karmen quickly interrupts, frowning at her new husband. 'We know that the water is warm there. He can last a long time in it.'

'Chantal says they're sending out boats. They're getting planes up there soon too.' This time it's Lulu trying to sound convincing.

'I think we should pray.'

It's Helene's suggestion and she moves quietly to where Anita is sitting and puts her hands on her sister's shoulders. Anita nods and drops her head. Then she slowly gets to her feet and gently takes the hands of her friends around her: Kirsten, Gaby, Katya and her sister.

The four women stand before the makeshift altar to Brett, and Helene begins to pray.

Those in the room, their heads bent, store the moment.

Helene wills Brett not to surrender. She calls on God to grant him strength. This is the time his crazy energy will save him, she says; he's a man who won't give up.

And for his friends on the *Naga Laut*, Helene adds, this will be a time of true valour.

There's a hush in the room.

A few metres away, Lulu quietly takes Louise aside and, sweeping a stray lock of blonde hair from her eyes, she whispers under her breath, 'Chantal says the weather over there is hectic. They've had a major storm. The seas are incredibly rough and the visibility is very poor.'

She shows Louise a text on her cellphone. It's from her husband Mark, sent in the morning, Indonesian time.

> Weather's not great. Don't tell Anita. We've turned back and starting a search. Losing signal so shall be in touch later on satellite phone. This doesn't look good.

'I know.' Louise looks through the door at the equally forbidding day in Cape Town. She drops her head. 'I've just spoken to CJ. He's been trying to get a private rescue going, but he's been told that planes can't take off because of the bad weather.'

'Something is happening. Chantal has assured me.' Lulu's

eyes dart across the room. 'But we can't tell Anita that the conditions are so awful.'

'I agree,' Louise nods sympathetically. 'We can't tell her anything that will cast doubt.'

'I need another cigarette!' Paula suddenly breaks the brittle mood. She stands up from the sofa and rummages through her handbag on the coffee table for her pack. 'Karmen, please take my phone.' She walks past her husband Loni, who is pretending to read the newspaper. 'I just can't talk to anyone any more.'

'I'll join you.' Louise grabs her lighter and square pack from the dining-room table and follows the older woman outside. Even under the patio covering, the two women aren't entirely protected. The rain is swirling in all directions. Out at sea, heavy clouds hide the horizon and the sky appears ready to rupture – a second wave in this storm appears about to hit.

Anita walks into the lounge. She seems uncertain how to act. The man she loves is in the sea somewhere on the other side of the world. She presses the digits of the *Naga Laut*'s satellite phone into the cellphone she's carrying around with her, glancing down at the number written on a piece of torn-off notepaper. The call doesn't go through. She realises she's misdialled.

She tries the other number, that of the boat's owner. Again, the call dead-ends. She decides to wait until her hands have stopped shaking.

She couldn't feel more distant – from Brett, from everyone else in this room, from her children, even from herself. She looks out the window at the drama of the storm: the vengeful wind and lashes of rain. As the water runs in rivulets down the windowpane, she imagines that she can hear the sea. Pulsing, like blood.

It's the sound of her breathing.

4.30PM TO 5.30PM
FIFTEENTH HOUR IN THE WATER

If I want to survive I have to make it through another night. I know that now.

The *Naga Laut* has sailed away without me. Again.

I enter into a state of mental torpor and a strange feeling unfolds: a numbness all over.

I feel simultaneously dead and alive.

Our boat is the only thing I've seen since falling overboard. I console myself that it has given me a sense of size and perspective in this boundless expanse. All the other things I'm convinced I've seen couldn't have been boats. They were illusions.

Anger is a powerful emotion. It takes command of both my mind and body. I've had a glimpse of rescue, a taste, a teaser. My boat came so close and yet it missed me. The absurdity of this fact both overwhelms and devastates me. There won't be another chance like that; it's madness to believe there will be.

God is taunting me, I decide, my bitterness rising. I lash out again, cursing the heavens. 'You made me believe I could get through this. If you know I'm going to die, why didn't you take me when I fell overboard? Just hit my head and drown right there? I don't want to suffer any more, God! End it. Let me die! Please!'

It's late in the day and bleak. Rain is still falling and I concentrate on the hideous din as it pelts the surface of the sea. Every time I think of the boat, I picture Anita, Jamie and Zara; it brings a new stab of pain. What are they doing now? I imagine them together, grieving, in an embrace.

I feel like I've overstepped some boundary. Taken some kitchen-cooked hallucinogenic that has left my brain on fire.

I've hit my breaking point and it feels as if it's threatening to upset my now teetering mental balance. I was feeling rational before, but now my ideas seem to be rushing, fizzing in my head.

Think of neutral things, I keep repeating, keep your mind in overdrive.

I have no idea how far I've drifted. I can feel the current around me, an underwater river of unstoppable power. But now all my hope has gone. There won't be another boat this late in the day; there won't be another crossing and fishing boats will stick to shallower waters, especially at this hour.

The *Naga Laut* has come and gone. That fact reverberates starkly like a series of aftershocks through my brain.

It's heading for nightfall. I really don't think I can make it through the night.

'God, I want to die,' I shout helplessly. My voice has changed. 'I can't carry on.'

Again I wonder where my body will surface. Where it will wash up, bloated with gases, decomposing. I can taste the sourness of my saliva.

Exhaustion is descending and my body is beginning to feel like melted butter. Death seems inevitable, something that can't be changed. The certainty of it reopens my regret and recriminations over a universe of things.

My eyelids flutter and I hover in that mysterious twilight territory between sleep and waking. The ocean around me begins to break up into refracted shapes of light and colour. The whole world seems to be liquefying.

I close my eyes.

'This is it,' I hear myself say.

Then a strange whooshing sound fills my head. I open my eyes to a plume of white water rising up some distance away

– I can't tell how far it is, but it appears to be hovering on the horizon, surging straight up out of the ocean. A colourless rainbow ascending upwards, it seems to connect the sea and the darkening sky above. I stop my gentle kicking, blink several times and rub my eyes. When I open them it's still there, a wall of white water shooting upward into the sky.

I'm suddenly lucid. Is this evidence of my irrational mind?

Then, within the cloud, I see the Virgin Mary.

I know it's her, even though I can only just make out a figure. Her form is full-length with white robes that fall down her legs and over her feet. She appears to be floating. Her head is bent slightly to the right with her veil falling around it. Her hands are clasped in prayer.

I can't see her face – she's too far away – but I am overcome by the feeling that she's here to watch over me. Odd for a man who has lost his religion.

I rub my eyes repeatedly, thinking she will disappear. I turn in the water to break my gaze, but as I come around again, she's still there. I move in a circle three or four times; each time I come around, the vision remains.

'That's impossible.' My voice is a raw whisper. 'There cannot be a figure in that cloud. You're delusional, Brett'.

But it remains. For what feels like five or ten minutes, the apparition stays.

I continue to stare and focus my gaze. The Virgin appears to be made out of Meccano. Her arms are long burgundy metal lengths with holes in them; an occasional bolt hinges her joints. It reminds me of the image of the Virgin in the stained-glass window in St Elizabeth's Church where I grew up. I think back to the church of my childhood. At the end of the nave, over the christening font, is the window featuring the Virgin Mary.

A sense of peace comes over me; it wafts over like a vapour.

'If you've come to take me,' I say. 'I'm ready.'

I wait. Nothing happens.

For several minutes, nothing happens.

The plume of water continues to rise out of the sea. My gaze tracks the vision of the Virgin and follows its length down to where it meets the ocean – and I see it. There, lurching around in the turbulent water, is an enormous buoy.

It looks like a channel demarcation buoy, like those used to direct shipping traffic. I've seen hundreds in harbours around the world. At its base is a massive red drum, with a pyramid of four arms that join above its hollow centre. An enormous bell, with an oversized yellow light above it, is hoisted on top.

Even at that great distance, I can hear the bell clanging. It echoes off the water.

Bizarre. I try to tame my mind with rational thoughts. Buoys are generally anchored, I think to myself.

But it can't be anchored in the middle of the ocean; it's too deep.

Even though I can't see land, I rationalise, I must be close to it. Perhaps I'm heading for a harbour and this is an early demarcation marker.

Okay, I tell myself, the Virgin hasn't come for you. She's come to show you the way.

I can still see the bright red buoy and its huge yellow light above it. The peal of the bell reaches me over the hiss of the water.

'Thank you, God. Thank you.' My tongue is so swollen my speech is slurred.

Suddenly I feel exhilarated, filled with renewed hope, a new belief.

Swim to the buoy, I urge my tired body. You can get to it. Buoys have beacons on them. You can strip the beacon and send a message in Morse code and someone will come to your rescue.

The buoy is very far away, but this is a powerful boost. I will have to get there before it's completely dark.

It's still drizzling from layers of cloud, but it's light enough. I'm unsure of the time, but I tell myself I can make it to the buoy before darkness truly sets in. It also means I'll have something to hang on to when I get there. Up there, I can make it through the night. Even if I'm freezing cold, I can hang on until someone finds me.

I have to pace myself, though. I don't want to implode half way.

The sea is still choppy, but the storm is moving away from me to the left. The Virgin still hovers in the cloud. The buoy is dead ahead. I can still hear the bell ringing.

I put my head down and start swimming.

THE NAGA LAUT
4.50PM

JM stalks to his spot on the portside of the *Naga Laut* where he sits down and resumes praying.

'Hail Mary, full of grace…'

He's been saying it all day. His prayer is interspersed with a telepathic message: 'Swim, Brett, swim.' The mental chant gets him through the hours that seem to be stretching out longer and longer. Am I in denial, he wonders? He closes his eyes. Will I have to prepare for a different outcome? For now, he holds his position: Brett is out there, waiting to be found.

Swim, Brett, swim.

The *Naga Laut* continues through the unrelenting sea. The atmosphere of focus and intent is exhausting and the men descend into a mournful funk as they depart the search zone. Drenched, chilled and miserable, they seem subdued and disorientated.

Craig looks down at the crumpled water. A quiet, modest man, he's grateful that others have taken the lead in this crisis. Like Niall, Banger, Weyne and Snowman, he is more comfortable in a supporting role.

Infected Mushroom's remix of 'Riders On The Storm' is riffing in his head. Craig often puts his thoughts to music. He's conscious of its power to define a moment, to transport a man in his mind. He's also famous for putting his surf photographs and video footage to suitable soundtracks. His thoughts drift back to how the Doors' song had been playing through the speakers last night – was it really only last night? – as the *Naga Laut* drew away from the mainland.

The boat had ploughed into the rising swells as they headed for the wide-open sea, while mainland Sumatra faded to a low, mangrove-lined smudge in the distance. Wobbling *praus*, the Indonesian fishing boats with long outriggers all lit up to attract their catch, looked like grand chariots roaming the sea.

The sea is starting to pound, Craig thought to himself at the time. He'd been sitting rather precariously with Brett and Niall on the foredeck, their legs dangling over the bow. It's not that safe, sitting up here, he thought. He wondered if he could make it to one of the *praus* if he fell in. He consciously leant back against the glass of the captain's wheelhouse, recoiling from the thought.

The mood had changed somewhat by then. The men had sobered up from their earlier drinks, eased off the banter and become more reflective. They'd talked about Rob de Beer, their school friend who'd died suddenly just before the trip.

'Life's too short to drink cheap white wine,' Brett had said with conviction as a tribute to their friend. 'We've reached a time in our lives where we need to grasp our reality and enjoy it.'

One by one, the men had left their huddled conversations and gone down to their cabins. JM and Tony had been the first to leave; they'd wanted to make an early start and be ready for the first day's surf at Telescopes. JM had made his way to the dungeon where, hoping he still had signal, he'd sent a text to his wife Tessa. Like the others, he had hardly slept for three days.

Tony had brought a couple of sea-sickness tablets and, as Craig noticed, took two 'to be safe'. After Tony and the two Marks had headed down to their bunks, Craig left the deck around 11pm. Settling into his bunk, he looked up to the cabin roof contentedly. Rod Stewart's 'I Am Sailing' was looping in his head. He thought about a *Vanity Fair* article he'd read on the plane about Johnny Depp and his life aboard his sailboat. 'This is the life,' he said to himself before dozing off.

Weyne feels suffocated by the uneasy silence around the boat.

No-one is talking, but a tense undercurrent is palpable. The only sound is the wind lashing the boat and the rain pounding in his ears. His vision has been so affected by the bad weather, he can't find a point of focus. He, too, can't help ruminating on his private exchange with Brett the night before.

He'd been only vaguely aware that the boat had hit the edge of the storm and that the sea was becoming rougher. The wind was howling and rain was falling in wide blurry sheets. Despite the fierce conditions, Brett and Weyne found themselves alone on the upper deck, swapping stories in the darkness.

Moved by their conversation Weyne decided to crack open the bottle of Jameson he'd brought along to celebrate his fiftieth. They each sipped a dram as they talked.

For an hour they were locked in close conversation, oblivious to the maelstrom out at sea. They shared anecdotes of their lives, joked about both being married to Greek women, talked of their children.

Weyne remembers now how Brett lit up when he talked about his daughter and son. The memory causes tears to well up behind his glasses.

It was an intense exchange, close and meaningful – about things they'd done well in life, of where they'd screwed up, of what they'd learnt along the way. Brett confided that his awning business was going belly-up and causing him great stress.

'I need to get a handle on it all,' he told Weyne, 'but right now, I'm in the best place in the world. The Mentawais are my soul place, you know. If, God forbid, anything should happen to Anita and the kids, I'd sell everything and come and live out here on one of these islands.'

The comment, made *en passant*, haunts Weyne now. He looks out again at the volatile conditions. Below him the sea moves madly, like a billion writhing eels. The task they face is a heavy one, he thinks to himself, and odds are it's a wild goose chase.

His spirits plunge further.

Ridgy is going over the mechanics of last night, slowly retracing his steps, replaying the events in his mind in case he's missed something.

Once the storm had woken him, he decided to go to the bridge to note the time, check their location in the Straits and assess the weather conditions. He didn't notice Brett and Weyne on his way up. Perhaps they'd gone to bed by then?

The weather had turned surprisingly nasty. Waves were crashing over the bow and the skipper had a spotlight beaming ahead. Ridgy could see how difficult it was to navigate through the pounding sea.

Shit, this is heavy, he thought before returning to his bunk.

With Niall fast asleep above him, he listened to the rain falling in torrents. The sea was chopping up badly and the boat was pitching in the heavy swell. It wouldn't have been difficult for a man to fall overboard in those conditions, he thinks to himself now.

The back-and-forth slamming of their cabin door as the boat lurched through the waves began to annoy Ridgy, but he couldn't work the latch when he got up to lock it. He pushed his bag into the doorjamb instead.

A minute later, there was a thundering crash and all the

cupboards in the galley sprang open, their contents falling out across the floor; tin cans, pasta and packets of cereal rolled back and forth across the room. He was all the more irritated when the crew didn't stir.

Grumbling, he got up again and went to wake the chef.

'Come on, Boi, let's get all the stuff back into the cupboards,' he shouted over the noise of the groaning engine. The two repacked cupboards and secured the doors, before they returned to their respective bunks.

It's going to be a long night, Ridgy thought.

Across the passage, the door to Craig and Banger's cabin had also been sliding to and fro. Theirs was noisy, too, rasping like a butcher's blade. Ever more frustrated, Ridgy eventually heard Craig get up to lock it.

He must have dozed off. Then, emerging from a cloud of sleep, Ridgy heard Banger shouting desperately. Hammering on their locked cabin door, his voice came out as a bleat. 'Hey, guys, help! Help, we're locked in here.'

Banger had been the first to feel the effects of the food poisoning. He'd leapt down from his bunk, but somehow broken the latch in the lock as he tried to open the door. With nausea consuming him, his timing couldn't have been worse.

Again Ridgy got up. 'It won't open!' he yelled, trying to force the cabin door. 'I think the lock's broken. Let me get Jaipur.' Then, almost as an afterthought, he added: 'Hey, guys – think of this as an adventure.'

Behind the door, Banger was moments from retching.

Ridgy turned on all the lights in the galley and went in search of the engineer. He returned with Jaipur and a 12-inch screwdriver. The two jimmied the lock to release the prisoners. Then pandemonium broke loose.

'What's going on?' asked Brett, emerging from the stairs just in time to see Banger dumping the contents of his toiletry bag and vomiting uncontrollably into it.

'Banger's sick,' Ridgy explained. 'Looks like Craig is, too.'

A glance at Brett indicated that the puking probably wasn't going to be limited to those two alone. He watched as Brett ran for the head, while Banger dashed out to the lower deck and was violently ill over the stern.

For close on an hour, chaos ensued. While the boat was being slammed relentlessly onto the sea Brett, Banger, Niall, Tony and Craig vomited violently. They also were struck with acute diarrhoea.

Ridgy was aware of the engine's oppressively cloying heat and the waves of diesel fumes that swamped the galley. After some time, he heard Brett comment to Banger, 'We need to get some fresh air', as the two men headed for the ladder to the top deck.

Ridgy gave Craig a couple of sea-sickness tablets and saw to Niall, who was lying in the main cabin unable to move, after which he went up to check on the two outside.

Gingerly he made his way up the ladder rungs and found Banger prone on the bench, clutching a small brown bowl. Brett lifted his head from vomiting over the port side. He was standing, holding onto the railing, his face very pale.

'You okay, Arch?' Ridgy asked.

'I'm not well, boss,' Brett said.

'God, this is terrible. Niall and Craig are also ill. There are sea-sickness tablets downstairs.'

'I can't go down there,' Brett replied.

Ridgy popped into the bridge where he found Skippy concentrating his gaze through his glasses, his brow furrowed. Yanto was beside him.

'How hectic is this crossing.'

It was less a question than a remark.

'Bad swell and pretty bad crosswinds making it much badder,' Yanto said without looking at him.

Ridgy noted the time on the instruments panel. The clock read 02h25.

Back downstairs in his cabin, Ridgy took a towel to his head, face and shoulders before climbing into his bunk. Almost instantly, he fell asleep.

I was the last to see him.

Ridgy keeps coming back to this admission.

I was the last to see Brett.

The time is crucial for him, an important logistical detail. It must have been just minutes later that the boat lurched and the unthinkable happened.

Ridgy stares, not blinking, as he looks out to sea now, where the conditions are still savage.

He tries to quell the frantic impatience within. He feels powerless against the consequences of last night's events. Despite his belief in Brett, despite their pledge to find him, a more cynical reality gnaws at him.

Are they doomed to disappointment? Will this be a tragic failure? One they'll have to live with for the rest of their lives?

5.30PM TO 6.30PM
SIXTEENTH HOUR IN THE WATER

I swim, alternating my strokes: crawl, then breaststroke, crawl, breaststroke.

Each time I put my head in the water, I'm terrified that the vision of the Virgin will disappear. Please be there, I think as I come up for breath. And as I surface, there she is. Magnificent. Mesmerising.

Equally, I fear the buoy will vanish, but I focus my gaze and can see it very clearly. What I'm seeing is entirely real. There is quite a distance to cover, and though I'm not conscious of the buoy getting closer I continue swimming.

I have to reach it before dark.

I swim for what I imagine to be an hour; the apparition stays ahead of me throughout. Sometimes she fades a little and the cloud threatens to dissipate, but I plead – 'Please don't go away. Please don't evaporate' – and she returns.

With each breath I keep the red buoy in my sights. After my earlier dream-like state I'm now struck by my clarity of thought. It's a relief after the dark period I've been through. If the Virgin has given me benediction, the buoy has become my talisman. Every now and again I hear the bell ringing.

The sea begins to calm. Although the swells remain colossal, waves no longer break around me. With each stroke, I feel myself being pulled up and over the upsurge and as I go down the other side, I seem to be going faster. I'm convinced I'm being helped along.

As I swim, I plot what to do when I reach the buoy. I'm going to climb up onto it, break into the beacon and use the Morse code I learnt as a Boy Scout to radio for help. Mad as the scheme seems, it does give me hope.

I think I'm getting closer, so I put my head down and put in a vigorous burst of freestyle. I swim as hard as I can. My lungs feel as weighty as granite and they ache; my arm muscles feel like an outstretched rope. As I come up to take a breath I notice that the buoy is now to my right.

It's because you're right-handed, I tell myself. Your right arm is dominant and it's making you swim off course.

I have to swim more consciously, I decide. Breaststroke will allow me to keep the buoy in my sights, but the light is disappearing fast and I want to kick out one last burst of freestyle. I put my face in the water and swim as furiously as I can for about three or four minutes.

It feels like forever and after a while I can hear a tinny ringing in my ears. On my last breath I lift my head and look up.

The buoy has disappeared.

There's nothing there.

I stop swimming. I tread water and turn a full 360 degrees. Again I go around and around, flopping about desperately as I look for the vision and the buoy.

'Oh please no. No. No! Where is it? Where is it?' I'm panicking, screaming as loud as I can. 'Have you swum in a circle? Have you gone off course? It was there! It was there!'

In every direction, all I see is wide ocean and flat, very dark sky. Nothing beyond.

Stupefied, I start babbling. It's almost incoherent.

'What are you doing? What are you doing to me, God?'

It's a fast descent into hysteria. 'Another red herring?'

My brain is screaming, blood feels about to explode from my veins. 'Now what have I got, God? Nothing! You've given me nothing. Nothing!'

Still I cannot cry.

Why?

Exhaustion drenches every sinew in my body. I stretch myself out, and because the waves are no longer breaking over my head I am able to lie on my back for the first time. My arms and legs sink beside me, but I take as much air as I can into my lungs and am still able to keep my torso afloat. I have to use my arms to scull beneath me, but agonising fatigue makes it almost impossible. I move upright again to avoid submerging completely.

'Is this your fucking plan, God?' Foul language will probably seal my fate. 'You make me swim so that I'm so fucking exhausted that I fucking drown? Is this a fucking test? Well, I can't fucking-well give you any more! I've done my best.'

I look down at my body. It's white. Almost luminous.

'Bob, Hilary, Emily,' I announce. 'I'm done. I can't swim any more.'

Silence.

I have nothing left. I put my head beneath the water.

I'll just sink, I decide. I want to go, but I still can't contemplate swallowing water. How do I drown myself?

Suddenly, a sharp pain shoots through the top of my right arm, followed by hundreds of needle-like stings. They feel like mini explosions all over my body. I look down into clearer water to see that I'm surrounded by tiny Portuguese men o' war. I've swum into a swarm of sinister stinging fire strings and they're everywhere! Transparent, with small blue centres, their tentacles float out like liquid cobwebs and give out a thousand electric shocks. Surfers call them 'ball biters' because they get into your baggies and sting your goolies.

They congregate around my neck, stinging my shoulders, upper back and chest.

'No!' I start thrashing about to disperse them. I desperately scoop the water away from me to move them from my path.

I'm going to be stung to death, I think. I have to get through them.

But just as quickly as they came, they are gone. I search the swirling waters around me but there is nothing. Not a single one left.

Were they even real or did I dream them, too?

The piercing pain and livid red stripes across my chest are the evidence that they were indeed there.

Stung, but not dead. I'm even a little disappointed. Why didn't the volley of little shocks stop my heart?

Instead adrenaline surges through me. My entire system feels charged. Nature has plugged in and given me a thousand volts. It's bizarrely restorative.

THE BYNDA LAUT
THE BARRENJOEY'S TENDER
20 MILES OFF TUA PEJAT
6.40PM

The northerly wind is howling, see-sawing between 25 and 35 knots. It's been pumping since they set out in a choppy, uncomfortable swell mid-afternoon.

Earlier, as they powered out to sea in the aluminium support boat, Colin, Jeff and Simon had quickly donned windcheaters and caps. They've pulled the latter ever lower over their eyes as they've ventured further into the tumultuous sea. Doris is still in a T-shirt, an accompaniment to his grimy red and white sports cap.

This is what the locals call a 'bad eye', one of the unforgiving storms that come from the north-west. It's black, rainy and windy, with white water everywhere. The men on the *Bynda Laut* are all proficient sailors, but these are not conditions to be out in a small boat.

From the outset, the Suzuki outboard engines have strained at 20 knots, ever since Doris carefully negotiated their way between the rocks and reefs of Tua Pejat's shallower waters. It takes someone of his experience, built up over decades, to understand the perils of the surf zone around these islands. In this weather, rip tides also make it hazardous, and beneath the surface menacing coral clusters lurk like the bared teeth of hideous sea monsters. The men with him now are witnessing why Doris represents the best of the skippers in these parts.

After two or three miles of motoring, Doris decided to change course, peeling off downwind for some respite from the punishing weather. The *Bynda Laut* was continually buffeted all the same.

195

Now, almost 20 miles out, whitecaps continue to jab them in peaky, short chops that come from all directions. Doris tries to take the tender fast, then slow, then side on, but it rocks and rolls through the swells. This is insanity, Jeff thinks to himself. He and Simon quietly confer and both confess to feeling seasick.

There has been no sign of the *Naga Laut* all afternoon, this despite that hapless boat's top speed of only five or six knots in these conditions. The tender is set low in the water and while the three Western Australians are holding on for dear life to the hard steel canopy in order to gain the highest vantage point, they're still only about two metres off the sea. It's pretty much the same height as the swell. They can't see anything through the sheets of grey rain and green, greasy sea. 'We'll have to just about run him over to find him in this,' Colin shouts over the wind.

Doris won't let the weather stall his progress; he leans on the engine's throttle with an obsessive determination. The wide arc of their travel through the ocean has taken most of the afternoon, but still the men see nothing. The bad light is beginning to fade further and as the day turns towards evening, the three men can see that their skipper is in some kind of mental turmoil.

Despite a rising concern for their own safety, they're silently impressed with Doris's indefatigability. Here is a man who runs towards risk when others would run from it. For them, Doris unselfishly scouring the waves around them strikes a heroic pose. He's like a commander charging unto the breach.

This is different from the impression some have formed over the first ten days of their surf charter. Their trip, which had started out on Doris's own boat, the *Rajah Elang* or 'Sea

Eagle', has suffered by a series of setbacks that has frustrated some in the party and infuriated others.

Simon Carlin had met Doris on his first surf trip to Indonesia in G-Land, one of the earliest surf camps on East Java, in 1995, but the others knew him by reputation only. He was part of surfing folklore, certainly, but they'd also heard that Doris was greatly esteemed in Indonesia. But their experience hadn't always corresponded with this reputation.

Like the nine men from South Africa, the nine from Perth had decided to celebrate their friend's fiftieth birthday by sharing a collective passion: surfing in the Mentawais. Some of them had been friends at school, boyhood buddies who'd pitted their talents against one another in territorial challenges off Perth's Rottnest Island, Trigg Point or further south at Margaret River. Serious and seasoned, most knew the power and perfection of Indonesia's waves, but for this trip they'd chosen to head for a set of islands to the north of the Mentawais. The Telo Islands are a wave-rich area, and still largely undiscovered. The area comes with an added appeal: a high danger factor.

Lyall Davieson, the trip's self-appointed director, had hunted online for a boat that was prepared to be more 'flexible' when it came to sourcing surf spots, one that would do 'dangerous' as opposed to the usual milk run. He found Doris Eltherington and the *Rajah Elang*.

The Western Australians were a motley crew. Lyall – called 'Cricket' thanks to his 60-kilogram body mass – was a waste manager for the City of Cockburn and was five years senior to most of the party; he'd been school friends with Simon Carlin's elder brother in Trigg Point and had dated his sister in their younger days, but his friendship with Simon had gone on to last much longer. Simon, somehow nicknamed 'Hank', was a chiropractor with two practices, one in Perth and the other in Margaret River; described by his friends as a 'gifted healer', he was also known for his musical talent, fluent Bahasa (he learnt it in high school) and dark sense of humour.

Pete Inglis was another man of the sea. A highly experienced skipper based in Western Australia's oldest port town, Albany, 400 kilometres south of Perth, he had a reputation for being able to fix anything. Then there was Colin Chenu, who grew up on Perth's Main Beach, a private man, a poet and quiet intellectual; he worked as a solicitor in a posh glass office in the city. Dave Carbon was a builder and 'the ultimate greenie'; he was also a talented musician and a volunteer life-saver, as was the extrovert and garrulous Jeff Vidler, renowned for his flamboyance. Justin Vivian, or 'Jug', was a Cottesloe-born urologist, who was also known for his way with words. Gary Catlin was a property valuer who, his friends say, 'doesn't suffer fools', and Mark Swan, or 'Swanny', was a successful stockbroker who had opted for a life in the country.

For most of the men, the trip couldn't have come sooner. It had taken Lyall some doing to get it together. Some had been financially under the pump after the GFC – as Australians cheerfully abbreviate the Global Financial Crisis – while others were having professional problems, and some had prickly relationship issues. They were all desperate to escape to the promise of great swells over their twelve days away.

Lyall was determined that this was going to be a happy time for the birthday boy, Simon. There were some very different personalities on the trip and his role, he felt, was to be the glue between them. A yoga practitioner, he felt that his on-deck meditations would offer a better chance at ensuring the energy was right.

The energy went haywire from the start.

In his haste to leave for the airport, Simon had reversed over a bobtail lizard, a beloved slow-moving species found only in Western Australia. He'd read it as a sign of bad luck.

The men had arrived in Bali at midnight and, with their thirty-three surfboards as excess baggage, endured the five-hour transit before flying to Jakarta and then on to Padang. When they landed at midday, a storm was brewing.

Doris, the ever-present cigarette hanging from his lower lip, had met his guests at the airport carrying a plastic bag of beers. Bintangs in hand, they'd made a quick stop in town for supplies and then Doris had shepherded them to the harbour where their bags and boards were ferried on dug-out canoes from the jetty to the *Rajah Elang*. Despite the rotten weather, he'd made the call to head out at 8pm across the Mentawai Strait so that in the morning his guests could look through their portholes at perfect waves. At $250 dollars a day, they would be wanting their money's worth.

It was Doris's first charter of the season. He'd been in the oil-rich Malacca Straits for the previous four months, running ocean-floor surveys on an oil and gas project for an Australian mining company. The *Rajah Elang*, the boat he'd bought a year before, was the support vessel to a seismic boat that took readings using a five-mile cable trailing a tail buoy. For 130 days straight, he'd been at sea, keeping fishermen and pirates at bay.

It meant that there had been less time for important boat maintenance.

The Western Australians chose their cabins, turned on the air conditioning and had a light meal. As the anchor went up, they knocked back a few tequilas to herald their holiday.

A few minutes into the crossing, Doris insisted that his guests gather at the stern. The Australians had already got a sense of the captain's mercurial nature. Reluctantly, they strolled to where he was waiting for them.

'I don't care if yer want to hear this or not, but there are rules on this boat,' Doris said without preamble, as if marking his turf. He knew his guests were all seasoned sailors, but he resented their bored looks, like airline passengers ignoring the crew's safety briefings.

'Life jackets are in there and the fire extinguishers are on the walls over there.' He stabbed a finger in both directions. 'The rest of the rules are up in the crapper. Read 'em.'

Later, while taking a pee off the side of the boat, some of the guys joked about the last line on Doris's rules board.

BE CAREFUL WHILE ON DECK. IF YOU FALL OVERBOARD, YOU WILL MISS OUT ON EPIC SURF. AND THERE'S A GOOD CHANCE THAT WE WILL NOT FIND YOU.

All the same, the thought of being lost overboard was sobering.

The first problem struck at 4am mid-crossing, when the main internal fuel tank, succumbing to unseen corrosion that had built up against the hull, ruptured and left the bows of the boat awash with hundreds of litres of diesel fuel. Later that day, as Doris and Pete Inglis tried their best to repair the damage, they discovered that the electrical problems weren't limited to the engine; the strain saw the air conditioners expire in rapid succession shortly after. Also the anchor was stuck, and because there was only one functional engine they couldn't power the motorised winch to take the slack off the chain and lift the anchor in the current.

The *Rajah Elang* was effectively marooned.

When the *Rajah Elang*'s desalination plant succumbed the following day, Doris was forced to capitulate. He offered to put up his guests at a nearby land-based surf camp, Wavepark, then take the boat back into Padang for repairs before returning to finish the charter.

While his guests joined the international visitors in Wavepark for two days of surfing the left-hander at the end of the point, eating beef rindang and drinking beer under thatch pagodas, Doris and his crew staggered back to Padang. Doris had everyone he knew look at his boat but it was his regular engineer, Herman, who broke the calamitous news: 'She needs a major overhaul, Doris. This ain't gonna take a day. More like weeks.'

Desperate and morose, Doris phoned another friend, John McGroder.

John was a surfing buddy and colleague of twenty-five years who had worked with him under Doris's great friend Martin Daly. For eight years, Daly, one of the early surf explorers in Indonesia, had Doris and McGroder captaining his *Indies Trader* chain of boats, steel-hulled cruisers that pioneered charters in the Mentawais, Marshall Islands and Bikini Atoll.

'Johnnie, I'm fucked!' Doris told him. 'I'm in the biggest shit imaginable.'

John and his wife Belinda ran charters off their boat. Named after the headland meaning 'small kangaroo' off Sydney's Palm Beach, the *Barrenjoey* was a two-masted steel ketch that for years had done supply runs to Lord Howe Island on the east coast of Australia. The couple had bought the yacht in New Port in 2002; they'd got her sea-worthy there, but had then sailed her on to Bali where they finished the fit-out. Also choosing a 'life of land and sea', they took their young children on the *Barrenjoey* on the long sail to the Mentawais.

John knew Doris well. He would trust him with his boat as he would his life. 'Don't worry, mate,' he said now. 'Our charter has just cancelled. You can go to sea in twenty minutes. The crew is ready and there's food on board. Bring your captain. We can get your clearance done now and you can be out of here in an hour.'

And then almost as an afterthought: 'Don't worry about the cost; we can square that up later.'

The mutual support in the Mentawai community was at work. This was a world unto itself with all its inherent rules. Here charter captains were forced to have one another's backs. It was an unspoken accord.

So Doris and John's crew sailed back out to Wavepark on the *Barrenjoey*.

'He did right by us putting us ashore. It shows his integrity,' Colin commented to Jeff. He believed Doris was a pretty solid guy, after all.

By then the swell opportunity in the Telo's had come and gone and, with the inclement weather, the consensus was to go south instead.

'The surf is smaller down there, but it's all right,' Doris said, putting an end to the dispiriting interlude. 'Yer can find some surf around Sipura while we anchor in Dreamlands. We have to visit the harbour master in Tua Pejat.'

It's past sundown as the *Bynda Laut* nears an outcrop known locally as Rockop.

'We can't really see anything out here any more, skipper,' Simon shouts across to Doris. The captain, still in commando mode, slowly nods his head; the day has been interminable and he knows that they still need at least an hour in the gathering darkness to get back to the *Barrenjoey*.

This weather is strange and capricious and Doris quietly starts praying for the south set, the conventional winds that blow from the south and would calm conditions somewhat. He hasn't seen currents like this in five years. Perhaps this guy's going that way, he thinks to himself. But the wind remains relentless, and realising that the *Bynda Laut* is being pushed beyond her reasonable limits, Doris is forced to T-bone the boat and head closer to the coastline to get out of the weather.

As they slowly come in to the more sheltered bay, darkness is almost upon them. It's 7.15pm when suddenly Jeff shouts above the drone of the engine. 'Look! Look up there!'

The dark shape of a small light aircraft is taking to the sky from the island to their left.

'They've started an aerial search!' Simon shouts. In the moment, he's relieved that someone has made this a less onerous burden.

'Unreal.' Doris squints. His vision is not that sharp in poor light any more. He tracks the silhouette of the inter-island plane taking off from the donkey track that is the Tua Pejat airstrip. It was built by the Japanese during the war. He watches the single red light blinking in the gloom. 'They're on it!'

He knows the little local passenger plane; it's old and small and flies tourists between the islands and the mainland – when it's working, which is mostly never. It doesn't have a schedule.

He watches and waits for the plane to start circling over the search area. Instead, it keeps going in a straight line, climbing up and flying onwards into the darkness, straight for Padang.

'Fuck!' Doris cries out. 'Fuck!'

With his left hand he pats his shirt for his pack of cigarettes, steering the *Bynda Laut* towards the lights of the *Barrenjoey* with his right.

The rain has stopped at last.

6.30PM TO 7.30PM
SEVENTEENTH HOUR IN THE WATER

The Portuguese men o' war have shocked me into action.

'Emily, Hilary, come on,' I rally the board members. 'We must keep swimming.'

Although the swells are still substantial, I can see that the ocean is flattening out. Without breaking waves, it's easier to maintain my big, wide strokes and I can keep going without expending the same energy as in my earlier torrent of freestyle.

I've stopped cramping and I've figured out how to lie on my back for short periods without sinking.

The buoy sighting was an imaginary promise of land, but now I can't see anything other than the pale line where the sea meets the sky. Be positive, I tell myself, a fishing boat might still come out in this calmer weather for some late-night fishing.

They'll find you.

I haven't done a paper test for a while, but the pull of the current is noticeable. Land. The current will take me there. I've been in the water for so long, land has to be close by.

I stop swimming and, treading water, take out my credit card slip. I'm down to a very small piece. I know I'll need to be careful with this.

I tear off a tiny corner and let it go. Because the water is calmer, I'm able to watch it for a longer time. It dances on the top for a few minutes, then sinks slowly, hovers beneath the surface and then glides deeper and then deeper still before it disappears.

I feel as if I'm moving at speed. After all this time, why haven't I seen land? The crossing is 100 nautical miles, 220 kilometres. I've hoped that the current will loop and tow me back to the mainland, but I never thought that I might be swept out the other way and hit the islands.

You don't want to hit those, I suddenly remember. The Indonesian coastline is littered with sharp reefs – the coral is as sharp as a scalpel. Wiping out on them is a surfer's biggest fear; you get shredded. On the second last day of our previous trip, JM had smashed onto a reef and cut his hipbone so badly he'd needed stitches. He could hardly walk afterwards.

My mind races. I picture myself, without a surfboard, grated up by coral and pulling myself, lacerated and bleeding, onto a deserted beach. The coasts are largely unpopulated and the chances of finding a homestead near a beach are remote.

You'll have to worm yourself into the jungle and hope to find a village deep in there. You'll be dehydrated. If you do find water on land, it might not be fresh. You'll get dysentery, and after all of this, you'll die on land…

My thoughts are illogical, a gut-level reflex to my circumstances.

If you do find someone on land, you don't speak their language. And even if they have a cellphone, you won't know the Indo emergency numbers. The phone won't have international roaming. How are you going dial out? How will you ask for help?

I won't make for shore, I conclude. If I see land, I'll wait in the shallower waters for fishing boats. They'll rescue me.

However, there is no hope of this during the dark hours. And just as surely, I know that I can't make it through the night. A boat has to come before nightfall. Until then I just have to stay afloat.

I start singing again – it's an escapist technique that has

kept me going all day. I don't know for how long I sing, but it feels like an eternity.

'Ten green bottles hanging on the wall...'

A fragment of weak grey appears through a break in the clouds. That must be where the sun is round about now. It will soon be setting.

Sunset, I know from previous trips at this time of year, is around 7.45pm.

I have about an hour.

I lie on my back to give my legs a rest, trailing them along as I fin again with my hands. After the earlier rush, the onset of exhaustion has begun again. New waves of lethargy sweep over me.

I wonder where I am now. How deep is it here? The ocean around me is an electric blue, iridescent. I sink down and put my head beneath the water.

Why aren't my eyes burning, I wonder, as I look around. For hours the salt has leeched my eyes, but now, mysteriously, I can open them under water. As if in a swimming pool.

It's another world beneath the platinum grey surface. A deep sapphire rises up from the depths, full of secrets from the bottom of the ocean. I slowly fin around – there are no patches of light or dark – just that extraordinary colour in every direction. It's magical.

I resurface for air, but it's getting harder to pull my strokes. Every few seconds, I roll over onto my back but just as quickly I have to turn over again. My head keeps slipping beneath the waterline; I can barely keep my nose and mouth out of the water.

Keep your head up. Don't slip down. There's no coming back from down there.

I say these words aloud. At least I think I do.

But an air of defeat overtakes me and surrender suddenly seems easier. I feel very calm. I'll never feel the earth beneath my feet again. I'll never again be on solid ground.

Perhaps death will come gently. I'll just sink and not be able to come up again. I think about the darkness that lies beneath.

Zara. Jamie. Anita. Their faces come to me and I start talking again to my wife.

'I've let you down, Neets. I'm not going to make it, after all. I'm not going to be there for you. You're going to have to be strong.'

Water laps around my eyes, creeps up to my nostrils, swallows my chin. Drained and dejected, I think I could be falling asleep. Each little breath, it strikes me, could be my last.

Then, a feathery feeling crosses my back, my arms and around my legs. Light, delicate, even pleasurable. I'm being tickled. Anita regularly tickles my back, my head and feet. 'That's wonderful, baby,' I hear myself saying. But then it starts on my stomach. I don't like being tickled on my tummy.

I open my eyes, blinking as if woken from that mysterious borderline place of unconsciousness. I look down. Hundreds of little silver fish, each a couple of inches long, are nibbling at my body.

How bizarre, I think, feeling weirdly detached. It instantly reminds me of a business trip I'd taken to Japan many years before where I'd seen people pay fortunes for a strange 'doctor fish' pedicure. They'd put their feet into bowls of flesh-eating fish that nibbled away at the dead skin.

Suddenly a sharp pain erupts from behind my knees. Short, sharp stabs of pain that precipitate a spreading ache that runs up to my groin and down to my ankles. I glance over my shoulder and down my back and see an entire shoal of what look like mini sardines in a frenzied attack on the back of my legs.

Jesus Christ! They're eating me!

My shorts have chafed the back of my legs raw. Two patches of broken, angry skin behind each knee provide a fishy buffet. I let out an agonising scream and kick maniacally around me to dislodge the creatures. They dart away, but as soon as I stop moving, they return.

Perhaps I should catch one to eat? Sushi, I manage a joke to myself. I kick my right leg and try to snatch a fish as a cluster goes helter-skelter. I plan to swallow it whole.

It makes me think of one of my first meetings with Anita. We were dating a set of twins. She was involved with the guy, another Brett, while I dated his twin sister. The four of us had gone to a black-tie event where they'd placed bowls of live goldfish on the tables as centrepieces. I like shocking people and so I got it into my head to pull a stupid stunt inspired by the film *A Fish Called Wanda*, which had just been released.

After the meal, Anita and her boyfriend joined our table and I asked if they'd seen the movie. I decided to re-enact the scene when Kevin Kline swallows Michael Palin's fish. My intention was to spit it out and put it back in the bowl. I dropped the fish into my mouth. It hit the back of my throat and slid straight down. I had two choices: to swallow or spew it out all over the table. I swallowed.

My girlfriend was horrified and got up and walked away. Anita's eyes were enormous. And a woman from the SPCA at the next table went ballistic.

I went to a vet friend who was at a table close by. The

fish had probably disintegrated in my gastric juices before it knew what hit it, he said.

'Will I be poisoned?' I'd asked.

'You're probably going to be violently ill later,' he'd laughed.

I remember the conversation verbatim.

I was indeed very ill later, so I'm not sure I do want to catch one of these things now.

My musing is interrupted by a sound. A distant, low moan. It's momentarily muffled but seconds later it seems louder. It dissipates again and I begin to wonder if I've imagined it. Then, yes, I hear it again. Unmistakable. The slowly ratcheting throttle of a plane's engine. I look up into the deepening darkness, scouring the sky. I rub my sore, puffy eyes and widen them to push through the pain.

I know from the sound that it must be a light aircraft, but I can't make out any form in the sky. I scan the arc above me, turning myself in a circle. Then out of the blackness, I see a red light. Blinking. And it's coming towards me. It must have taken off from over there, I think to myself. It's come from land. I flip over onto my back and trace the light, pulsing. Like a heartbeat.

A rescue plane? They're coming for me. They're coming for me.

My stomach wrenches within, but at the same time a realisation descends. Part of me knows that they'll never see me – not at that height. Not at this hour. I imagine someone up there in his winged sewing machine, looking out of the window. I lift my arm in a wave as the amorphous shape whirrs overhead.

'Hey!' I hear my strangled voice. But I know that it's futile. 'Please. No.'

My words seem to float on the air around me.

The red light gains height and continues to the east. I watch as it goes, its engine now taking on a higher pitch. Like the whine of a mosquito. And then it's gone.

Grief coils up inside me and I'm swamped by a tsunami of melancholy.

Once more I'm alone.

FISKAAL ROAD
CAMPS BAY
11.23AM

'Do you want this to get out to the media, Anita?'

Kirsten Horn asks the question tentatively. Tremors of uncertainty run through the room. Everyone is gathered around the dining-room table as if in conference, sensing another daunting decision.

Time has slowed to a leaden pace. Nothing further can be done. The search for Brett, everyone believes, is under way: the *Naga Laut* is retracing her course; several boats are to set out in an organised grid, and planes will take to the sky. All facts have been investigated, discussed, dismantled, classified. The practical has now given way to the most challenging task: waiting.

Only Anita's father Loni seems somewhat removed from it all, determined that nothing will breach the armour of his defences.

Kirsten, who had been a local television personality in her youth, still has contacts whom she thinks can help spread the message that Brett is missing. Half an hour ago, Shelly Griessel, Steve Griessel's sister-in-law, who lives in the US, called; the news had found her too via Facebook and she asked if she might set up a dedicated Facebook page, something that could link JM's posts and the updates they're getting from Chantal in Hermanus.

'It's a way for people all over the world, those who know Brett and those who don't, to follow what's going on,' she said.

She posted the page and calls it 'Searching for Brett Archibald'.

'What must I do?' Anita tries to maintain a façade of composure, but she's pale and dark rings have formed around her eyes.

'We should do whatever we can,' Louise says patiently. 'What if Brett's injured in some way? The sooner we get this news out there, the greater the chances of someone finding him.'

'We've got to let the world know that there's a man missing in the Mentawais.' Helene stands up as if to shake off the lethargy. It shifts the mood a little. 'The people on the islands, all the damned boats that are out there – they all need to know what's happened, what Brett looks like. It should be front-page news. And with modern technology...'

'A friend who's been to Indonesia has told me about a small news website in Padang. I'll ask them to put it into their local news report,' Lulu offers. 'We'll have to deal with the language barrier, but...' He voice tails off as she scrolls for the details in a text message on her phone.

'So many people are calling to find out what's going on.' Karmen also looks tired. 'It would be better if we directed them to Facebook or a media website.'

'An email accidentally went out from here with the boat's satellite phone number,' Lulu adds. 'Mark sent me a text complaining that people are calling them. We must tell everyone not to call. They need to keep that line open...'

'Right, I'll get hold of someone I know at News24.' Kirsten is grateful for something to do.

Paula puts her arm around her daughter's shoulders. Anita's eyes convey the depth of her despair. 'Perhaps you should go up and change.' Her voice is gentle, as if Anita is a little girl again.

'Our story's not over yet, Mom.'

'No, not yet.' Paula's words are barely audible as Anita turns to go up the stairs.

'I need to go.' Lulu starts gathering up her handbag. 'My boys are sick at home. I must check in on them and I have a site meeting at midday.' She's cancelled most of her decorating business's meetings for the day, but couldn't change this one. 'I'll come back later.'

'I have to be off as well.' Katya wipes her eyes, which are red from crying, and then quietly blows her nose. She turns to the group of women huddled at the kitchen door.

'I've told Anita that I'll fetch the kids. Jamie and Zara can come home with me after school and have a sleepover with Alex and Katarina. I think it's best if they're not here. Besides, they'll love it – especially on a school night.'

She manages a tepid smile. For Katya, the day's emotion is sublimated into these details.

'We'll let you know if we hear anything,' says Helene, stirring a production line of coffees. 'I'll come around later with pyjamas and clean clothes for them.'

Lulu shrugs to lift her coat over her head and Katya opens a small green umbrella. They skittle out one after the other into the stiff, wet wind. Another downpour has begun.

'Oh God, what's going on up there?' Gaby points towards the ceiling. 'It's about to collapse!'

In the far left corner of the study a dark, menacing mark is spreading like Gondwanaland across the ceiling. A section has given in and buckled under the weight of the water. The sound of falling drops has gone unheard all morning and is now a steady trickle into the room.

'Shit!' Louise and Kirsten scramble to remove papers on the table under the widening wet patch.

'I'll get up into the roof and sort that out.' Luke's chair

screeches across the tiles as he gets up from the table. 'Where can I find a bucket?'

Letti waves him into the kitchen. 'We can't let everything fall apart,' he says under his breath.

At the foot of the stairs, Helene stops to listen. She looks up into the stairwell, like the darkened architraves in a cathedral. There's a lull in her sister's weeping upstairs. It reminds her of their childhood when their bedrooms were side by side. Anita's crying pattern of love and loss, her grief's rhythm, is the same. When upset as a child, she would give a long, loud nose blow that would precede a wail. Long silences would always follow.

Despite the silence, Helene knows that Anita is still crying.

The two women are highly attuned to one another, this despite having spent many years in different parts of the world, living different lives and, more recently, on different sides of Table Mountain. Residents of Cape Town joke how the great wonder of nature can also be a divide; it can separate people who become too complacent, too lazy or just too damned comfortable where they are to take the drive to the other side.

For some, 'the other side' might as well be another country.

It might also partly explain the veil of recent reserve between Helene and Anita. Still, the sisters share most of their emotional life over the phone. They talk every day.

For a moment, the worst outcome crosses Helene's mind.

How will my sister cope if Brett is dead, she thinks? Anita depends on Brett for so much. As far as practicality goes, she's in la-la land. He does all the banking, the house payments, cars, school fees, insurances. She couldn't deal with day-to-day fundamentals.

Her mind moves quickly. Would Anita move to

Johannesburg to live with their parents? Would Paula and Loni move to Cape Town instead? How would that affect them? How would life – all their lives – change if they had to forge a support network around her sister?

No, she switches back to her innate response. This is going to be a victory over tragedy, a victory over tragedy. And she begins to pray.

'I think she wants to be alone for a while, Zendi,' she tells her aunt when she feels a presence beside her. Zenda, normally immaculately groomed, has just arrived from Stellenbosch in a tracksuit. 'Don't go up just yet.'

Upstairs Anita is outside on her bedroom balcony once again. The wind is whipping around her, sending hair flying about her face. She looks out again at the bay, the waters a vortex of seething whorls and swirls. The sea and sky have merged on the horizon in a cloudy communion, as if they're hiding something.

I can't see anything out there, she thinks, staring at the white horses colliding in a frantic dance. I wouldn't be able to see a boat, never mind a man's head.

The onslaught of dark, sceptical thoughts is overwhelming. She has tried so hard to keep these feelings buried, but they descend now.

Please, God, please, she prays, feeling slightly dizzy. She watches the sea. It feels strange, foreign, uncontrollable, but with a curious mesmeric quality.

Suddenly she steps back and shuts the sliding door with force. Her unwieldy thoughts must be brought under control. She decides to return downstairs, still in her pyjamas. She doesn't want to be alone. She wants to avoid the look of dread that stares back at her in the glass.

Wayne Grieveson meets her on the stairwell. He embraces

her without saying a word. When he'd eventually picked up his wife's desperate messages this morning, he'd cancelled his business diary for this day and the next.

Anita is grateful for Wayne's presence. A quiet man, he is clear of thought, accurate, methodical, organised. Brett had, for years, been his business mentor, an older-brother figure for him, and a strong personal friendship has grown out of their professional one.

Wayne returns to the armchair he has secured in the lounge and opens his laptop. He has removed himself from the fatigue and tedium in the dining room. He has the air of a loner's steely self-reliance.

Paula and Zenda embrace Anita as she comes downstairs and goes to stand sorrowfully before her makeshift altar.

'Nana had a weird superstition.' Zenda takes out a tissue from her handbag. Her mother-in-law was a Russian nurse who'd escaped the Nazis and fled to Ethiopia before ending up in South Africa. 'She always said that if you lost something, you should knot a hankie and it would soon be found.'

Anita takes the tissue and folds a knot in the centre of it.

Tears stream down Zenda's face. She has a vivid flashback to the weekend wedding. Brett had been sitting opposite her; he'd been at the heart of the party, swinging the girls on the dance floor, '*Impi* dancing' with the boys.

Amazing for a man of fifty, she remembers thinking.

'You're not going to do this to me, Brett!' Anita suddenly shouts angrily at the altar photograph.

Her outburst heightens the already amplified electricity in the room. After a brief silence, Helene walks over to her.

'This is not your husband's death, Anita,' she says. 'He has lived the most amazing life, done the most extraordinary things. He's not going to go out with a bang. He's going to have the most boring death of all of us. And this is not it. He doesn't deserve to go out this way.'

A phone rings.

There's a sharp intake of breath in the room. Each time anyone's phone rings, they all look at one another, unnerved; it could be 'the call'. A lumbering silence follows.

Karmen answers.

'It's the school, Anita,' she says quietly.

'I'll take it.' Helene reaches for the cellphone. She walks outside to escape the pressure-cooker quality around them. It's the Bishops school counsellor, who recommends that Helene chat to a child psychologist regarding the children. Her phone number is passed on.

The psychologist tells Helene that she's heard about a Camps Bay man missing overboard in Indonesia on a radio news report. 'Weird. I happen to be looking at the "Searching for Brett Archibald" Facebook page. I'm staring at your brother-in-law's face right now.'

They talk about counselling Zara and Jamie. It's better that they sleep away from home, she agrees. 'But Anita must tell them the truth in the morning. Whatever the outcome. They need to hear it from their mother, not from one of the kids in their class.'

Inside, another phone rings. Again, the anticipation is like a plunge down a rollercoaster. This time Karmen hands the phone to Anita.

'Craig Lambinon of the NSRI.'

'How are you doing, Anita?' Craig asks cautiously.

'Not great.' She tries to keep the equanimity in her voice. 'My husband is out there waiting for us to find him. Who have you got to help look?'

Craig has been trawling the international sea rescue networks in Australasia.

He can't bring himself to give his intended message: that with Brett missing now for more than ten hours, there is just a one percent chance of finding him.

THE NAGA LAUT
7.02PM

The *Naga Laut*'s radio is out of operation; the satellite phone has fallen silent. The only sound is the strumming of light rain on the boat's synthetic deck-covering.

Doubt is beginning to creep into Weyne's heart. He has spent this desolate day with an uncomfortable thought sitting like a stone in his chest. He keeps mentally replaying part of his conversation with Brett from the night before. It's driving him crazy.

'This is my soul place. This is where I'd come to escape. To opt out. This is where part of me belongs.'

The words have looped in Weyne's head all day, bringing with them a rising tide of emotion. He has remained silent, grappling with the personal turmoil. Could Brett have done this on purpose? Could his comments have disguised a more intense despair? Could he have chosen his 'soul place' to take his own life?

Weyne can't bear to voice his suspicions and keeps hoping that he might have misunderstood or misread Brett.

He wouldn't commit suicide, he rationalises. And not out here, not like this.

Still, he hasn't seen his old classmate for many years. Could there have been clues in their powerful encounter last night that had more significance than he'd realised? Outer facades often hide a complicated inner wiring.

As darkness falls, darker thoughts come with it. Weyne's fretting is unbearable. He needs to unburden himself. He makes his way to JM, who is hunched on the portside. JM's legs hang through the railings like a marionette's. Weyne crouches beside him, his manner quiet and intense.

'I need to say something privately, JM. I need to share this.' It's like he's speaking in church. 'Was Brett happy at work? Was everything all right with his business? He sounded a bit depressed about it when we chatted last night and I don't know if he was in such a good place.'

His speculation, once spoken, is carried away on the wind. 'Could it be a possibility?' he asks finally, clearly concerned.

He's met with a Sphinx-like expression. Then JM is gently emphatic.

'No, Weyne, don't worry. I know Brett. There's no way. It's just not like him.'

A wave of relief washes over Weyne; it's reflected on his face, upturned to the sky.

'Of course, I know that. But I've been going mad remembering our conversation.'

'It's okay.' JM can see the conflict that has raged inside his friend.

'We've all had terrible thoughts. This morning Tony and I went through Brett's bag looking for travel documents Anita wanted. Tony found a note. "You are my hero. I'll follow in your footsteps until the day I die," it said. Tony thought Brett had written it. A suicide note? It's bullshit. Why would anyone travel with a note like that?'

Weyne puts his hand on JM's shoulder. 'I just had to say it. Get it off my chest.'

They both look up to the east, where the bow is still belly flopping through the chop. Everything seems blurred at the edges, but JM can just make out the low bank of grey looming beside them. It's the mainland, like the back of some giant sea creature breaching its watery home.

'Sumatra,' JM announces, his tone flat.

A shout suddenly comes from the stern. Jaipur is calling

to Yanto, but what he's saying is inaudible. They follow his pointing finger. The men see a small precarious-looking wooden fishing vessel behind them, materialised out of nowhere. It has ventured out to the shallower water in this mad weather, but is being tossed about the agitated sea.

Yanto waves to the solitary man, a local, requesting him to draw up alongside. Shouting in Bahasa, he tells him that a man is out there in the water. The fisherman's long face remains immobile. Saturated, he nods in acknowledgement. His vessel is barely afloat.

'This is not looking good, Ridgy.' Niall joins Mark Ridgway on the bridge. He speaks softly. 'It's pretty dark; the sea is still very rough. I don't think he can see through the night. We have to consider that he's gone and that we might be looking for a body tomorrow.'

'We do have to think about those things, I suppose.' Ridgy is calm. 'This holiday has turned into a fucking hell. How would we recover the body?'

'Where would we keep it?' Niall looks behind him dejectedly.

'There'd be an inquest. We wouldn't get out of here in ten days. We'd have to fly the body home. Consulates. Officials. Oh, Christ, can you imagine? And what about Anita and the kids? It'll be chaos.'

Craig comes up behind JM and Weyne.

'Brett will have to make it through another night.' He's had the same thoughts. 'That's another eight hours or so of pitch darkness.'

For a moment, the idea hangs in the air. Banger moves in beside them.

Morale has reached its nadir.

Helplessness and guilt leave the men devoid of words.

7.30PM TO 8.30PM
EIGHTEENTH HOUR IN THE WATER

Darkness is falling fast. It must be after 7pm and the sun appears to have set through clouds that are now just smudges of smoky vapour. It indicates, at last, where west is. For the first time, I realise that the islands must be in front of me. The current will regurgitate me onto them. Eventually.

There can be only thirty minutes or so of this half-light left.

The water has calmed now; it's smooth but still, with big, undulating swells. The ocean seems to be breathing – gently inhaling and exhaling. I feel quite peaceful, but for my arms. They feel so heavy, like grandfather clock weights hanging off my torso. I no longer have the energy to swim. I try to turn on my back again and arch myself as far as I can to stop my body from crumpling in.

'Shirls,' I wonder aloud, 'how the hell did you float like that?'

I try again, as I've done a thousand times, to lift my legs parallel, but I have to keep my arms moving to do so. They are so utterly useless to me now that whenever I stop my legs sink, taking the rest of me down with them.

I resurface, coughing. I've swallowed what seems like a gallon of water.

As night looms, the hope of fishing boats appearing is fading away. I briefly recall the long out-rigger pirogues that we've seen come out occasionally in the evening to ply their trade in the shallower waters. They looked like giant dragonflies: a flimsy construction of two canoes joined by a strut that the fishermen rig with industrial lights. They cast big pools of light into the ocean around them and scoop up the catch attracted into it. Moths to a flame. Would one come out at dusk?

It's a last-ditch wish, but I'm afraid to wish for anything any more.

I imagine the rays of light from a rig. Like enormous haloes. I imagine becoming a fish – growing gills and webbing between my fingers and toes. I'm in a fisherman's net and I see the shock on his face as he pulls me from the water. A glowing white, crinkled man trying to breathe through holes in his neck.

He'll shit himself. The idea amuses me.

But another fate awaits me – and that thought causes a squeezing in my guts.

I can't make it through ten hours of darkness. I shake my head. I can't do it.

These thoughts are echoing in my head when I feel a massive wallop against my back, like a punch, slightly above my left kidney.

What the hell was that? I swirl around.

A barracuda, is my first thought. When we aren't surfing on these charters, we fish, and we've often caught barracuda – big inedible killer fish, with large sharp teeth like an Alsatian's. They're the wild dogs of the sea. If there were ten of them, they'd strip a man's flesh to the bone.

They've sniffed the blood from the holes in the back of my legs, I reason.

Then – bam! Whatever it was hits me again in exactly the same place.

That's not a barracuda. I'm filled with horror. That's a shark.

I know from the many television documentaries I've watched that some sharks bump their prey first to identify it. Sharks are not a common sight any more in these waters, but my intuition is pretty certain. Fear and desperation bubble up like vomit. I try to convince myself that rationality must rule.

You've got to see what this is, I tell myself. You can't wait for an attack to come from nowhere, for jaws to crush your body. You have to face it!

I sink beneath the surface and slowly fin around. Through the deepening gloom I see it. It's a few metres away. Sleek and, when a brief burst of light catches it, silvery. A shark is coming straight towards me. It's the size of a bus!

Oh my God! There's chaos in my head.

It moves through the water as if in slow motion, gliding towards me, its massive tail weaving its entire form left to right. I can hardly make out where its body ends and the dark water begins. Its black-centred eyes are as opaque as the water around it. They look dead to me. Its jaws are slightly open in a sinister sneer.

Fuck! Fuck! Fuck!

I recognise the black edgings of its vertical fin like an ink mark. It's a blacktip reef shark. I've dived in the Maldives, where they're common. It's not actually the size of a bus, but at two metres or so it's big for a blacktip and the effect is magnified underwater. Even though this one might have a go, I know it would have to be starving to attack a human.

I feel my heart hammering in my chest. Blood is coursing through my head, thudding in my ears and pounding behind my eyes. My thoughts are split-second. I switch to practicalities.

Blacktip reef sharks don't swim miles out to sea. They keep close to reefs. This one might be a little bit out of whack, but there has to be a reef nearby. I must be near land.

As it continues towards me, a powerful surge rips through

my body. My survival instinct, primal and raw, takes over and a truly absurd idea forms.

You can take this guy, I tell myself. Try to get him to come at you. As he opens his mouth, move your body out of the way and ram your left arm down his throat. When he slows down, throw your right arm over his tail and hang on. He can take you into shore.

I might lose an arm, I reason, but at least I'll be towed to land. Out of this ocean. Out of this wretched watery wasteland. I'm about to ride a blacktip reef shark to salvation…

Bear Grylls comes to mind; his show is a favourite of mine. Could he do this?

'Step aside Bear Grylls, here comes Arch! C'mon, buddy', I mentally shout at the shark. 'C'mon!'

But in the next moment, it's gone.

'Where are you? Where have you gone?' I shout, coming up for air. It's lunacy. Instead of relief at not being shark bait, I feel disappointment. My plan has failed.

'Not again,' I hear myself whine.

I spend the next twenty minutes finning around in the water, wondering if the shark will return. Whether he'll attack me. Wait for night. Bring friends.

My hand explores my lower back and I cautiously touch where the shark hit me. It's very tender.

That was no hallucination!

I feel recharged, though. Revived. And, importantly, I have hope again that I'm near land. Hang on, I think. You'll see it soon.

Slowly, gently, I start swimming.

'Oh Lord my God,' I start singing, 'when I in awesome wonder…'

I feel Anita's presence all around. 'Talk to me, baby.'

I open my mind and my heart – and from somewhere deep inside, I believe I hear her voice.

'Swim, Brettman, the love of my life. You can do this. I'm not letting you leave me. Swim!'

THE NAGA LAUT
7.55PM

As the *Naga Laut* slowly motors into a small bay south of Padang, the rain lets up at last and the sky seems strangely translucent. But it doesn't lift the mood on board.

The South Africans are dazed, introverted, somnambulant after their angst-ridden day. When they do speak, it's in quiet tones and about evasive generalities, never about the reality of their circumstances. There's an aura of loneliness.

The boat takes safe anchorage in front of a chokka village squatting beside a long sweep of beach. Communications are restored and almost immediately the satellite phone begins to ring.

A local radio station in South Africa has got wind of the story and wants an interview. Ridgy gives the handset to JM.

The sun has set and in the west the sky looks rubbed out. Clouds above are moving hurriedly in the gathering gloom. Night hovers like a bird of prey.

Red-eyed and haggard from their fruitless search, the men move to their phones where 3G connections deliver text messages all at once. The tri-tone alerts sound like an orchestra warming up.

Phone calls and texts begin to flit across the globe – fragile threads that link these men to home. They cast out and reel in information, grasping for a lead out of this torment.

A text from Chantal Malherbe in Hermanus beeps on Tony's phone. He reads it aloud: 'Calculated that the current is going west to Sipura, about one or two knots. He will have found land already. Trying to get boats to search outbound of the islands. They'll sail with bright lights so that Brett has something to swim towards. The hope is he finds a tree to hold on to – and the current.'

Tony looks up. 'He's got a chance.' The idea of Brett on land buoys him. 'Guys, Arch is going to do this thing. He's going to do it.'

'Of course he is.' JM rubs his burning eyes.

Ridgy bends down over the charts once again.

'With us sailing back down towards the islands and those other boats coming upwards, does it mean we'll criss-cross the sea? Surely we'll now get better coverage?' JM asks.

'Yes, theoretically,' Ridgy nods. 'At two knots, the current should have carried him to about here.' He slides his finger in a line across the blue of the chart. Powder blue on paper. Very different in reality. 'The line for our crossing tomorrow morning must be a little further down.'

He looks at Yanto, whose face looks wrinkled, like un-ironed laundry. As with the rest of the crew, he is utterly exhausted. Mark can tell he doesn't believe Brett will be found alive. It has been too long.

'We're going back out there tomorrow morning. We'll start early.' It sounds like an order from JM as he sits down in the galley with his iPad. He calls up his Facebook page and updates it with a post. 'We're heading back through the Straits in the morning,' he types. 'WE WILL FIND HIM.' As if by willing it, it will happen.

'I think I should phone Anita again,' JM says, standing up. He walks slowly to the bridge to retrieve the satellite phone and moves to the prow of the *Naga Laut*. He takes a moment to gather himself. It's deep twilight now and scattered lights are appearing on the mainland, blinking like fireflies.

JM is nervous. Slowly he sits down on the deck, inhales deeply and dials Anita's cellphone.

Karmen answers. 'She's not taking calls, JM.'

But he hears Anita moving closer in the background, and her voice: 'I must speak to him.'

It's an awkward phone call for he has nothing new to tell her. Anita mentions that she, too, has received news that the current could possibly have taken Brett to land.

'My dad says he's on an island having a cocktail with an umbrella in it.' The joke is laced with apprehension.

'Listen to me, Neets. Brett's mind is strong. He's fit. He knows the ocean. He will get through this.'

'What if he's hurt?' she asks quickly.

'We don't know that. Try not to think about it. Here's what we do know: it's been cloudy and raining hard all day so he would have been able to get some fresh water down his throat. And he won't be burned to a crisp.'

His words seem to be coming out all wrong and Anita doesn't respond.

'Promise me you'll be strong. Have faith. I have. Don't believe the negative sentiments... I'll phone you again tomorrow when we have him back. *Believe*, Anita.'

'I do believe.' He can barely hear her whisper over the crackling line. He's impressed by her dignity. 'I do.'

JM hangs up and drops his head. It's been an incredibly energy-sapping day. He begins to search for Shirley Archibald's number on his cellphone. He has known Brett's mother since he was a boy. She will be beside herself. He takes another breath and dials the house number. It just rings.

He tries Shirley's cellphone. No answer.

He opens the internet browser on his phone. Logging onto Facebook, he messages Brett's sister Sandra and asks for their brother Greg's number. Greg and JM have also known each other since boyhood; his younger brother was in Greg's class and they'd all played sport together.

This one is a terrible call.

'Toast, have you found him?' Greg sounds like he's had a couple of drinks.

'No, my bud. That's not why I'm calling.'.

'Then what are you phoning for?' Greg spits back. 'What's going on there? Had he been drinking? Was he pissed?' Questions fly like machine-gun fire.

'Hey, just slow down, buddy,' JM says firmly. 'Give me a chance. Let me tell you what I know.' He inhales again, slowly. 'We haven't found him. We've been searching all day. It's been a long day and we're all exhausted, but there are enough reasons to believe that Brett's alive.'

JM goes through the same reassurances he's given Anita.

The Archibalds are in the Drakensberg, awaiting news. What no-one knows is that Greg, desperate and alone, has secretly been calling his brother's cellphone – simply to hear his voice. And to leave messages. Wistful, pleading, like prayers offered in church.

'You have to be all right, Brett. You have to come back home.'

'He didn't fall overboard because he was pissed,' JM continues into the phone. 'He went over because he was extremely sick. Puking his guts out over the side of the boat. We can only think that he passed out. We've checked the boat, wondered whether he slipped backwards, but there's no blood, we've checked every angle. He must have gone over the top and passed out. And if he did, he'd wake up and swim. I know that –'

Greg cuts him short: 'Please just phone us when you have better news.'

It's sharp and curt. Then Greg hangs up.

JM is rocked by the dismissive call. His confidence wavers. He knows that Greg is in pain and is just venting, but the rebuff upsets him. There are many theories circulating and circumstances are open to interpretation, he knows that, but no-one really knows what happened to Brett.

JM clambers down from the front deck and moves below, where he finds Tony.

'Greg's just crapped all over me. Asked why I hadn't called with better news.'

'Forget about it,' Tony tells him calmly. 'He's scared. Like the rest of us.'

The men fall silent for a moment.

'It's been a very long time already, JM.' Tony's next words are almost a whisper. 'We have to consider all outcomes. The crew has been telling us that when a man drowns at sea, the body stays beneath the surface for seven hours. Then it fills with gases and floats up much later.'

'For God's sake, we aren't looking for a body.' JM also speaks in a low tone. 'We're going back out there to find him alive. We're on the right track; we just have to follow the chart.'

8.30PM TO 9.30PM
NINETEENTH HOUR IN THE WATER

Wham!

Something hits me on the back of my head.

I must have fallen asleep for a second, but the wallop forces me wide-awake.

I feel a rush of air over my face first, followed by an odd rustling in the gathering darkness. It moves so fast over me in the near night that I can't see what it is. A menacing presence. Then, focusing as much as I can, I just make out the silhouette of a bird – a seagull. It's circling above me in the last minutes of light.

Again it swoops at speed and this time misses my head by millimetres.

'Hey!' I shout. 'Hey! What the fuck are you doing?'

He returns to dive-bomb me a third time from behind. My natural instinct is to duck and I submerge, coughing as water fills my ears, mouth and nose. I'm under attack.

For a moment, I think I'm dreaming.

'Fuck off, fuck off!' I shriek. Then I realise: it's trying to pluck out my eyes or rip off my ears!

It keeps coming at me, screeching maliciously as it hovers in the darkness above. I sense more than see its kamikaze trajectory down towards me, its beak like scissors. All of a sudden, it strikes me how thirsty I am. I haven't thought about it before, but I suddenly feel desperate. Thirsty. *Thirsty*. Water now would be a godsend.

As the gull screams and squawks over me, I hatch another outrageous plan: I'll coax it to land on my head. Reach up and snatch it. Break its neck, bite off its head and squirt the blood down my throat.

I'll eat the fucking thing, feathers and all. I'm defiant.

Then my face feels like it explodes. Distracted, I haven't seen the second – and larger – bird come from my left. He hits the bridge of my nose; it feels as if it's been sliced clean off my face. I remember the pain from when I was once head-butted in a bar fight.

He was going for my eyes, but I'd turned my head at the last second and thrown him off his aim. My eyes water, as blood pours from my nose over the rest of my face. Blood, heavy and sticky, also fills my mouth.

'You motherfuckers!' I scream at the birds.

They shriek back, as shrill as the harpies I'd read about in books as a boy.

'I hate you! You disgusting pieces of *shit*!' I swivel my head around furiously, trying to see where the next attack will be coming from. 'Since when do seagulls attack humans?' I ask in a fury, as if they'll answer back.

I lift the skin up off my nose and feel blood trickle down to my lips. But again, my mind is questioning: seagulls don't spend the night out at sea. They land and float on water but they don't sleep at sea. They sleep on land. The shark and now the seagulls… I have to be close to land.

Then they are gone. Off to my right, I watch two dark shapes disappear into the mysterious night.

I have to see an island soon.

'I'll hang on, Neets. For you and the kids. Anita, can you hear me?'

A deep black is suffusing from the surrounding ocean. I'm very cold, shaking uncontrollably. It will soon be pitch dark. And I have to make it through the night. Another nine hours. My mind circles around the vast emptiness of the idea.

'How are you going to do this?' I can barely keep my head up and am continually swallowing sea water. Sometimes speaking aloud, I find, helps me focus. Despondency keeps dragging me down.

'Bob!' I yell. I hear his grunt, as if also woken from sleep. It isn't the voice of anyone I know, but I have an idea of the kind of man Bob is; one I'd want beside me in the heat of battle. 'Guys, this is going to be our darkest night. We have to work together. Talk to one another. Work as team.'

I try to take deeper breaths, but it's an immense strain.

'Pump those lungs, Bob!'

The girls are a cacophony, talking simultaneously. 'You have to keep your head above water, boss. It's the only way production is able to breathe.'

I sweep over the sea's rolling swells. There is no light anywhere around me. There are clouds above but oddly the night isn't completely black, which fascinates me. Instead I begin to notice a strange light coming off the ocean, a luminous glow that makes it look as if the water could come to life any minute. It's eerie, but exquisite. As the glowing swirls come towards me, I realise that it's phosphorescence, living plankton on the water's surface, a moving continent of microscopic creatures come to light my way. Their luminescence is like nothing I've seen before, a magnificent sight of liquid blue-green, like a swathe of stars that have fallen to earth. For a moment, this marine miracle makes me feel less alone. I'm exhausted and slowly I roll onto my back as I run my hands through the neon fairyland before it disappears into the wake of the undulating waves.

I feel incredibly small after the encounter. Imperceptible. A drop in the ocean. I come upright and turn very slowly in a small circle to look around.

I might as well be in the Arctic or in the Sahara, also dying of thirst. Either way I'm at the mercy of the elements. We are nothing against nature's wonder and might, I think.

My chances of surviving, of being found now, are minimal. I accept this and for a time I feel utterly divorced from myself, my mind just a deep blank.

The mysterious phosphorescence has calmed me and I'm suddenly reminded of a special ocean experience I once had with my wife.

Anita. I feel a union with her now.

'Neets, remember our ride with the dolphins?' I speak to her as if she's beside me.

We'd gone on a cruise to the Caribbean some years before. Part of the package was a life-jacketed swim with trained dolphins. We lay, tummy down, in the water with our feet arched. Two dolphins swam up underneath us, gently put their noses beneath our feet and pushed us up out of the surf like water-skiers. They swam holding us up like that for several metres. We'd both said it was the most exhilarating experience of our lives.

I imagine two dolphins coming up beneath me now. I hold on. Allowing them to tow me to safety. Saved by dolphins. Rescued by fish.

My heart is racing, but I don't have the strength to swim right now. I gently scull to keep my head above water. I'm just able make out my arms in the murkiness.

The paper test I'd done just before it got dark showed that I am still in the current, still moving well. 'It'll take you to land in the night,' I whisper consolingly.

The backs of my legs, rubbed raw by the edges of my shorts, are stinging now, welling into a crescendo of pain. I can't twist around to get a good look at the wounds, but I can feel the open flesh with my flaking fingers. As I bend my knees, I imagine the tendons stripped bare.

You're aware of pain and that's a good sign, I decide. It'll keep you awake.

I feel bloated and a little nauseous from all the salt water I've swallowed. I need to pee badly now, but I know from the pressure on my bladder and the sting in my groin that it's going to be excruciating. I have no strength to drop my pants so I close my eyes, anticipating the agony, and simply urinate.

The pain is intense and the urine so hot that I think it might burn me. I pull my shorts away from my body as the hot liquid slowly moves around me.

The agony somehow loosens my bowels and I defecate – it, too, is a hot liquid.

The sense of loneliness, of remoteness, is immense.

On top of it I feel incredibly tired all over again. It's a recurrent thought. Can you keep your head up? Can you make it through the night? An anthem in my head.

You should listen to your body, not your pride.

As darkness deepens, irrational fears overtake me again. I'm on a razor's edge. Thoughts of man-eating sharks and barracudas play on my mind and I begin to wonder what strange creatures of the sea, less benign than the phosphorescence, might emerge at these strange hours. I envision a giant octopus coming up from the depths to surface and swallow me whole.

I put my head under the water to see what's down there. I can't see beyond the waistband of my shorts. It's as black as death. I'm trapped in an ocean of thick tar.

THE NAGA LAUT
9.32PM

Yanto comes out onto the lower deck.

'Dinner.' He gestures for the men to come in. His eyes have that thousand-mile stare reserved for the condemned; he stands watching them file in, emotionless.

The men huddle into the galley, as the boat sways to a gentler ocean rhythm.

'Guys,' Tony breaks the silence as the men shift into the benches around the table, 'we need to mark this moment. Arch is still out there. It's going to be a long, cold, dark night. I think we should say a prayer.'

The gesture recalls the days when Tony was vice head boy at school.

He turns to Benoit. 'Banger, will you do it?'

Banger looks solemnly at each of the dazed men for a moment and then nods. They bow their heads and close their eyes. Banger pushes out his barrel chest and starts to pray: first a formal grace and then a prayer for Brett – asking God for his safety and for calm for his family. His words are clear, strong, reverential; they resound in the small cabin as it if were a basilica.

Many of these men haven't prayed in a long time, if at all, but somehow it seems appropriate, even important now. It's a powerful moment. Some fight back tears, their throats thick with emotion.

If God does exist, Weyne thinks to himself, this is the closest I've come to feeling it.

Dinner, a lamb dish on rice, is laid on the table in silence. The men sit, shoulders hunched, eyes red and glistening. They eat in a strange, ethereal silence.

But then the hiatus is over and they begin to mutter about their frustration with the day, of facing another protracted crossing, of being so far away from the zone and of the time it would take to get back there, at least another seven or eight sailing hours. They feel trapped in some kind of nether world, wishing, willing time to pass.

Craig's cellphone rings. His sister, who has also known Brett since childhood, has heard the news and puts a call through from London. He gets up from the table and moves outside. 'Craig, if anyone is going to make it, Brett will,' she says reassuringly. She, like so many others, knows Brett's larger-than-life reputation.

Below, Tony receives equally pacifying text messages: one is from his awning business's sales rep in Durban. It's afternoon there now. 'Tony, we had a hundred people gathered at church today praying for Brett.'

He's relying on the power of prayer.

Another is from his wife, Barbara: 'My darling, Brett always gets himself out of shit. We'll be hearing this story for years to come.'

Tony relates this part of the message to the others.

'It's true. The bugger's got nine lives,' says Ridgy managing a smile.

'And by God, we'll never hear the end of it.' Banger's chuckle eases the tension.

'He's going to be in such shit when we find him,' Snowman jokes, 'putting us through this.'

Yanto appears at the galley door again.

'Mr Ridge,' he says breathlessly, 'captain of *Barrenjoey* on radio. They also searching in the morning. He wants to talk to you.'

Niall stands up to allow Ridgy to slide out of the bench.

'We've been tryin' to reach yer all bloody day, mate!' Doris's exasperation is clear, even if the line isn't. 'Yer bluddy radio's been off.'

'I've been trying to work out frequencies all day.' Ridgy scowls as he looks through the bridge window at the pitch dark outside. 'It's been a nightmare.'

'We had to get hold of yer on fucking Facebook to tell yer to put on yer radio!'

Doris's gravelly voice booms through the wheelhouse. He doesn't wait for an explanation. 'Okay, so we know about yer mate out there. Yer reckon he's swimmin'?'

'Definitely. He's tenacious. It's not in his nature to give up.'

'What's his name? How old is he? Where d'ya reckon he went over?'

Ridgy carefully answers the questions, giving Doris their speculative theories and telling him more about Brett. He feels reassured. It's clear that the man knows these waters.

'He coulda well drifted to land by now,' concludes Doris. 'But even if he hasn't, he's got young kids. When you've got small kids like that, yer don't give up. Yer never give up.'

After co-ordinating their prospective courses, Ridgy returns downstairs where JM is ending a call on his cellphone to Durban's East Coast radio.

'They wanted a live update,' JM shrugs, putting his phone back in his pocket. 'Everyone back home is talking about this story. Apparently, the news has gone global through the Facebook shares. The whole world is waiting for information. Everyone everywhere is praying and rooting for Archie.'

'What did you tell them?' Ridgy asks.

'I said the same thing I've said to Anita and Yanto: that we will find him.'

The crew moves silently around the boat, preparing it for another run across the Straits. It will be the *Naga Laut*'s third crossing in 24 hours.

'What do we do now?' Niall looks back at JM.

'I think we should turn in,' Banger pipes up. He glances at his wristwatch. 'We're all shattered and we'll be needing our strength tomorrow.'

'I agree.' Craig needs no further persuasion. He rises and moves immediately down the passage to his cabin. One by one the others follow.

Weyne goes out to the lower deck of the *Naga Laut* for a few moments. The night is calm at last, like a broken-in colt. The clouds are beginning to break up and the moon casts silver outlines to their ghostly shapes as they move across the sky. He takes out an old Nokia – he's forsaken his iPhone on this trip – and begins a text to his wife Tatiana.

> Hey Baby. I'm sitting on the deck alone where Brett and I chatted last night. This is just too tragic. Not the way to end. We will find him. Xxx

Minutes later, the response beeps:

> This is a story about a man's will to survive and the friends who never lost hope. You endured the same mental anguish today. You are correct. This will be Brett's tour de force. Xxx

As Weyne returns to his cabin, he passes JM, who has just ended a call with his wife Tessa. Yanto has his back to them both in the galley.

'So we'll set out at 3am?' JM calls to Yanto. 'Please make sure we're all awake when we get to the zone.'

Yanto turns to face him and nods in silence. His face looks like a death mask. JM puts his hand on Yanto's shoulder before he makes his way down the passage, past the cabins where low muttering indicates that the last of the men are readying for bed.

Niall is already lying in the dark. His thoughts have darker currents flowing beneath. It must be terrifying out there, he thinks. Not a boat in sight, no lights, just darkness suffocating the breath out of him. Brett, how are you going to do this? It's an unanswerable question. He's relieved the darkness is hiding the hollow feeling in his heart. Brett must be dead. After all this time. What a way to go. What a horrible way to go.

He turns to the wall and squeezes his eyes tightly shut as if to shut out these malevolent thoughts. Instead sleep envelops him with anaesthetic speed.

On the bunk below him, Ridgy is also grappling with conflicting musings: I'm lying here in my bed, and Brett's out there, after a day and a half, still swimming. And there's nothing we can do.

The water may be warm, he reflects, but hypothermia has surely set in by now. He thinks about Brett's mental strength. Then Doris Eltherington's words echo in his head: 'When you've got small kids like that, you don't give up. You never give up.'

Never give up. They're the last words he remembers before sleep swamps him too.

JM approaches the darkness of the dungeon, a place he's been dreading. He can hear faint echoes of Brett's voice in the blackness. He relives their arrival; Brett joking and fooling around. The triviality of it all now feels momentous.

He switches on the light and turns to Brett's backpack. It's neatly packed, a reflection of the owner's tight, organised personal world. In a side pocket, he finds a collection of notes. Ten of them. They're in a child's hand.

'Tony,' JM whispers as he puts his head out of the dungeon; in his hand is the 'You are my hero' note they found earlier. 'This is Zara's handwriting,' he says as Tony stoops through the door. 'She's written notes for him – see, they're numbered? One for each day. Anita puts notes in the kids' lunchboxes when they go to school. Zara's done the same thing for Brett. Written him a note for every day of the trip.'

Tony drops his head. And then after a moment's silence, he says simply, 'He has another nine to read. We have to go get him.'

'Get some sleep.' JM turns away and gently replaces everything neatly in the backpack.

Slowly, quietly, he readies the cabin. He makes Brett's bed, repacks his bag and puts his shoes beside the bunk. Just as he'd like it.

After flicking the light switch, JM climbs into his bunk. Lying in the dark, in the bow of the boat, he grapples with an image of Brett in the water.

His phone, on silent, lights up in the dark. A text message has come through from his mother, Estelle, who is an ardent Christian. Tessa told him earlier that Estelle had fallen to her knees when she got the news, and together with her housekeeper and friend of thirty-five years, Gladys Gwala, had prayed all afternoon. She'd also organised countless prayer groups.

JM takes a moment to focus on the text.

I've been praying 'Bring him, Jesus' repeatedly. Two hours ago, I opened my Bible to Isaiah 48.15. It reads: 'I have called him, I will bring him, and he will succeed in his mission.'

9.30PM TO 10.30PM
TWENTIETH HOUR IN THE WATER

For the first time since I've been in the water, the clouds break and clear to reveal a patch of star-strewn sky. The moon, almost full tonight, has just risen and is now slowly climbing. Swollen, it's a magnificent sight, with a huge yellow halo glowing around it.

The stars are jewels on black velvet. They offer an ancient tool used by centuries of seamen to navigate the sea. At last, a way to orientate myself.

I find my old favourites, the kite-shaped Southern Cross. And Orion, the hunter. The distinct constellation delineating his belt is unmissable, as is the red tinge of Betelgeuse, marking his shoulder. Sirius, the dog star, shines brightly nearby. They're familiar friends from my southern skies back home and, to my relief, are a means to get my bearings.

I use my old Boy Scout method of establishing south. I draw a mental line down to the horizon from the intersecting point of the Southern Cross's extended long axis and the perpendicular bisector of the two Pointers, and realise that in fact I have not been swimming south. I'm going in the opposite direction. It means the islands in the west are to my left and not my right as I had thought.

Although it's a very rough guide, it still feels better knowing in which direction I'm headed. It seems to add purpose to my predicament. To make it feel less meaningless.

So, with the back of my head in a pillow of water, I look up at the night sky. I pick a star, and for as long as I can, I track how far I move. I truly believe that I'm making ground. It gives me hope.

It also distracts me.

I recall boyhood afternoons as a Cub and later as a Boy Scout with JM and his younger brother Pierre. We learnt so many things through that organisation that have proved useful throughout my life. Scouts made me resourceful and inventive – and many times got me out of trouble.

Our scoutmaster's face comes to mind. Mr Stead, a lovely guy who took us on a weekend survival camp down the coast to Pennington when we were thirteen. We had to bivouac in the bush, armed with nothing else but a penknife, a compass and a box of matches. That weekend we were caught in torrential rain. Most of the boys were soaked and wanted to go home, but I loved the adventure. I set up camp, built a fire and was warm and dry.

Survival techniques. I think about them now. I cast my mind back to what I learnt in the army. South Africa had a conscripted army in those days and I did my compulsory national service in the early '80s. I was an officer in a tank squadron. I was sent to the Angolan border, and as horrible as those experiences were, they taught me to get through tough times.

I've been a can-do kind of guy since childhood. I've always fixed things, made things work. It comes easily to me and is a kind of therapy. I still tinker around the house. I even go on holiday with my toolbox, for God's sake, fixing people's broken windows or unhinged doors.

But I have nothing on me now. No box of tools to help me out of this one. Nothing can save me now.

A long burning lash of pain sweeps across my chest and around my neck, blistering my skin. I cry out in agony and raw rage, but my voice is so hoarse that the cry is unrecognisable to me. I cannot see anything but I immediately know what they are: the tentacles of jellyfish. This isn't like the searing sting of the earlier Portuguese men o' war; this is pure electricity, burning, throbbing all around my torso, cutting up my back. Over and over again, I am shocked, a razor-like cat o' nine tails swirling its stinging fingers against my scarlet skin. I feel the gloops of the jellyfishes' enormous gelatinous heads suctioning around me, sticking to my neck as I try to make my way through the shoal, away from the pain. I shake my limbs, scramble through the thick watery forest of fire, trying to dislodge the strangling defribillator-like trains. I rip off the tentacles that seem to be trying to claw the breath out of me and throw them as far away into the ocean as I can. I hear them plop into the water and give off a slight gurgling sound as they sink. I imagine the water all around me as a sea of blood. My blood. Seeping out of me.

I'll die. And it will be quick, I console myself.

But then, just as suddenly, I find myself out on the other side of that dark, sluggish river. My skin is still burning, but the creatures have done their devilish work and have completely disappeared. I'm panting from the pain and exertion.

Even in the darkness, I can make out the deep, darkening welts they have left on my skin. Like clear-cut contours all over my chest.

THE BARRENJOEY
DREAMLANDS
9.38PM

A few beers are being opened on deck, ostensibly as a preamble to Simon's fiftieth birthday tomorrow. The weather has lifted and the clouds are finally dissolving to reveal the full moon. Doris is alone, brooding in the wheelhouse, lost in silent thought.

He'd refused dinner with an impatient shake of his head as he came off the *Bynda Laut*, walked purposefully to the bridge and immediately tried the radio.

'*Naga Laut*, do you copy?' he repeated into the mouthpiece; his voice was weary, but his body was like a rocket ready to launch.

He was confronted with the same silence he'd had to contend with all day. Frustrated, he flicked open his laptop and used his forefinger to hammer a blunt message onto the *Naga Laut*'s Facebook page: 'Turn on your fucking radio!'

An hour later, Pete, Colin and Simon join Doris in the wheelhouse. The captain looks strangely removed as he squints into the light of his laptop screen. He seems to have turned inward, as if he's in his own private capsule.

'You okay, skipper?' Pete asks tentatively.

Doris looks up – his blue eyes are red and tired, but commanding. 'I failed today. I don't like failin'.'

There's a long silence. It's a direct statement, without any embellishment, and it catches the three men off guard. They're uncertain how to approach this dark mood.

'Um, Doris, the boys are talking downstairs,' Simon ventures. 'We're all happy to help, to do whatever we can, but this bloke's been in the drink a long time. It's likely that he's gone by now...'

'We've been talking about the currents, trying to work out where he'd be,' Colin continues. 'Realistically, what are the chances of finding him tomorrow morning – or of finding him alive?'

'I'm not interested in yer chit-chats downstairs.' Doris stands up. His body is shaking with emotion. A low growl comes from the back of his throat. 'We'll find him!' He's shouting. He's suddenly imposing in the small wheel-house.

'We've got to keep at it!'

There's manifest surprise on the faces of his guests as they assess his reaction. They're bewildered at how this incident has escalated to upset Doris to this extent. How has it become such an all-consuming challenge?

The captain is more controlled when he slowly sits down again. 'I talked to some *bule* on the *Naga Laut* when I eventually got hold of 'em,' he says. 'This guy's a Saffer. He's fifty, a bike rider. If he's fit, he's probably still alive.'

Doris exhales heavily and closes his eyes after his rant; he seems suddenly exhausted. Then he looks up again.

'He has a wife. Two little children. Nine and six. For Chrissake, he'll want to see 'em again. They're somethin' to stay alive for.'

No-one says anything. The timbre of Doris's voice changes again. This time it's low, hardly audible. 'Brett Arch-somethin'. That's his name. Chantal also gave me some co-ords that they think are more accurate.'

He looks out into the darkness, eyes wide, but unseeing. He speaks slowly.

'The water's warm. Hypothermia is going to kill him faster than anything else, but it's warm. Also, there's been no sun. I'm tellin' yer, he's alive.'

The three Australians stand in awkward silence. The captain seems to have taken the lack of action – from the authorities, from those around him – as a kind of a personal betrayal.

'I lost my best friend yesterday.'

The statement comes entirely out of left field, but the three guests quickly realise that Doris is attempting to explain his erratic behaviour.

'My buddy, Dave Kinder…'

The conversation is clearly a painful effort. 'We've been friends for many, many years. I got a call yesterday that he died. Cancer. And hard livin'…'

Doris snorts; it's a half-chortle, half-sob. 'I wanted to get down to Perth to see him…' He studies his hands as his words trail off.

The men look down at their feet. They're uncomfortable with this keyhole glimpse into the captain's emotional world and they stand in uneasy silence. It does at least explain Doris's odd demeanour over the last day or so, though. Pete quickly steps across Doris and silently pulls out the ocean chart tucked behind the dashboard.

'Right, mate. Let's decide on a course for the mornin'.'

Doris lets out a wheezy cough and instinctively reaches for his packet of Marlboros.

His hands are shaking a little.

'My brother and sister-in-law work for the Department of Foreign Affairs and Trade in Canberra,' Colin pronounces. 'I'll ring them, see if they can talk to someone who can help.'

Doris simply nods as Colin and Simon leave the wheelhouse. The two captains are left to consider the night's tides, the weakening winds and fading currents. They start to map out the following day's search area.

'I'm goin' north tomorrow,' Doris announces after a few minutes. 'We'll go north-east towards Padang, but at 99 degrees, we'll turn. Here...'

Pete lengthens his tall frame and shakes his head. 'Nah, Doris, we should head due east.' His finger runs along a line of latitude. 'If we head out along here, he'll be under you... the current goes south...'

'Jesus Christ!'

Without warning, Doris asserts himself again. This time there's an another dimension at play, a delayed reaction perhaps to his surrender of leadership to Pete the previous day. 'I'm skipper of this fuckin' boat! We're going north. When we get there, I'll jump in the tinny and check things out.'

Pete says nothing. He slowly shakes his head.

'Fuck you, I'm goin' back on my track. This is the line and we're doin' it.' Doris's words hang in the air for a moment, like smoke rings.

Pete decides to stand his ground: 'I disagree.'

'I'm tellin' ya. The tides were runnin' south yesterday as they do most other days, but things are different today. I've been thinking about it. On the way back in on the *Bynda Laut* tonight, we had to stop to take a piss. It was rainin' and we were gettin' wet, but I noticed two coconuts in the water. The wind was blowing south – yeah – but those coconuts were goin' the other way. I tell yer, the current's moved north.'

Doris is resolute about his instinct; his seafarer's sense has been ingrained since he was a boy sailor. He's grown up reading the weather. Living by it. And he still stubbornly eschews technology in favour of it. Doris is known for ignoring internet weather reports – 'I prefer to look out the window,' he says. For some, it substantiates the mythology of the man: both practical and visionary.

Doris throws Pete one last look. 'We go north. My gut's not wrong. And we'll set off early. I want to make the search zone by daybreak.'

'I still think we should go east.' Pete stalks out, also flushed with anger, but he grudgingly keeps it in check. He calls out over his shoulder: 'It's your ride, skipper, your decision.'

10.30PM TO 11.30PM
TWENTY-FIRST HOUR IN THE WATER

My body is burning – but now with a kind of cold fire, a triumphant pain. Instead of life flowing out of me, it has flooded into me. As the Portuguese men o' war did before, the jellyfish have somehow nourished me, jump-started my heart. They've proved there are things in front and that more might come. I am back on this tightrope; depthless chasms opening up beneath me; one false step and it's down into the darkness.

Fortunately, the moon is my companion. I feel comforted by her presence. Her hazy aura, the storm's afterglow, makes her seem especially blessed. I watch her constantly, trying to work out what time it is. I settle on around 11pm and the thought cheers me. It means I have only six or seven hours left of darkness.

'Then it will be light. I'm better in the light.'

The lack of cloud cover has made it so much colder, and as hard as I try I can't stop my teeth from chattering. The clacking reverberates in my head.

I put my hand over my mouth. My lips are cracked and enormous.

I tell myself with soft persuasion that I can make it through those hours. I can wait until the fishing boats come out, I say. Now that I know my direction, I can hang on.

Yes, hang on.

The sea is calm at last, a line of moonlight trips on the tops of the waves before me. Rivulets of liquid mercury run all over the surface. Slowly I move through the small swells, trying to measure my progress against the stars.

Slow and steady, I tell myself.

Just keep moving. Keep moving.

Clouds scurry across the moon, swirling in her crown of light. As calm as it is below, it's furiously busy up above.

My mind wanders. An image forms. It's afternoon and I'm lying out on the grass in our back yard with my grandfather. I'm six or seven. We're playing that children's game, looking for shapes in the clouds. I'm laughing excitedly as magical white creations morph before my eyes out of the piercing blue.

I look up now. With the moon's backlighting, the sooty clouds become other things: a dragon, a butterfly, a horse, a heart. A cloud moves over the moon, and suddenly it's Apollo, the Greek god. The archer. His bow and arrow form across the moon's face.

Apollo. A god of strength. You're married to a Greek. You have to be Apollo to get through the night.

Slow movements. Just keep moving. Keep moving.

The clouds scatter and dissipate into nothing. I'm so cold, so tired, I ache everywhere. I roll onto my back and try to relax, try to stretch my legs.

As I do, I realise that I'm not in pain. Why hasn't it occurred to me before?

For the last eighteen years, I've lived with constant back pain – all day, all the time – a residual throbbing that has plagued me through my sports, through everyday activity, even watching TV on the couch.

I broke my neck in 1996 when I dived off the roof of a three-storey building into a swimming pool at a friend's house. Tequila was involved. The pool was beside the house and had only a metre's depth at the shallow end before it sloped down to its deeper end.

I stood on the roof with thirty people watching. Concerned,

they all shouted at me not to do it. But I was a fool and looking for attention.

I swan dived off the roof and on the way down knew I was in major trouble. I'd miscalculated and I hit the water in the shallow end. My outstretched arms took most of the fall.

Someone jumped in just as coils of blood formed in the water; he pulled me up by the hair. 'I made it,' I gasped as I came up.

'Arch,' he said. 'You didn't'.

I was rushed to hospital. Doctors told me that I'd dislocated both shoulders, broken my collarbone and dislocated my jaw.

I was a lunatic. I made the nurse stitch me up without an anaesthetic and I pestered her to allow me to go back to the party. Which I did.

At 3am, I seized up. I called Anita – we'd just started dating – and asked her to come and take me home. The following morning I couldn't move. At the hospital, they did further X-rays and tests. I'd broken my neck, with eight fissure fractures in my C2 and C3 vertebrae.

But here, in the water, I'm pain free. After all the hours I've been swimming, it amazes me. Has the floating released the pressure on my spine? Or has my body lost all feeling?

Is my brain shutting down? Is this a state of perdition?

Must keep moving. Keep going. Just keep going.

I feel so weak, I can barely move. And tired. So very tired. I stop talking. Stop talking to God, to Bob, Hilary and Emily. I summon up all my strength and mentally shout to Anita: 'Help me! Help me stay awake!'

Keep moving. Move.

A strange tinnitus is ringing in my ears, like the low hum of fluorescent lights. The moon begins to blur and the water around me feels like lead. It's as if icy arms have taken me in a ruthless embrace.

I can barely keep my face out of the water and I can no longer feel my limbs. I close my eyes. The tinnitus turns up to full volume.

Move, move, move.

Then. A little boat. A canoe. Coming towards me out of the night.

I lift my head when I hear the water lap as it paddles towards me. I see the prow first – clear in the darkness. It isn't quite on the surface of the water, but seems to be floating a couple of inches above it.

Two small Indonesian boys are sitting in the canoe. Both are about six, Jamie's age. They're the children who come out from the islands' shallows for local trade. They sell carvings, masks and island trinkets to the moored charter boats.

I've hit land!

Elated, I shout to them: 'You've come to see me in?'

The boys have long oars and they keep paddling towards me. The one in front paddles to the left and the other to the right. I'd always been fascinated by these kids' speed and technique: they never lift the oars from the water, they swirl them around instead.

The child at the back is beautiful. Black wavy hair and, oddly, blue eyes. He has a bright smile with magnificent teeth.

I've always had a thing about teeth. Mine have been terrible. They've been knocked out in fights and been the source of all sorts of problems. For a while I considered having them cosmetically fixed, but vetoed it eventually as the height of vanity.

The kid in front is the opposite. Not normal. He has

a misshapen face, spiky hair and teeth that stick out in every direction.

'You've saved me!' I shout. 'Thank you! Thank you, boys!' I focus on the one in front.

'I'm going to take you with me to South Africa, to the best dentist in Cape Town. We'll get those teeth fixed.'

They are both smiling at me, but they don't say a word.

I swim up to the canoe. It's a few feet away and I reach out to put my hand on the prow. As I'm about to grab the wood, my hand passes through air and into water.

Gone.

The canoe and the boys have disappeared.

Down I sink. I close my mouth. Close my eyes. Try to keep from going under, but water fills my head.

It wasn't real.

A trick of the mind, a dream, a phantom. Another crushing disappointment.

A thought flashes through my mind. These are souls of those lost at sea, ghosts of the ocean who have come for me, a drowning man.

I'm in an eerie, unknown place. Far from the living and very close to the dead.

THE BARRENJOEY
11.07PM

As his guests retire one by one to their bunks, Doris returns to the radio and over the next hour he hails other boats in the area.

Earlier Colin came upstairs to tell him that his brother had contacted the Australian Maritime Safety Authority as well as diplomats in the South African consulate. 'They all seem to know about it,' was all he could offer.

'Didn't think they'd help,' Doris sniffed but he appreciated the unreserved support now coming from his guests.

He considers how he's going to co-ordinate the coming hours. Again, he calls John McGroder, then Martin Daly, the man they call 'the bull', who agrees to radio the captains of his two other vessels, the *Indies Trader II* and *Indies Trader III*. *Trader II* is further south so for them it will be an early start, and *Trader III* will have to sail out of Padang. The crossing will take several hours.

'I'll organise their clearance from here and get them to deploy,' Daly explains. '*Trader IV* won't make it – she's too far away.' He's at Jakarta airport – he's been at Dave Kinder's funeral, in fact – and is about to board a midnight flight to Padang.

'No-one else is going to do this, mate. It's up to you,' he tells Doris over the humming background terminal noise.

The comment is like a chisel through the captain's head. 'You know what you're doing. If anyone's going to find this guy, it'll be you.'

Daly has always believed in Doris when others didn't. It emboldens the captain, makes him feel a little less isolated.

Doris calls a colleague in emergency management who worked the search and rescue detail with him on their recent oil and gas project. His boat is demobilising in Padang.

'I've had no support from SAR, the TNI or the harbour master,' Doris tells him. 'They don't care. They don't care about one guy.'

'How far out did this happen?' his friend asks. 'What were the last co-ordinates?' But after a few minutes' consideration, he concludes: 'Ah Dorie, he's dead. In today's conditions? Thirty knots of wind, slop seas, no life jacket? You can forget it.'

'Thanks for fuckin' nothin', mate.' Earlier he'd had similar unhelpful responses from oil-rig rescue acquaintances currently based in Vietnam. 'It might happen to yer one day and no doubt you'll expect our help when the shit hits the fan!'

He hangs up abruptly, grumbling to himself. 'Go on, just drink yer coffee as the world goes by.'

Doris looks again at Belinda McGroder's Facebook page. After his earlier conversation with John, she has posted a Mayday message that makes his heartbeat thud in his throat.

Hey fleet and camps. Naga Laut lost a passenger around 4am this morning. Last known co-ordinates: 99 degrees, 55' East and 1 degree 40' South. According to Doris on Barrenjoey, there is a lot of debris out there. Weather conditions, horrible. We need every boat out there at first light to form some sort of grid. We will be out, along with Huey, Indies Trader 3 and Kuda Laut. We need more. Please factor in the current and strong West Nor West winds. Please communicate on VHF 16 and HF 8.17.9.0 MHZ. Come on surf community, we have to try! He's a surfer. Imagine if it was one of you. Team-work time!

At around midnight, the *Huey* and the *Kuda Laut* come in to Tua Pejat. The *Kuda Laut*, under the captaincy of another Australian, Bryan Jacobs, has been informed of the morning search by radio and has sailed up from the southern Mentawais. Both vessels drop anchor a couple of hundred metres from the *Barrenjoey*. Doris is grateful for the company.

'I'm coppin'g it here from my guests,' Steven Sewell tells Doris from the *Huey*. 'They're asking "Why are we here?"'

'Fuckin' shit. Did you tell them that we're goin' to look for a human being, Suley?'

'Yeah! They say, "But we're on holiday…"'

'Jesus. They can sit on the beach all day, I don't care,' Doris rejoins, 'I've got a Mayday.' He adds, 'I've been havin' my own shit here.'

He tells Suley about his disagreement with Pete Inglis.

'I won't sit on the fence and watch two captains spitting it out at each other, Doris.'

Suley's relationship of trust with Doris goes back years. 'You and I just don't do that. What do you want to do? If you want to go out at 99, I'll run out at 99.05, right? *Trader III* is coming down the track from Padang and we'll meet in the middle.'

'Yeah.' Doris inhales deeply on a cigarette. His reply wafts out on a billow of smoke. 'Matty's comin' south in *Foxy* from Burger World. He'll head down on 99. I've asked him to zigzag in front of us. I want to get all our boats in a line, with a mile between us eventually, running parallel on this track. It's where I've roughly estimated this bloke's gonna be…'

After a short pause, Doris adds, 'Matt asked me about the

fuel. Don't worry about the fuckin' fuel, I told him. Just do it, get out there, mate! Keep zigzagging.'

'Have you heard from the *Naga Laut*?' The question, by association, annoys Doris.

'I made contact. They've weighed in Padang, I think. I have no fuckin' idea what they're doin'.'

'Listen, Doris, it's 1am. I'm going to get some sleep.' Suley pauses wearily. 'We'll deploy at 3am, right?'

'See ya, Suley. And thanks, mate.'

Doris considers the time it will take Daly's two *Indies Trader* boats to make the distance. The McGroders will also join the search, with their sons Fynn and Duke, on their catamaran, and Matt Cruden, another of Martin Daly's skippers, will deploy at dawn from Burger World, a surf spot to the south west of Siberut. He will motor south in *Foxy Lady*, the aluminium speedboat belonging to the charter boat *Mangaliu Ndulu*.

It's eerily quiet in the wheelhouse, but Doris can't even contemplate sleep. He continues to pace up and down, unsettled and anxious.

We've got to find him, he keeps thinking. He's got kids… I've got kids. I've also got my three gran'kids. God. Allah. Ganesh… Doris starts praying – he believes in God but has no time for preachers. Prayer seems appropriate now.

'Help me find him.'

FISKAAL ROAD
CAMPS BAY
4.37PM

Luke leaves to run errands. Wayne fields calls from Chantal. Outwardly calm and pragmatic, he is dealing privately with his pain.

He Googles the *Naga Laut* and finds online photographs of the vessel. He zooms in on details: the deck, the railings, the tender. How or where could Brett have gone over? He's determined to solve the puzzle.

Anita wants to call the *Naga Laut* for another update.

'Please limit the calls to the sat phone,' JM stressed earlier. Wayne couldn't miss the frustration in JM's voice. All round, emotions are running high. He can't let them run roughshod over reason.

'We can't keep calling the boat.' He is firm, but gentle with Anita. 'It's not helping. We need to let them just get on with what they're doing out there. Besides, it's the middle of the night over there…'

He remains silent regarding a particularly worrying element in JM's reports – they haven't seen any planes or other boats at all in the Straits.

Wayne asks Gaby to Google the number for the South African embassy in Indonesia and he makes endless back and forth calls to them and to High Commission officials in Pretoria trying to confirm whether an official search is indeed under way. He's met with the classic diplomatic response: 'We're going through the official channels. We're doing everything we can…'

When Brett's brother Greg calls from the Drakensberg, Wayne filters the information once again.

'The *Naga Laut* is going back out there. I've also Googled all the surf camps around those islands and I'm making contact, asking that they look for Brett by boat and on land. People are looking – it's just a matter of time.'

Loni walks out of the kitchen. He's made a platter of open pastrami sandwiches and silently puts it on the dining-room table. They go untouched.

A strange quiet has descended. The rain has stopped but the day is plunged into an alien afternoon fog.

Inside, another haze is building. Paula and Zenda have chosen to ignore Brett's no smoking rule and sit silently together on the couch, immobilised, exhaling plumes in great waves. Ashtrays overflow before them. Lulu has returned from her meeting, and she and Louise join them periodically. The smoke silently snakes and curls through the room. No-one talks.

Paula prays the Our Father softly. It becomes meditative. I can still feel him, Louise convinces herself. 'Brett has such a strong life force. He hasn't left this world.'

Loni moves to look over Wayne's shoulder at his laptop screen. The younger man has become a scribe, the notary, systematically dealing with detail, quietly challenging officialdom, carefully collating fragmentary bits of news. He walks outside to conduct conversations that he doesn't want Anita to hear.

In the dining room Helene and Kirsten quietly read posts that flood the 'Searching for Brett Archibald' site. Thousands of hits, likes and shares reveal that people from across the world are following the story. They offer compassion, counsel, their prayers and unwavering hope. The women avoid the insensitive posts like 'He's long dead,' or 'He's a goner. No-one can survive in the sea for that long.'

Cruelty in times of adversity is an unwelcome surprise.

Earlier in the afternoon, CJ called Wayne from Jakarta. Night had come to Indonesia and he confirmed that the bad weather had kept all planes grounded. He couldn't say whether a single rescue boat had gone out.

Wayne sits with the news, a heavy weight on his heart.

'Why hasn't anyone phoned? Why has no-one picked him up yet?' Anita has been asking, desperation beginning to infiltrate her voice. Wayne decides to add on another hour to the time difference so as not to frighten her.

Chantal has, however, called Louise with the same information. And Lulu's text messages from her husband repeat the sentiment.

Babe, it's not looking good. We can't see within one metre in front of us. We have to be strong.

Then:

It's late here. We're so tired. Mood is not good.

The women break the silence in the house to deliver the news.

'Planes haven't been able to leave and all boats have been recalled... the sea is too rough.'

Louise's voice is metallic. Lulu uses the opportunity to deliver her bad news, too. 'And the *Naga Laut*'s captain has also said that they must head for port. They have to anchor in Padang for the night.'

Anita stares back, wide-eyed.

'JM has said that they'll start out again at 3am, though,'

Wayne is quick to sound reassuring. 'They're hoping for calmer waters by then.'

The news strikes a chill that spreads like ether. Anita slowly sinks back down into her chair.

'They can't leave him out there. When the storm passes they'll go back out, right? Indonesia's five or six hours ahead of us, so it's around 7pm... the sun only goes down at around 10pm in Indonesia, doesn't it?'

Kirsten types into the Google rectangle: 'Sunset, time, Indonesia.' Her face blanches.

'What?' Anita reads her dismay.

'It's already around 10pm there, Anita. The sun set a while ago...'

Anita recoils and then begins to sway and rock. She emits a low wail as she clutches at her belly. Her mother is instantly at her side, but she, too, cannot disguise her fear.

'They can't leave him there! They can't!' Anita's voice has a high pitch. 'He's alive, I can feel it. But he won't be able to get through another night on his own! He's been out there for hours. He can't get through the dark.'

There's an uncomfortable silence as Anita becomes prisoner to a crying spell.

'The guys on the boat are gutted that they have to leave the zone,' Lulu reports defensively. 'Mark says they're devastated.'

'It must be so hard for them too.' Helene shakes her head.

Wayne steps forward. 'Um. Martin Daly, one of the ship owners, told me that he has three charter vessels that he'll lend to the search.'

He needs to say something, anything, as a palliative to the desultory mood sweeping the room.

'They're bigger vessels. They'll plot themselves on a grid, put on their lights and follow the current so that Brett can see them. Even if it's pitch black, he can swim for the lights. They're also going to turn off their engines so that they can hear him if he shouts…'

It's far-fetched, Wayne knows, but there's a flash of gratitude on Anita's face. She needs something to hold on to for the long, uncertain journey ahead. But nobody has the true measure of the situation, Wayne knows. The little knowledge they have is dangerous. Illusion, even ignorance, is better.

Gaby puts her arms around Anita. 'My friend,' she says and buries her head in Anita's shoulder. Then she emerges, resolute. 'Enough with the tea and coffee. It's time to open a bottle of wine.'

'Great idea.' Lulu jumps up from her spot beside Paula. 'I'll get glasses.'

While Louise and Kirsten move to the low set of cupboards against the lounge wall that serves as Brett's liquor cabinet, Wayne returns to his laptop. He searches the international clock and notes the time of first light in Indonesia the following day.

Will we find him? he contemplates privately. Will we *ever* find him?

'Give me some of his Chivas,' Paula says, breaking her silence. Then she smiles. 'That'll bring him back in a hurry.'

Louise takes her glass outside to take a call from a friend, but the concentration of emotion finally cracks her self-control. She stands, a solitary, rain-soaked figure, and for the first time today cries copiously.

11.30PM TO 12.30PM
TWENTY-SECOND HOUR IN THE WATER

From darkness. Through darkness. Into darkness.

I muster my last strength to push myself up to the surface. I emerge coughing. Salt water dribbles over my plaster-cast lips. My tongue is so coarse and distended I can't swallow. My throat closes of its own accord. The stars above me seem to fall from the sky, others dart off as if they've been caught out for being there.

Is this a dream? My eyes are open, but very heavy-lidded. I cannot keep them from closing. I can barely see over the granite waters.

Then, above the waterline, three lights. Three lights are lined up in front of me.

The boys on the boat weren't real. These aren't either, I think gloomily.

I look again. I see the three lights – far in the darkness, quite a distance apart. One there. One there. One there. Orion's belt fallen to earth.

I keep staring at them, waiting for them to disappear.

I turn myself around slowly. A full 360 degrees. Slow movements. I look back. They're still there.

'Land.' I know it instantly, but I'm not entirely sure if I'm dreaming. 'It's land. Those lights are three villages spread out quite far apart.' The shark, the seagulls and now the lights – all evidence that I'm near the islands.

How far are they? Ten miles? I'd swum the popular Midmar Mile dam race in KwaZulu-Natal in my younger days.

You can swim there, I instruct myself. You can swim there. If you start now, you can get there by daybreak.

Another life ring. A crumb of hope.

I have to take it slowly. I have hardly any energy left and what I have I must use sparingly. I pick the middle light as my destination and start swimming breaststroke towards it.

Small strokes. Slow and steady. Keep moving. I hear the hypnotic, syncopated rhythm of my hands through the water.

I watch the light, but after a few minutes I realise that I'm drifting from the middle light towards the one on the right. I turn again and swim for the others, but always end up being swept past the far one.

You're swimming against the current. I can feel it. Unless I get out of the current, I'm not going to make it.

I keep going, arms out together in little praying movements. If you swim across it, you'll break out of the current.

Land. You have to get to land.

Focus. Swim. Conserve energy. I repeat these things over and over again in my mind. It feels as if hours pass.

But hard as I try, I'm not getting anywhere. The lights keep moving away.

Disoriented. Disabled. I'm out of my depth. Out of reach. Going nowhere.

FISKAAL ROAD
CAMPS BAY
5.42PM

A light drizzle has started again when Anita's aunt Zenda begins the drive back to Stellenbosch, promising to return in the morning. She will spend the night crying in her bed, her cellphone on her pillow.

In Fiskaal Road, Paula Nicolopulos calls Shirley Archibald again. She has spoken with Brett's mother and sister periodically throughout the day. Both mothers feel a need to connect, to unite as parents in this time of fear and uncertainty.

The day is ending, but its persistent gloom has made it feel like one interminably long night. The house lights, which have been on all day, have taken on a strange aqueous quality. It makes the house feel more like a place in a dream.

'Surely, if there was bad news, we would have heard it by now?'

Anita is flagging. There has been no further word from the *Naga Laut*, except a text from Mark saying that Brett should no longer be in open water, that by now he should have drifted onshore with the current.

'The fishing boats will find him.'

The idea lifts her mood a little.

Helene takes Zara and Jamie's overnight bags to the Laspatzis house in Sea Point. She sits with the children on the bed and tries to reassure them, still revealing nothing. Jamie plays with Lego on the carpet, unaware. Zara, her knees drawn up to her chest, is quieter, a little sullen even.

'Have they found the boat?' she asks. Her tone has a sceptical edge to it.

'Yes,' Helene replies, her back straight. 'But we still haven't made contact with it. All the wives are going to stay at the house tonight trying to do just that, but it's been tricky because of the time difference. Mom will be busy so it's best that you sleep over here.'

Helene is still uncomfortable with the falsehood; perhaps more so because she can feel Zara's eyes on her, assessing the truthfulness of the statement.

Ari, Katya's husband and a friend of Brett's, is standing in the doorway. He is suddenly overwhelmed. He's been watching the children playing together all afternoon, entirely unsuspecting of the saga. He turns and leaves the house to break down in the garage. Katya enters the room with her cellphone. Their mother has called to say goodnight.

Back in the Camps Bay house, Anita curls up on the couch in a foetal position as she talks to each of her children. Quiet and composed, her pretence at normality only heightens the fragility in the room. The others listen to her attempts at innocent diversions. It's the hardest thing Anita has ever had to do.

12.30AM TO 1.30AM
TWENTY-THIRD HOUR IN THE WATER

I try.

Try to keep my face out of the water. My nose keeps filling and my throat closes in. I can hear myself snorting, fighting for breath. I attempt swimming, but my body is failing me. I can't feel anything from my chest down. I'm disconnected from my limbs, my emotions, my will to keep going. Totally numb.

I attempt to lift my head once again to see the lights. They're still there – like sirens calling. Land is within my sights but I don't have the physical ability to get there. The realisation is shattering.

'Bob, Emily and Hilary,' I pep-talk my team, 'we've got to make it to the lights, we've got to get there.'

I can't go on, however. Exhaustion has won. Death is the forfeit.

I've failed. Failed myself, failed my family. I'm a failure.

I can't keep my eyes open any longer. I can't keep my neck straight. I feel my head plop into the water.

I think I fall asleep.

The sound fills my head before I see it. Old beams of teak creaking as they shift in sync with the movements of the sea, great ropes stretching and twisting as the wind fills a mainsail. I'm unsure if I see it in my mind's eye first, but it's a clear picture: a 1634 Dutch East India Company sailing ship is broadside, about twenty metres away.

It's not an enormous vessel but it's imposing enough. I made a model of one as a kid. I lift my head and there it is. Quite clear. Despite my earlier disappointments, I'm convinced this *is* actually there, that it's real.

271

Five or six sailors walk across the deck towards the edge of the ship: raggle-taggle men, longhaired and bearded, with rotten teeth and wounded eyes. 'Come on, lad, you can make it.' They talk over one another in rough tones but I hear what they say.

'You can make it. You can make it.'

Two of them throw a rope over the side of the ship and a wooden stepladder unravels down into the water. The clunking of the timber steps against the ship's hull as it unfurls echoes in the stillness.

Slowly, so slowly, I start swimming for it. My hands feel like dumb-bells. I know I'm hallucinating – they're the souls of drowned sailors – but somehow they seem so real.

'Swim, lad,' I hear them say, 'swim'.

I was enamoured with pirates as a kid – I read every pirate-inspired book I could get my hands on and watched them in old movies. These men have those same faces – rough and hewn and folded up like socks. One of them looks like my grandfather.

I swim up to the side of the boat. As I look up to those weathered faces, I reach up to grab the ladder.

Again nothing there. Nothing. Nothing.

Down I go. Yet again.

This time, I submerge quite deep. Water rushes over my head and I can hear bubbles popping with deep, resonant plops around my nose, ears and mouth. I swallow half the ocean. My chest wants to explode and my throat feels flayed open to the elements.

I don't know what's real any more.

I'm hallucinating. I know it now for certain.

My head lolls in the water, my face submerged. I don't have the energy to lift it. I try not to breathe because I know I'll swallow salt water. I can't help myself. It races up my nostrils and down my throat again. After what seems like an aeon, I manage to raise my head so that my chin is on the surface. I have no strength in my diaphragm to cough up the water so I just let it run from my mouth.

I'm freezing. Numb all over. My teeth are chattering and I can feel chunks of my tongue coming off in my mouth. Could I bite it right off? Like in a seizure, unable to control my own body.

I spit the pieces out into my hand and look down at them. Slivers of raw, bloodied muscle. I put my hand into the water and watch the pieces disappear into the darkness.

That was a mistake. I regret it instantly. The blood will attract sharks.

I put my fingers up to my mouth. My lips are splitting into great fleshy canyons. I touch my alien tongue. How much have I bitten off?

I look down at my fingers: they're enormous, puffy and white in the moonlight. I can barely make out my wedding ring. I lift a piece of flaking skin in my fingers and an entire sheet peels off in my hand.

'Aargh!' I shout. I'm not sure if it's out of pain or panic.

I feel amphibian. Perhaps my body is liquefying? The sea is slowly reclaiming me. I'm not even dead yet and the ocean is taking me back.

Don't bump your hands, Brett. You don't want blood in the water.

I have to control my teeth chattering, to make them stop. I put my left hand under my chin to force my jaw shut, but discover that I can't swim with one arm.

'Stop chattering,' I scold myself. 'Stop your teeth chattering.'

Stop it.
Stop it.
Stop!

FISKAAL ROAD
CAMPS BAY
8.52PM

Lulu leaves shortly after someone has ordered takeaway pizzas. It's a little before 9pm.

She's torn, but she also knows that she can do no more this evening. The uncertainty of events has been exhausting; it's been all rumour and speculation. She walks out, her sadness a heavy cloak. All day, she's been trapped in a coma and there is a long night ahead, several more hours of little context and no meaning.

The rain has stopped and the black roads steam in the circles of light that surround the streetlamps. Tomorrow morning she will return early and Mark will have news. This infinity game will come to an end. There'll be resolution.

Lulu sits in her car at a red traffic light, eyes closed for a moment. She feels utterly drained by her swirling thoughts and she prays out loud that the outcome is not the fear that has so far remained unspoken.

Louise, Kirsten, Karmen and Gaby stay on at Fiskaal Road. They take their wine and join Paula and Loni in the lounge, where they all sit in a close huddle around Anita.

The women have continued to field calls, people desperate for updates, but things are quieter now. 'Everyone's an expert,' Wayne comments when Kirsten recounts someone's theory of what might have happened.

He grabs his coat and passes the pizza delivery man at the front door. The helmeted moped rider has been driving up and down the road, unable to see the house number in the dark. The pizzas are cold.

Wayne briefly returns home to Hout Bay, where Gaby's

mother has spent the day attending to their children, but it's not long before he returns to Fiskaal Road. Waiting at home will shatter his unyielding exterior.

As Helene returns from Sea Point, the family embraces one another again. It's beautiful to see, Louise thinks as she watches their closeness.

Time slows right down again. The group is silent. There is nothing left to say.

'Anita, you need to rest,' Paula suggests at around 10.30pm. 'You must sleep so that you're ready when the sun comes up.' She opens her bag. 'Here's a sleeping tablet. Take it and go lie down.'

She also gives Anita a small dram of Brett's whisky.

Louise decides to go home as well. She gathers her things to drive down the hill to their house in lower Camps Bay.

'Anita,' she says with conviction as she straightens up and wraps her scarf about her neck, 'phone me when they've found him.'

1.30AM TO 2.30AM
TWENTY-FOURTH HOUR IN THE WATER

Crushing pain. Legs. Arms. Back. Toes in a vice. All the bones in my feet are in a spasmodic grip. Pain rips through my entire body.

I'd forgotten about the cramps while my mind was lost to me, but now they take revenge. As they intensify, they remind me that my body is still connected to my head.

I hunch over. A cripple. Broken. A broken man. I bend my knees. An excoriating burn flares behind each kneecap. I pull my toes back. No change. No relief. For a long time, no relief.

Eyes close. Teeth clench.

This must pass!

Instead, the weight of sustained, excruciating pain. I sink down several feet each time I try to release the agony. It must pass.

This too shall pass!

'Wake up!' I hear screaming. 'Come on, boss, wake up!'

Hysterical. High-pitched. Urgent. It's Emily and Hilary. 'So typical of the boss! Sleeping on the job. If you don't lift your head, we can't work.'

They sound as if they've multiplied.

'Girls, I can't do it any more,' I hear myself say. Strange animal sounds come from my throat.

'Lift your head!' they shriek.

I try but sink under again. Barely resurfacing, I cough and retch.

'Make saliva, make saliva!' Their shouting is cruel, punishing, furious.

But I can't move my tongue. I can't even close my mouth.

'Come on, boss,' Bob admonishes me. 'I can't breathe if I'm underwater.'

'No more,' I say. 'No more.'

I don't want to go on any more.

THE BARRENJOEY
THURSDAY 18 APRIL 2013
1.18AM

As the night deepens, the wind drops completely and an unnerving calm settles, bringing with it the familiar cloying humidity. The small swell gently slapping against the hull of the *Barrenjoey* is the only discernible sound.

Suddenly the wheelhouse feels small and airless; Doris feels trapped, like a convict in a cell. He takes a near-empty bottle of vodka from under the dash and moves to the deck. There, in the silence and darkness, he sits entranced, emitting puffs of smoke and watching the moon pierce its way through fast-moving clouds.

He feels an ache in the pit of his stomach. He's had it since yesterday. He recognises it as the strange free-floating grief for Dave Kinder that has been hovering since he got the news of his passing. He hasn't allowed himself to think of his friend until now.

'You're the man, Dave.'

Doris voices his solo tribute out loud as he lifts the bottle and swigs the last of the fiery liquid. His eyes are brimming as he remembers his eccentric, imaginative friend. Kinder was a kindred spirit who seemed to recognise and accept Doris's sometimes graceless interpersonal skills. They'd met years before when the former was the fleet manager of the *Indies Trader* chain and Doris was first mate and later second captain of *Trader I*.

Kinder had taught Doris much.

Flashes of events take Doris on a nostalgic roller-coaster ride, but it's the mental picture of Kinder, a deepwater diver, shipwright, welder and engineer, marching out of a yacht's toilet area in filthy, foul-smelling shorts and a T-shirt, that forces a smile. With a putrid macerator pump in one hand and a cigarette in the other, Kinder had cursed his way though his cocktail-swilling guests, flicking them with faecal slop as he went.

Doris had cherished that moment. It typified his disdain for pomposity and pretentiousness.

Doris was always in awe of Kinder's toughness. He recalls a ghastly accident that Kinder had had one year in the island dockyard off Padang, where Martin Daly had kept his boat maintenance workshop. It had become a tale told (and embellished) in the expat bars around the islands.

Kinder had been busy with an angle-grinder in a confined space in the carcass of a boat, when he'd slipped. The blade had sliced through his leg and severed it almost entirely at the knee. The man beside him fainted at the gory sight.

'Wake up! Get up and get me a bandage,' he'd shouted at the queasy man. 'Get me on the tinny!'

'But you're going to lose your leg, Dave. You have to go to Singapore to get that sewn back on.'

'I'm not going to Singapore,' Kinder had shouted defiantly. 'Take me to Padang hospital.' In the end, Kinder had driven the tin boat himself back to the mainland. He was back in the pub a couple of weeks later with a pretty sci-fi scar.

Doris wipes tears from his crumpled cheeks. Gruff exterior, big heart, he thinks. The most amazing friend I've ever had.

The loss, like the others in his life, is searing for Doris. He misses Kinder's presence more than ever now and talks to him out loud.

'Mate, tell me. Tell me where this guy is...'

He knows Dave Kinder would understand. He was a

man who would have walked through hell to do the right thing.

Doris also talks to Denise, his hippie sister who taught him how to surf all those years ago. Despite his wanderings, they had remained close, and her death in 2009 from motor neuron disease had taken a massive psychological toll on Doris. Denise knew Doris's inner conflicts and fears, understood his misgivings about life, forgave him his weaknesses. She'd helped him through his dark times – and still does. Only now from the grave.

'I've gotta go get him, Denise,' Doris whispers.

2.30AM TO 3.30AM
TWENTY-FIFTH HOUR IN THE WATER

'Come on, Jetman, listen to me. Swim, Arch. Swim to me.'

I open my eyes.

It's Banger. His smile gentle, his eyes encouraging, his arm reaching out. He's on his haunches on the platform at the back of the *Naga Laut*. His hand, big and reassuring, is stretched out towards me.

They're here. They've come back.

Just in time.

I lift my head. It feels like a block of marble. I'm dizzy. The vision seems to oscillate just a little, like heat off the tarmac on a scorching day. My eyes are small slits and I try to fix my stare to stop the wobbling.

'Well done, Brett, well done!' the girls yell.

I'm battling, but I can get to the boat, I think.

I swim for about twenty metres. The edge of the boat is in front of me and I grab Banger's hand. I feel his grip in my own. I lift my foot. Like a cripple, I try to force it onto the platform.

Instead I collapse into the sea, and sink.

I come up retching, but I can still see the back of the boat. Ridgy is now standing on the platform.

'Swim to us, Brett.'

Real or imaginary, I can't abandon this call. I have to try.

I attempt to lift my arms to pull me forward but end up flailing. It's as if I've never learnt to swim. It takes forever to make a few metres.

I look up to nothing there.

Again, I sink. Again I resurface. This time I see JM on the boat.

'Come, my buddy. Come to us.'

One by one, the boys join him on the platform: Tony, then Weyne, Niall and then Snowman. I swim to them, but as I reach for a hand it evaporates.

Still slowly, incrementally, a few metres at a time, I keep going.

Led on.

Craig is left standing on the platform. The last one. I hear his soft-spoken voice.

'You can get to us, Arch,' he says.

'Craigie, I can't,' I say aloud. 'I can't.'

'Yes, you can.'

I remember the surfboards on the deck of the boat. Perhaps I can grab one for something to hang on to.

I lift my arm to grasp Craig's. He brings his face down level with mine and I look into his forlorn eyes.

'You haven't come to get me,' I say to him, 'you've come to say goodbye.'

He nods slowly.

I hear the splash of my arm on the water.

Down. Down. Down.

FISKAAL ROAD
CAMPS BAY
10.53PM

The duvet is like a concrete slab across her body. She feels claustrophobic under the debris of the day. Anita is on her husband's side of the bed, burrowing her head into the pillow, trying to breathe in some of his smell.

She shivers as she looks over to the bedside table at another of his photographs. It seems oddly magnified somehow. She can clearly see his eyes in the darkness, the flash of his teeth. She remembers a crown he had fitted two months ago – such a random, ridiculous thought.

She tries to make out the time, but her wristwatch has stopped. About the time Brett fell overboard, she remembers. The hours have been liquid anyway. Anita is exhausted, but she avoids sleep.

If I sleep, I won't be able to hear him.

Her feelings are again showing signs of rebellion. Dark ideas feel like shadowy spectres skulking beneath the bed.

What if I'm left on my own? What will I do? How will I tell our kids?

Life without Brett. It would feel like a limb had been amputated.

She's always described Brett as her 'one', her 'can't-breathe-sweaty-palms' first love. 'I couldn't be with anyone else,' she still tells anyone who will listen – this after ten years together. Most of her girl friends find her infatuation adorable; others secretly admit it's annoying.

'You've broken my heart before, Brett,' she says, thinking back to a break-up during their courtship. Her exhaustion fuels another surge of angry defiance. 'You don't get to do that twice.' But her outrage quickly dissolves into recrimination and she begins to sob, hiccupping into the linen.

The bedroom door opens a little. She sees the outline of her sister against the light from the hall.

'I thought you might be asleep, but I heard you crying.'

'I have terrible thoughts every time I close my eyes.'

'Did you take the tablet?'

'No.'

Helene lifts the duvet and climbs in beside her sister. The two women lie facing one another, their knees drawn up.

'You really should sleep,' Helene says, stroking her sister's hair. She begins to sing a hymn they loved as children. It brings a strong sense of familiarity.

'This little light of mine, I want to let it shine…'

'I need to keep talking to him, Helene,' Anita interrupts her. She is calmer now. 'He's my soulmate. You know that we have an unbelievable connection.'

'Yes, I do.' Helene says it slowly, carefully. Then, as if making a quick decision: 'Pray out loud. Put all your positivity out there.'

'Please, Lord…' Helene goes on to say a prayer. Afterwards, she opens her eyes and gives Anita a fixed stare.

'Everything is going to be okay.'

She then shifts onto her elbow. 'I forgot to tell you: Katya called earlier. She asked me to tell you that a medium phoned her this evening with a message for you.'

She moves to sit up and props the pillow against the headboard. 'This woman was at school with her, but Katya says she doesn't know her very well. The medium said she could feel Brett. That he is alive. She had visions of a man in the sea. He's strong; he's stubborn, she said, and he's a fighter.

He's floating. He's exhausted and hurting, but he's still alive and can see land.'

There is a long pause. Helene slowly blinks, then stares at her sister with concern. She has always been cynical about clairvoyance. It goes against her reason. And her religion.

'She said that he's talking to a small boy with blond hair, but she can't feel the boy.'

Anita's eyes close and a single tear trickles down her nose onto the pillow.

'You know I don't believe in this stuff,' Helene continues falteringly, sensing her sister's fragility. 'Neither does Katya, but we know that you do. We thought you'd want to know…'

Anita opens her eyes. Like an unlucky gambler clutching at one last desperate throw of the dice, this is a belief that she can cling to. And she's reluctant to let go of it.

'You don't understand, Helene. That's going to get me through the night.'

Helene kisses her sister on her forehead and lies with her for another half hour.

Their eyes close, but neither of the women sleep.

Gaby peeks in a little after midnight.

'I think you should take this to help you sleep, Neets,' she says, bringing in the sleeping pill that Anita had left downstairs. She puts it on the bedside table with a glass of water next to Brett's picture. Anita ignores it.

Gaby and Helene swap places for a time and the friends lie in silence in the dark. Words are useless now. When she presumes that Anita has drifted off, Gaby quietly goes back downstairs. She finds Kirsten in Zara's room and climbs into the double bed beside her.

3.30AM TO 4.30AM
TWENTY-SIXTH HOUR IN THE WATER

Air. Air. I need to breathe. Black. Black water. It's everywhere. Am I going up or down?

I need air but I can't find it. I can't breathe.

Kick. I cough underwater and bubbles leave my nose and mouth. My ears are about to explode. It feels as if my tongue is being ripped out of my head.

I try to move but I'm in slow motion. It takes forever to surface. Then miraculously: air. Gasping, I take it in in painful, rasping grunts. My lacerated throat makes the salty taste of the sea that much sharper.

My lungs ache. Charred by life-giving oxygen.

I'm in a dream, navigating the zone between life and death. My thoughts, too, are fluid, disappearing just as quickly as they form. There are momentary flashes. It must be when I open my eyes.

Broken shapes form in front of me, but before I can identify them, they're gone.

There are raucous, scrambled noises in my head; voices, crackly with static, are trying to reach me.

I'm light-headed. Lost.

Stars rush overhead in a high-speed race to the horizon. Their light signals their orbit in long comet tails behind them. I'm the centre of everything. I am the earth's axis.

Everything rotates around me.

The moon. I haven't been conscious of it for hours. It has dropped in the sky and punched a hole in the veil of mist around it; in the glow of lunar light, it's wobbling and bouncing around. Like Peter Pan's shadow, it won't be pinned down.

It gets bigger and bigger. Eventually I'm swallowed by the moon. I'm in a whiteout on a snowy mountain, lost in a blizzard.

The water around me feels like liquid cement, pressing in on me from all angles.

Squeezing the life out of me, like the doors of hell closing.

My eyelids flutter like a trapped moth and all memory melts away.

Once again, I sink slowly down.

THE BARRENJOEY
5.34AM

When first light flickers over the masthead, Doris turns his back on a night of sleepless emotional wrenching. He's been drinking black coffee since 2am and has already been on the satellite phone and radio to the four boats homing in on his search zone.

He is quiet and calm. Liberated even. He's operating with a sense of certainty and a purpose that has replaced the complex, ambivalent feelings of the night. He has been through some kind of mental evolution, re-energised and reassured by his talks with the dead.

When dawn comes, it's a perfect day, ordained perhaps by Lyall's pre-sunrise meditation.

Lyall was woken at around 3.30am when the anchor was pulled up through the belly of the boat and the motor rumbled to life. He felt the vessel's small, slow movements, a rhythmic cradle-like rocking. The ocean was at peace at last.

He got up in the dark, made his way to the bow to practise yoga and then, as the others slept, returned to his cabin to meditate for another hour and a half. Now at first light, he returns to the deck to greet the sun.

'A day for a miracle.'

It's a whispered wish.

Behind him, Doris is alone on the bridge, coffee cup in hand. He is looking out to the horizon, but staring past it somehow. He is also offering one last prayer.

'Denise. Dave. Give me some love. Please.'

At around 5.30am the rest of the Australians emerge on deck. Doris glances ahead and notes a couple of them starting to get their boards ready. It flicks a switch.

'Yer yuppies waxin' up?' he says under his breath, to himself. 'Still wanna get in yer last day's surf, huh?'

Jeff and Colin, who are standing at the stern, hear the captain's annoyance. They join him on the bridge.

'I see some of yer are keen to get off surfin'. We'll drop the dinghy and then go out lookin'. But I'm not givin' up. I'm goin' to find this guy, dead or alive. I'm not goin' in until I've found him.'

Colin's reply is unruffled.

'Don't be ridiculous. We're all going out.'

'Tell that to yer buddies over there.'

'We all know that this is about a man's life, Doris.' Jeff looks at his friends through the glass. 'There's not even a choice here.'

The two duck out the bridge. Subdued, he watches as Suley steers the *Huey* down their portside. The faster boat will reach the designated co-ordinates first. He picks up the radio.

'Yer might have to put a fire extinguisher on yer guests, Suley, but I have a couple of skirts here who wanna go surfin'.'

'You're shitting me,' Suley replies.

'Yeah, well, they might've had a change of heart.'

Suley smiles and salutes the captain of the *Barrenjoey* from the wheelhouse as they pass. His troops have fallen in.

Doris touches the brim of his cap and hangs up the radio. He watches the *Huey* for about a mile. Ten minutes later he is still staring ahead to some imagined vanishing point. He is in his own world once again. He hardly notices how the coral sky is slowly turning very clear, and overhead, very blue.

He also barely registers that the sea is the colour of shimmering silver in the path of the rising sun, its surface only slightly creased from yesterday's storm. Instead he watches the bow of the *Barrenjoey* cutting through the *Huey*'s now settling wake.

Suddenly all sound seems to stop. Doris hears the blood coursing through his brain and the world seems to shrink to the size of a pinhole. Then, out of the void, an idea slowly forms. It's like a flower bud gently opening. He's instantly certain of what he must do.

He grabs the radio again.

'Suley, I'm peelin' off at eighteen degrees further north. I'm droppin' it by ten.'

It's a pivotal moment.

'Roger that. Whatever you think, mate.'

'Turn it up eighteen degrees,' Doris turns and instructs one of the crew, a man with whom he'd scouted in the northern Sumatran province of Aceh.

The *Barrenjoey* slowly turns. She glides like an ice skater through the oily, still water.

4.30AM TO 5.30AM
TWENTY-SEVENTH HOUR IN THE WATER

'Brett!'

A shout. It's Anita's voice.

I open my eyes. The water around me is brightly lit. Everything above is gun-metal blue. Dawn has come without announcement.

I force myself to the surface. I blink repeatedly. Try to gather myself. I concentrate on focusing on the real things around me. Conscious thought forms and takes shape.

I'm still alive. Still in the water. I can't feel my body.

The sun has risen.

Light.

The word comes up like an electronic sign in my mind. The night is over. Over. Over the worst.

It takes several minutes to recover myself. I turn slowly in a circle.

And then I see it.

The shape of an island rises up out of the water before me. I can see a blur of green foliage and distant trees disrupting its skyline. I can't compute the distance, but it feels very close.

It's real. I'm convinced. The cold light of day has conquered the tricks of my mind. I've woken from a dream world to normality where there's clarity. Definition.

It's land! Land. An island just over there! The voice in my head is shrieking.

A surge races through my body, as if rocket fuel has been injected through my veins.

Relief. A private elation.

No witnesses.

Immediately I know that I can stay awake for a full day to reach it.

I turn around, and there – there again, more land. It's much further away, but it's another island.

I begin to swim, making for the closer one. It doesn't take me long to realise that I'm not making any headway.

Forget it, I say to myself. I must stop, assess this situation and choose my best option.

So I turn and decide to go for the island behind me. Even though it's further away, I must remain with the current.

Slowly, feebly, I take out the last of the paper from my pocket. My hands feel like wet papier mâché.

There's only a square centimetre left. I tear it in half. I can't face the idea that I'll soon have nothing left to guide me. The current, it reveals, is going north, so I turn and swim with it.

It carries me north. Perhaps I imagine it, but the land mass seems to increase in size; the other is further away. I'm getting somewhere.

Then. A speck in the distance.

Moored between the islands. It breaks the dark line of the sea where it meets the sky. A boat? I stare at it for an eternity and eventually establish the outline. It's unmistakable.

A boat. It's a boat.

Am I trying to convince myself?

The first fishing boats are out for the day. My throat is closing, this time with excitement.

I don't care. A boat is excruciatingly close by. The idea is like a tick, sticking fast. It's probably anchored, I think, but it will spend the whole day fishing there.

I must swim to it.

As I had in the night, I imagine becoming a fish – forming gills and webbing between my fingers and toes. It reminds me of a fishing prank we'd once played on Banger; we'd secretly dived under the boat and tugged dramatically on his handline from below. He'd truly believed he'd landed a big one.

I fantasize now about grabbing the end of the fisherman's line – I imagine his surprise when he sees what he's caught.

I put my head down and begin to swim.

It will take me a long time to get there, but it will be the summit of my achievements.

5.30AM TO 6.30AM
TWENTY-EIGHTH HOUR IN THE WATER

My limbs feel frozen. Stiff and arthritic, I'm swimming, but remain focused on saving energy. I try not to think of the time – or anything – ahead.

Instead I reach forward as far as I can to pull big, sprawling breaststrokes. My arms and legs are burning.

I'm too afraid to close my eyes, terrified that I'll lose sight of the fishing boat. I start to count my strokes yet again.

The sun is rising on my left and a soothing salmon pink is spreading across the eastern sky. It's a beautiful day. The ocean is like glass, reflecting massive glowing cirrus clouds. It's glorious. Minutes later the sun's rays set the water alight. A Turner painting.

I pee frequently now, which is excruciating, but even that cannot deter my purpose. My mind is razor-sharp again. All I can think about is swimming for that boat.

It doesn't have masts so I know it isn't a sailboat, and I can't see any outriggers, but I'm convinced it's a fishing boat. A good old Indo fishing boat coming out to throw nets. I swim, very slowly, for what feels like forty-five minutes, counting my strokes as I go.

The sun that started out as a welcome caress now feels hot against my left cheek and temple. But I'm making ground. Each time I look up, the boat, while still far away, seems to be getting closer.

Then, the dark shape against the skyline changes shape momentarily. I stop to make sure I'm not imagining it. Had they got sight of me? The sound of an engine starting up, although barely audible, is carried to me on the stillness of the morning.

The fishing boat turns sideways against the horizon, its

outline clear against the dawn sky. It's maybe a hundred metres away. It sets its course going east – away from me – and starts to move off.

I watch in mute horror.

The sight causes an inner disruption so great that my first impulse is to ignore it, deny it. But I can see it clearly, cruelly, retreating into the blue. It disappears. Like a mirage in the desert.

Something in me snaps. I even hear the sound. It's another shock to my system, but I cannot absorb this blow.

I cannot make it to the island – the current, the distance, my level of exhaustion. It's beyond my reach. That boat was my last chance.

I slowly tread water, considering my options. There's not going to be another boat – certainly not for a long time.

Not in time for me.

I have a flashback. I'm in bed with Anita about a month ago. She's reading a magazine article about a man who'd come close to drowning in a swimming pool. He'd knocked himself out, and while his brain knew that he was drowning, his body wouldn't move. Semi-conscious, he couldn't push himself back up to the surface.

Anita's reading me his description of drowning. Lying on the bottom of the pool, his eyes open, looking up at the glorious blue of the sky above. He breathes water – in and out – as if breathing air. It hadn't hurt, he'd said, and he'd slipped into unconsciousness.

Someone had pulled him from the pool. It hadn't been his day.

This is my day. This magnificent, sanctified morning.

I imagine looking up through the water at the sky. This, my painless, peaceful death.

I slowly submerge and concentrate on the waterline as it trickles past my face. I breathe in, but the water hits the back of my throat like a punch. I choke and vomit it out as quickly as I've taken it in.

I lift my face to the surface. Desperate now.

How am I going to do this?

I want to die.

Fury rises from deep within me, from the blood in my veins, the marrow in my bones. I'm *livid* with God. There's no grand plan, no predestination. I'm a bad throw of the dice.

I begin shrieking. Smacking the water with impotent arms.

'Fuck! Fucking hell! Fuck, fuck, fuck! I've made it through the night. You gave me signs, things to believe in, but now you're washing your hands of me. Fuck it. God, take me, I am done!'

Still, even in this state, drawn to the final edge of my living resolve – that undefined point I've wondered about throughout my time in the water, when the last traces of my will to survive are consumed by the ocean – still, tears do not come.

'Anita, my love of my life. Zara, Jamie, my precious children I can't. Mom, Greg, Sandy, I just can't. I am so sorry! I have to go.'

I cannot control my shivering. I'm close to hypothermic. Drowning myself will be a release.

In the moment, I make a conscious decision to do it.

The article said you have to take water into your lungs.

The solitude of the last day and a half has prepared me for the solitude of death. It's not a great way to go, I think. Fighting, believing, determined... then sinking down, defying every instinct to surface, simply too spent to carry on.

Go.

The voice in my head is quiet and calm.

Let go.

I sink under the water and float there, suspended.

I'm like an acrobat, a high-wire artist frozen in mid-flight.

I look up. The day is becoming ever more beautiful – not a cloud in the sky – and a dome of magnificent blue shimmers through the water as the sun radiates from the east. There's a bright focal point that moves between the patches of light and shade and subtle reflections oscillate in between. It holds the promise of warmth and comfort.

For a millisecond, it seems to me that this is the apex of existence: of serenity, perfection, of understanding.

'Neets, Zara, my little Jamie. I love you more than you will ever know.'

I take a deep breath and fill my lungs with the salt water that has crashed against and beaten me since it ensnared me.

The article is right: it's not painful. I breathe out and warm liquid streams from my nose and mouth. I keep looking at the light above.

I breathe in another lungful of salt water.

Suddenly an agonising pain burns around my tongue, as if a torturer is cutting it from my mouth with a dull knife. The salt in the water is cauterising every open wound.

It doesn't go all fuzzy, as the article said. I breathe in salty water again. This time the water feels even warmer as it surrounds my face. It feels as though my head has been dipped into a bucket of molten lava. The water escapes yet again.

I try a fourth time, but the pain around my tongue is

intolerable. What is left of my raw tongue cannot tolerate the searing salt water. Black spots dance before my eyes.

What the fuck do you think you're doing?

The mental scream is a sound I've never heard before.

You can't do this! You can't kill yourself!

I kick up through two metres of water and burst through onto the surface like a champagne cork. I collapse back down onto the sea, choking and snorting. As I cough up salt water, I detect the faint metallic taste of blood.

I stretch out my arms and try to scull. Try to keep my head up.

The piercing blue expands above me. My eyes move across it. I groan from the energy expended to surface. From the decision made and then unmade.

I turn my head. My right cheek rests on the water and it laps over my right eye, tickling my nostril.

Then. Floating above the water, I see it. A black cross.

'Take that cross and shove it!' I scream skywards. 'I'm done with all the signs of hope. Just done!'

Yet it draws nearer.

A small crucifix. Rising over the gentle swells.

THE BARRENJOEY
6.58AM

The sun is climbing into the sky and it's already starting to bake. The *Barrenjoey* has reached Doris's predicted search zone. The Australians have all taken up positions on the main deck and the bow to look out across the immense stretch of water; they pass a single pair of binoculars around. All acknowledge now that this task will require a united team effort. Everyone seems to have dismissed the earlier tensions between them.

Pete Inglis is sitting on the bowsprit of the *Barrenjoey*, the highest point on the yacht, his lower legs catching the soft spray coming up off the hull. His gaze moves across the blinding water, trying to find a point of focus.

Doris calls Anas and another crew member, Wilson, to join him on the deck. He hands them each a set of binoculars. 'Yer guys gotta get up high, climb onto the roof of the wheelhouse. No smoking *gulags* or talkin' shit. I want one of yer portside, the other starboard. Look up and down through yer binocs, from the boat up to the horizon.' He demonstrates a vertical patterned scanning movement that he'd taught his own crew on the oil and gas project.

'If yer look straight, you'll look right over him. Got it, guys?'

They nod in unison and Doris returns to the wheelhouse. He pours himself another coffee and, after a minute's silence, puts a match to another cigarette.

They've long been out of signal range for cellphone calls and text messages, so he turns towards the satellite radio, mentally readying himself to call the other vessels. He breathes deeply, in and out, then advances two steps to the dash.

In the stillness of the morning he hears Anas's voice through the roof.

'Boss.'

It's almost casual, nonchalant.

'There he is. He's over there.'

At that same moment, Pete shouts from the bow: 'There! Fucking *hell*. We've got him!' He's scrambling to his feet and pointing to the north-east. 'He's over there!'

For a moment the men on board the *Barrenjoey* stand still, staring with a shocked curiosity. It's as if no-one truly believed this moment would come. Then a loud gasp of amazement sweeps across the deck. Then shouting. Cheering. Rushing. Whooping.

The hair prickles on the back of Doris's neck. He looks out to the portside, narrowing his eyes to focus. It's difficult to see with the naked eye but after a few seconds he can just make out a tiny speck in the water.

About a hundred metres away, just off the port bow, he glimpses a man's head glowing like a beacon in the early light, and beside it, a ghostly white arm raised and waving.

A warm pulse shoots up Doris's spine as he furiously spins the wheel. He points the nose of the *Barrenjoey* towards the man in the water, then drops his head into his hands.

While the others scramble to the side of the boat, Doris weeps. He wipes his eyes with the front of his T-shirt as he picks up the radio receiver.

'Suley, mate,' he says softly. He clears his throat and then says in a more powerful voice, 'We've got him.'

The reply comes back: 'Dead or alive, mate?'

'Alive.'

FISKAAL ROAD
CAMPS BAY
1.39AM

The clock on the DVD player reads 1.39am when a car alarm goes off across the road.

Its piercing siren destroys the peace that has eventually come to the neighbourhood. The wail, punctuated by long pauses of false hope, persists for ten minutes.

It's too much for Kirsten, who gets up and returns to the lounge. Helene follows shortly afterwards. Then Gaby, Karmen and finally Anita. All are secretly grateful that they're not alone in needing comfort and wanting to keep vigil this night.

'I'll make coffee.'

Karmen shuffles to the kitchen, switching on the unforgiving fluorescent tube lighting that Anita loathes. The others follow, squinting, as Paula makes her way down the stairs. Wretched thoughts have also filled her head since it touched the pillow. She shakes out her hair as if to dispel them.

In the lounge, Wayne is also awake. He lies on the couch listening to the low murmuring coming from the kitchen. He counts the hours that separate South Africa and Indonesia and knows that it must be daybreak over there.

Did you get through the night, Brett? he wonders. He keeps his eyes closed. If a call doesn't come through soon, it's not going to come at all.

He briefly imagines breaking the news to the children later this morning, a dread that has been building steadily. It's left a pit in his stomach.

Gaby brings Wayne a mug of coffee. He sits up as they all

302

congregate once again in the lounge. A table lamp emits a diluted light and they sit disconsolately, edging closer to it – for warmth and comfort.

The harsh ring of a phone on the dining table makes everyone gasp. They stare at it as the piano ringtone punctures this strange hour and the luminous face reflects in the glass tabletop. It's the first call in hours.

Anita stands up and quickly walks around an armchair to answer it. This is the moment for which she has been mentally preparing. Her heart is hammering, hands shaking. She rips the charger from the base and lifts the phone to her ear. Her tentative 'Hello' is difficult to hear.

The others quickly move around her.

'What? What did you say?' She's shouting into the mouthpiece. A rasping noise comes from her throat, then there's a second of silence.

'He's been found? They've found him?'

'Jesus Christ.' Wayne says it first from where he has remained standing beside the cabinet in the lounge. The women have their hands over their mouths as they stare, stupefied.

Is Brett dead or alive?

The moment seems to exist outside of time.

'He's alive?' Anita is screaming. 'Say it again. Please, say that again. Did you say that he's alive?'

Her knees give way and she collapses, pressing the phone to the side of her head with both hands as if to absorb the news. She begins to convulse with sobs.

The room erupts and relief spreads like a kind of ecstasy. Kirsten, Gaby and Helene all burst into tears and start screaming as they jump up and down. Karmen puts her head in her hands and Paula stands momentarily and simply gapes. It's the second shock call of the day, almost as unbelievable as the first.

Wayne quietly sinks to his knees on the beige carpet; the hard rock inside begins to crumble and his hands go to his face as he begins to weep.

The ruckus brings Loni, in sleep shorts and a T-shirt, running down the stairs.

'They've got him, Daddy. He's alive.' Tears are streaming down Anita's cheeks.

'Oh my God!' Loni yells; he begins to cry. His body starts to shake as the full breakdown comes and his wife Paula takes him in her arms.

THE NAGA LAUT
APRIL 18, 2013
7.15AM

JM lies in the darkness of the dungeon. Despite his exhaustion, his night's sleep has been fitful. He was aware of the engines coughing to life at 3am and the gentle sway of the *Naga Laut* as she made her way back out once more into the Mentawai Strait. The storm had lost its fury at last, leaving the morning calm, as if equally drained by the previous day's exertion.

JM turns onto his shoulder, uncertain of the time. With no portholes, the cabin gives no clues as to the dawn of the new day.

He listens as the captain cuts the motor. 'We must be at the search zone,' he muses, his eyes still closed, his feelings conflicted. Noise of movement from the neighbouring cabin signals that the others are stirring.

A loud scream shatters the calm.

JM sits bolt upright; the start causes him to hit his head hard on the low ceiling. Mark Ridgway is shouting. Holding his head, it takes JM a second or two to make out Ridgy's words.

'They found him! They found him!'

Shouts suddenly erupt from all over the boat. JM unfolds his frame and is up in a single movement; he takes long strides through the narrow passage to where the friends all come together at the stern. It's early morning and the dawn is transforming into the start of a perfect day; every second is changing the colour of the sky.

Ridgy is standing in the doorway of the bridge above, the satellite phone still in his hand. Yanto has collapsed beside him, sobbing unashamedly.

'They found him. And he's alive!' Tears brim in his eyes and his face looks suddenly changed. The tension is visibly draining from him as he speaks. A pulse of warmth shoots up JM's spine as he takes the ladder in two steps and embraces his friend.

'Fuckin' no way!' Someone shouts it across the morning – one they'd approached with dread – and the words seem to gather acoustic momentum. After a stunned moment, there's a sudden cacophony of yelling, hugging, high-fiving. Relief. Elation. The men have never known such release.

'Alive,' says Weyne bowing his head quietly. 'That's ridiculous.'

'Bring out the Bintangs!' Snowman yells out amongst the rousing whoops and howls. Despite the early hour, he moves quickly towards the bar fridge. His hands, shaking with emotion, battle to unclasp the elasticated belt around it.

'This nightmare is over! A toast to Archie,' Tony is weeping openly as the beers clink in unison. Ridgy has brought down the crumpled chart and is slowly repeating the co-ordinates that Doris has given him, still a good seven hours' sail away.

'From now on we'll call him Bob.'

Banger's joke seems funnier than it should, and it dissolves the tension that has charged the last twenty-four hours. The men feel licensed to joke again. To fast-track back to 'normal'. Their hilarity is at fever-pitch.

Once again it's Banger who calms them. 'We should thank God,' he says simply. The group lowers their heads for a few moments to stand in silence; each says his own private prayer.

'You never stopped believing,' Weyne says quietly to JM as he takes him aside by the arm. The others are embracing the crew who are just as emotional. JM cannot trust himself to speak; his throat has closed. He smiles softly instead.

A shout from Craig is a welcome diversion.

'Now let's go get him!'

6.45AM TO 7.15AM
TWENTY-EIGHT-AND-A-HALF HOURS IN THE WATER

Spewing up salt water, I look up again. It's still there. The black cross.

Is it the angel of death? God coming to get me?

My lungs are constricted in a vice and I'm gasping for air, but I instruct myself to stay calm.

The cross is getting bigger. Please, God, tell me I'm not dreaming…

Mustering my last strength, I tread water, sculling quietly. My heart is hammering against my ribcage as I watch it get bigger. And bigger still.

A crucifix. God's sign. I suddenly realise it is the mast top and spreader of a yacht – I can see its rigging now. And it's coming my way.

Then the prow of a boat rises up into my line of sight. Her hull on the portside catches a dart of early morning sun and flashes like a distant spyglass caught on a turn. I'm low in the water and I can't see her mainstays, but that prow is indisputable. It's far away, but it's a boat. Of that I'm certain.

'Don't get excited. Don't get excited,' I keep repeating.

Then her whole length comes into view. I clock the distance at about 400 metres. There's activity on deck. The men look like ants.

It seems to take forever – but it's undeniable that she's coming straight for me. I'm determined to keep my emotions in check. I won't survive another disappointment.

I decide not to swim for her. Instead, I tread water, opting to follow her with my eyes. After a few minutes, she turns away from me – just slightly to starboard.

'NO NO NO!' I scream. It can't happen again.

She continues on that course.

One degree. The difference between rescue and my watery death. If I put my head down and swim freestyle as hard as I can, I'll cross that course, I realise. The current is still in my favour.

'This is it, God,' I say, not taking my eyes from the yacht. 'This is my last shot.'

I have to give it my best. Either I'll intercept that boat or drown doing it, God. Are you with me?

My pep talk stirs my mind and I feel adrenaline slowly seeping into my limbs. Oddly, I think of Chad le Clos, the young South African swimmer who recently became a national hero by taking gold in the 100 metres butterfly in the 2012 London Olympics. He'd beaten his idol, Michael Phelps.

Chad and I went to the same school in Westville – only 30 years apart. 'Chad,' I say, 'you have to help me get to that boat.'

I do a quick mental calculation: the yacht is about 300 metres away. About three-hundred strokes.

That's what it will take to get you into her path, Brett.

I say a quick prayer and call again on Anita to give me the strength. Three hundred strokes, baby. That's all I need.

I make a pact with myself. This is it, Brett, your last stab. You are going to give it everything you've got. You are not going to lift your head for the count of three hundred. One of two things will happen. You will either intercept the boat when you look up, or if they have sailed on you will be so burst that you will have no more energy and you will sink to the bottom with no more will to fight.

I put my head down and I swim.

I feel like I'm flying. I imagine I am a dolphin, racing

through the ocean, propelling myself faster and faster toward my rescue. All the time the voice in my head is screaming.

Please be there. Please see me. Please let me connect with this boat.

I count with my head down: one, two, three, four, five, six, seven, eight, nine, ten...

When I get to three hundred I stop. I look up. The boat is coming straight at me, only a hundred meters away.

'Hey! Hey!' My voice has left me. 'Here, over here!'

My words come out weak, pathetic, but I've never felt more determined to be heard. I give it everything my lungs and throat have got. I don't stop screaming.

I can now see the entire hull of the boat. In the full glory of the early morning sun, she's aglow, as if on fire. I give one last final scream and propel myself out of the water as high as I can, using my last traces of energy.

I hear yelling from the foredeck, and through my stinging, swollen eyes I sense more than see a flurry of movement. The boat veers directly towards me. I see a man in the prow of the boat jump up and gesticulate, arms waving. The shapes of men running; someone tearing off a T-shirt; a splash as someone dives into the water, as still as a millpond. The sound comes to me as a hush.

A perfect dive.

Just like Chad le Clos.

I see a life ring thrown from the rail and more bodies diving over the side.

I feel the relief spread through me like a warm glow yet my last swimming effort has drained me of all my faculties. I realise I have nothing left in me to even stay afloat.

I start sinking down, ruefully aware that I am going to drown before they get to me.

So close… So damn close…

And then an arm comes up beneath my ribs and moves across my chest.

Someone has me. I feel his strength in an instant.

For a moment, I'm too afraid to let go. To believe that there's a man beside me in the ocean.

I look up to see the visual swirl of a bright orange life ring sweeping in an arc around me.

Then I hear him. His words are a little breathless.

'We've got you, mate. We've got you.'

EPILOGUE

Brett Archibald was rescued at 7.15am on Thursday 18 April 2013.

He was found at 99° 46′ E degrees longitude, 01° 53′ S degrees latitude, drifting unaided on the current, in the exact area that Tony 'Doris' Eltherington had predicted.

He had drifted approximately 50 nautical miles, more than 70 kilometres, in the open water of the Mentawai Strait. Found a long way out off the north-east coast of the island of Sipura, wearing nothing but underwear and a pair of cargo shorts, he'd been in the water for 28-and-a-half hours.

After first spotting his sunburnt head from a distance of a hundred metres, and then hearing his frantic screams, the men on the *Barrenjoey* took another ten minutes to swing around to port and come up alongside him. Dave Carbon threw a life-ring into the sea and he and Simon Carlin, both powerful swimmers and trained life-savers, dived into the water. Dave Carbon reached Brett just as he was sinking down under the water. Colin Chenu ran down the deck and dived in afterwards, as did Indonesian crew member Aroziduhu 'Elvis' Waruwu, who leapt onto a surfboard and paddled out to offer assistance.

As the four men circled him in the water, the rescuers were immediately struck by how lucid and talkative Brett was. He was making quips and shouting to the others on board as they assessed his condition, pulled his arm through the life-ring and guided him to the boat. When they reached the vertical ladder on the starboard side of the *Barrenjoey*, Simon assumed Brett would be a dead weight after his tremendous physical ordeal. He took the back of Brett's boardshorts to lift him up the ladder, but was astonished to find that the

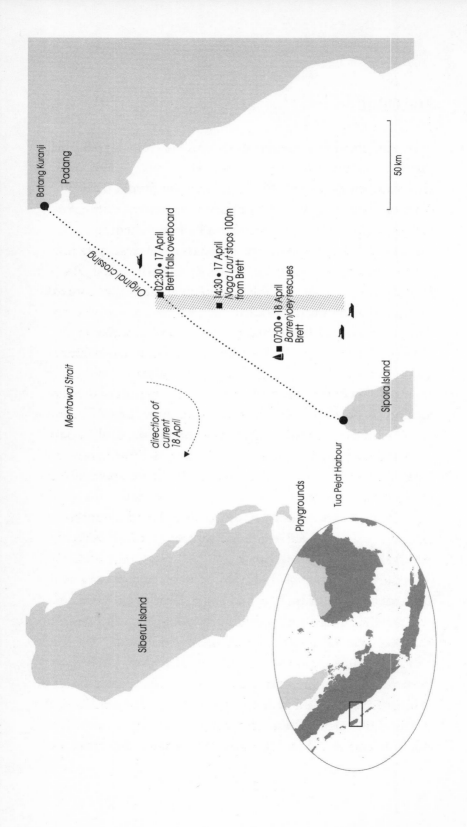

Batang Kuranji

Padang

Original crossing

02:30 • 17 April
Brett falls overboard

14:30 • 17 April
Naga Laut stops 100m
from Brett

07:00 • 18 April
Barrenjoey rescues
Brett

Mentawai Strait

direction of
current
18 April

Siberut Island

Playgrounds

Tua Pejat Harbour

Sipora Island

50 km

man did not need the help. Brett's body was responding with one last surge of adrenaline.

On deck Brett was shaky but otherwise in surprisingly good condition. They wrapped him in towels and made him sit on a board bag. His immense thirst was the immediate concern. Brett pleaded for a Coke, but Justin Vivian, the urologist, advised that they slowly rehydrate his body instead. After examining Brett's painfully swollen tongue, Justin gave him a mug of warm salt water and sliced segments of apple which he told Brett to move slowly around his mouth and chew without swallowing.

Brett continued to jabber nonstop, but it was not the gibberish his rescuers expected. He was remarkably coherent, describing everything that had happened to him.

The men who had found him were somewhat overwhelmed by the turn of events. Although Brett was a stranger to them, they all attest to experiencing a sense of wonder and elation at his recovery. Finding him, and finding him alive, was a privilege, they explained afterwards. It caused their spirits to soar.

Up in the bridge, Doris Eltherington was a reluctant hero. He retreated again behind the *Barrenjoey*'s wheel to radio the other search boats and notify them of their miracle find. He remained reticent until his guests insisted he come forward to meet the man whose life he had just saved. Doris made his way down from the bridge, beer already in hand and cigarette on lip, to shake Brett's bloodless, shrivelled hand.

Brett Archibald's rescue was exceptional in many respects. What began as an ordinary tale of easy accidents and a run of rotten luck became a human drama with all the hallmarks of the extraordinary. The tangled stories came together in an ultimately glorious confluence on that April morning.

First, it was a statistical long shot. The odds of finding a man lost for a prolonged period in the middle of the ocean are remote at best. The proverbial needle in a haystack. If Doris had not taken the *Barrenjoey* north or steered the vessel to starboard at precisely the moment he had – guided, he believes, by his late sister Denise – it's unlikely that Brett would ever have been found alive.

Second, the survival of a man in the water for that length of time is uncommon. There are factors that aided Brett through his extreme plight: the warm ocean temperature, the lack of sun and the opportunities he had to take in fresh water during the rainstorms. Nevertheless, it remains a feat of remarkable stamina and endurance. Brett would not allow himself to fail, and in extremis he pushed himself far beyond what he thought he was capable of.

Third, the tale bears strange elements of synchronicity. Two boats, each with nine guests on board, both sets of friends celebrating fiftieth birthdays, form separate pieces of a single puzzle that fit together in a way that sometimes feels perfectly logical, yet at other times it seems as if something more than coincidence is at play. One example is that at almost the exact time Anita placed her altar on the dining-room table in Camps Bay, Brett was seeing visions of the Virgin Mary in the plume of watery cloud after the *Naga Laut* had sailed away for a second time. Another was the unsolicited call from Katya's medium to say that Brett was alive.

Hope was an essential strand in the saga. In a world where people die every day in tragic ways, a man facing certain death was given a sudden reprieve.

On the *Naga Laut*, Brett's friends felt morally duty-bound

to find him, to believe that he was the kind of man who could survive a test like this. And back in South Africa, his wife, friends and extended family also refused to give up hope. Determined that he was still alive somewhere in the sea, they continued to pray, to believe and to will Brett's return home. When news of his rescue reached them all, there was a frenzy of celebration. The collective joy was immeasurable.

And then there was the man who found Brett. The man who would not accept that he had perished. Doris Eltherington's stubborn determination, fuelled perhaps by personal events and emotions and guided by his intimate knowledge of the environment, led to the truly miraculous rescue of a complete stranger. His refusal to abandon Brett is a profound example of humanity at its finest.

It was a day that should have ended in tragedy, but it concluded in triumph.

Not long after being brought aboard the *Barrenjoey* and rehydrated, Brett was led below deck. He was seated in the saloon where his rescuers spent the next hour getting him warm. Throughout, he continued to recount his experience in the water, often with remarkable detail.

He talked incessantly. Some of the Australians described his condition as a little manic. 'He was as red as a rooster and high as a kite,' Doris commented afterwards, remembering jokes about Australian and South African sports rivalry. They were astounded at his physical strength and stamina, but more significantly, his unbreakable will.

Brett's blood pressure was dangerously low at 68/44, a reflection of his severe dehydration. Since the only IV fluid on the boat was out of date, Justin Vivian opted for caution and decided not to administer the drip. A brief discussion whether to contact an emergency physician for further medical advice ensued, but after careful monitoring Justin was satisfied with Brett's overall physical condition. His face and head were significantly burnt, even from that morning's first hour of sun, his tongue was still engorged, his eyes red and painful from the hours in the salt water and his nose had a gaping hole in it where the seagulls had pecked him. The backs of his legs had been rubbed raw, grazed by the constant chafing of his shorts; his underarms were also raw, his lips chapped and chafed. Despite all of this, the consensus was that there was no need for Brett to be evacuated to a hospital.

News of Brett's rescue spread rapidly. Calls were made to the *Naga Laut*, to the search boats that had mobilised that morning, and to Anita and her children back home.

In Tua Pejat, port authorities requested that Brett be brought ashore, but Doris blew them off, insisting that the doctor on board the *Barrenjoey* had advised Brett to rest. He was not about to allow officialdom to take over just yet.

Brett had a tepid shower, was given a new T-shirt and a clean pair of boardshorts and was shown to Lyall's cabin to lie down. Even though he had not slept properly for around eighty hours, he was unable to sleep. Instead he stared vacantly at a magazine, his brain churning as he came to terms with the realisation that he was no longer in the water. He then furiously scribbled pages and pages of notes in an attempt to remember all the emotions and thoughts he had experienced while swimming. He was still unable to cry, not even tears of relief.

All the while, the *Naga Laut* steamed as fast she could to reach the *Barrenjoey*'s co-ordinates. The South Africans were eager to be reunited with their friend, but it would take another seven hours of sailing before they'd get to him. The Australians, meanwhile, decided to get in the tinny and head for Icelands to surf. It was, after all, their last day. Dr Vivian and a few others stayed behind to monitor the patient.

At around 2pm the *Naga Laut*'s tender pulled up alongside the *Barrenjoey*. In order to catch up to the faster ketch, Mark Ridgway, JM Tostee, Tony Singleton, Niall Hegarty, Mark Snowball and Yanto had decided to take the tender to collect their friend. Weyne Mudde, Benoit Maingard and Craig Killeen stayed behind.

There was a strange moment of tension when the South Africans first boarded, an awkward unspoken questioning of whether the *Naga Laut* had, in fact, put up a respectable search for Brett the previous day. Once the misconception was cleared up, however, a rapturous reunion ensued with hugging, joshing and secret tears all round.

Brett returned to the boat from which he'd fallen overboard, but not before once again embracing the man who had saved him. He also repeatedly thanked the Australians for playing their part.

'I love you guys,' he beamed.

As the vessels parted, both parties were left contemplating the events of the last day and a half. On the *Naga Laut* Brett followed up an emotional call that he'd first made from the *Barrenjoey* with an equally charged second call to his wife. Later Anita would describe both calls from her husband as frenetic. He talked full-tilt, recounting his saga. She was just as overcome, sobbing with joy and relief. Brett also spoke with his mother and brother in rousing exchanges. Afterwards, he sat down with his friends to commemorate a miracle – and discuss what to do next.

Seated around their cabin table, Brett spent several hours

once again vividly evoking what he had been through. At the end of it all, he made a surprising announcement.

'I don't think we should go home just yet, boys. I've talked it through with Anita and I think we should continue our holiday. I think we should go surfing.'

Many, including some family members, thought he was crazy and acting selfishly. After such a traumatic event, surely the best place to be was at home with his family, they believed. But Anita was fully supportive of her husband's decision. 'He was physically okay and he needed to get back out there, to get back on the horse. If he hadn't, he would have snapped,' she would say later.

That afternoon John and Belinda McGroder sailed into Playgrounds with their two young sons, keen to meet the stranger they had helped save. Brett spent an emotional two hours with them on the upper deck of the *Naga Laut* as John and Belinda detailed the massive efforts that they, Doris, his guests and crew, Martin Daly and the Malherbes had all gone to during the previous 24 hours.

Along with the men from the *Naga Laut*, they then all went across in their dinghies to the *Barrenjoey*. A celebratory feast of canapés and prawn sandwiches was brought out at sunset and all charged their drinks in a show of warmth and admiration for the *Barrenjoey*'s captain, saluting him for his resolve. Brett, still fragile from his ordeal, could not contain his emotion; its greatest display was in the constant hugging of Duke McGroder who'd turned six that day – the age of Brett's own son, Jamie.

Soon after their return from the *Barrenjoey*, Brett passed out utterly spent. After just a few hours' sleep he awoke to a deathly still boat; all crew and guests had collapsed in deep sleep following their last harrowing day and a half. Brett quietly made his way up to the point from which he had fallen and sat staring into the perfectly calm and moonlit sea. His mind was in turmoil, trying to assimilate the events of the previous three days. Tears suddenly started coursing down his cheeks as he contemplated his miracle rescue. Unexpectedly, a thin wiry arm reached out from the cabin and embraced him around his shoulders and neck. It was Skippy, the captain of the *Barrenjoey*. The two men sat in silence, Skippy's tears falling onto Brett's shoulders and Brett's tears falling to the deck. Both men silently rejoicing in life. After a long while, Brett quietly said to the older man, 'Skippy, you have to put me back in the water.' There was a gasp followed by a horrified silence, then a croaked reply: 'No, no, no, Mr Blett. Me not put you back water, man no get second chance.'

Craig Killeen has a video of Brett and two of the guys boarding the *Naga Laut*'s tender the day after the rescue. It's very early morning, well before sunrise, and they're heading out for the first surf of the trip. It's Brett's first venture back into the sea. The camera catches him unaware as he climbs into the tinny: the expression on his face is one of sheer terror.

Beneath the daily headlines of death and destruction, good-news stories still capture world attention. The rescue of Brett Archibald was no exception. For the 28-and-a-half hours that he was missing at sea, people across the globe followed his story with commingled horror and fascination. Technology has changed how people experience another's ordeal, so many followed it in real time on Facebook and Twitter, and those closer to him through SMS. There is an obvious irony: Brett could not have felt more alone and isolated during those hours in the water, yet all the while thousands of people around the world were reacting and responding to his plight. Like a pebble thrown into water, the ripple effect was felt in the furthest parts of the global pond.

Over the following ten days that Brett stayed on in the Mentawais, the media storm grew. The story of his rescue found its way onto the front pages of newspapers across the globe. Surf legend Shaun Tomson said in an interview, 'If it had been me out there, [instead of] the air force or navy searching, I would have rather had Doris.'

International journalists, reporters and writers from news publications, magazines, surf titles and television news shows jammed the *Naga Laut*'s satellite phone line and hounded Anita in her home. In retrospect, it was probably a wise move for Brett to stay on the boat in relative isolation; otherwise he would have walked straight into a frenzy of publicity.

News attention also followed the Australians after they landed in Jakarta and then later back in Perth. 'It was all about selling a paper that day,' Simon remembered later.

Television documentaries that were screened worldwide followed. The media focused primarily on the 'miracle at sea', but there were also a few questions about culpability.

Tony Eltherington was reluctantly interviewed for the Australian documentary *60 Minutes*.

'I'm stoked for Brett, Anita and the kids,' he told interviewer Charlie Wooley. 'Yeah, I was able to give someone back her husband. And children, their father.'

Despite his almost monosyllabic answers, the event caused him to become something of a minor celebrity.

'Why did I go looking for him? Because I reckon I'd want someone to be looking for me…'

True to form, Doris was not even remotely caught up in

the publicity. He continues to live in semi-seclusion and run his surf charters out of Padang. Although he attracted further respect and praise, those close to him attest that he remains unchanged by the admiration. He has never been a seeker of the limelight – it's just not the man's style. 'For him, it isn't about counting karma credits,' says Kirk Willcox, his friend and director of marketing and communications for SurfAid.

Doris himself claims to have calmed down. 'I've been really Irish over the years, but now I don't get as angry as I used to. Just don't steal my girlfriend, my surfboards, my boat or my money. Anything else, you can knock yourself out,' he laughs wryly.

He continues to head down to the Gold Coast with determined regularity to visit his children, Taryn, Jarrah and Madeline – a goofy-footer surfer like her father – and three grandchildren, River, Chase and Kymani. 'I want to spend more time with my children,' he explains.

'When Dad called and said, "I just saved a guy," I thought, Oh, okay cool,' Taryn, Doris's eldest daughter who helps run his charter bookings from Australia, relates. 'But then magazine writers, bloggers, journalists from all sorts of TV channels started calling me trying to organise interviews. Wow, I thought, either he's done something really good or really bad. You have to be open to both.'

On a trip home in February 2014 Doris was notified that he'd won two Australian surfing awards from Surfing Australia, the sport's representative organisation in Australia and internationally. One, the Peter Troy Lifestyle Award, is effectively a 'lifetime achievement' award; it was bestowed on Doris for his part in pioneering surfing in Indonesia and generally opening the sport to the world. The other is the

Waterman of the Year Award, an acknowledgement of his heroism in rescuing Brett.

Despite his visits to Australia to see family, Doris remains in his soul place, a place that doesn't fit into the 'nine to five'. It's where he can make his kind of living, one that can give him what he lives for: 'water time'. 'When I've got a six-pack of beer, a carton of cigarettes and the surf's pumping, I'm at my happiest,' he says.

Like other surf charter captains in the Mentawais, he donates his time to the United Nations and charities like SurfAid, ferrying medical supplies and mosquito nets to the poor villages around the islands. Knowing the bays and waterways as well as Doris does, charter boats like his have logged GPS co-ordinates of even the most remote village locations over the years so that primary healthcare and malaria and cholera prevention programmes can reach them. In emergencies, they're usually the first on the scene.

'I'd go straight out there if I got any kind of call again,' Doris says matter-of-factly. 'Of course I'd go.'

Brett Archibald's ordeal, having to pit all of his strength and ingenuity against the forces of nature for more than 28 hours, is something very few people could have survived. So says Professor Tim Noakes of the Sports Science Institute of South Africa in Cape Town, who has retrospectively assessed Brett's physiological responses throughout his time in the water.

'If you put 1,000 people in the sea in those circumstances, 999 would die,' Noakes says.

Even though significant factors worked in his favour, Brett showed astonishing tenacity and a powerful will to live.

The ocean's temperature – at 28°C – was critical, says

Noakes. It meant that Brett was able to keep swimming for longer than would have been possible in even marginally colder water.

The human core body temperature is stringently maintained at 37°C. Our bodies continually generate metabolic heat, however, which is then brought by convection to the skin's surface where it gets lost to the surrounding environment. When we're clothed, a layer of heat is kept close to our skin, but if submerged in water it rapidly gets lost to the surrounding liquid and our body temperature begins to drop. Every individual has a critical temperature tipping point, Noakes explains. Above it, one can survive for some time, but as one's body temperature drops, hypothermia starts to set in. In 28°C water, this would be expected to happen after 10 to 15 hours.

While Brett was certainly losing heat down the temperature gradient to the water, this was limited to some degree by his body shutting off the blood flow to his skin and diverting it to his heart and brain. In addition, he was still able to generate some heat through the movement of his swimming and through shivering. It's likely that his body temperature had already dropped by one or two degrees in the first 15 hours in the water, but after 28 hours he was heading for serious trouble, explains Noakes.

Had the water in the Mentawai Strait been half a degree colder or had Brett remained in the water for much longer, his body temperature would have eventually plummeted. At around 33°C, his brain would have cooled, he would have been unable to control his thoughts and he would have lost consciousness. Drowning would have been the inevitable result.

Brett's severe dehydration was also a significant threat. At the time of going overboard, he was already considerably dehydrated. He'd undergone around 54 hours of uncomfortable travelling, had had less than two hours' sleep and, departing South Africa off the back of a two-day family wedding celebration, his body was already under pressure. Add the aftereffects of a tainted meal – a long cycle of vomiting and diarrhoea so severe that it caused him to black out – and his dehydration was extreme.

Brett also swallowed copious amounts of salty sea water, an emetic. Once in the system, the osmotic effect of the highly concentrated salty fluid would only intensify the overall dehydration.

'Humans have a huge capacity to cope with dehydration,' Noakes explains. 'It's ruled by genetics. The world's best runners, for instance, can dehydrate by between 12 and 15 percent.'

Brett's incredibly dry mouth, severely swollen tongue and spasms indicate that he was at about 16 or 17 percent – severe dehydration. 'If he'd got to 20 percent, his kidneys and liver would have begun to fail. Even if he'd washed up on an island later on, full renal failure would probably have killed him.'

When we are dehydrated, our blood pressure starts to fall. In compensation, the vessels that perfuse the kidneys, liver and gut constrict. Ultimately, severe dehydration can thus lead to extensive damage to the entire gut. Dehydration also resulted in Brett's urine becoming highly concentrated and the formation of small salt crystals in his urethra – the reason why relieving himself was so terribly painful.

Extreme thirst can also drive a man insane, says Noakes, which could partly explain Brett's hallucinations. While his self-instruction to 'generate saliva' did not necessarily help combat the dehydration, it did give Brett mental focus. The rainwater might have helped, too, but again, more mentally than physically.

Although Brett had no food in his system, no fuel to burn for energy, his brain was metabolising his body's glucose reserves in order to keep going. 'If there aren't enough carbohydrates in the digestive system,' Noakes explains, 'the liver generates glucose from protein or fat that gets used by the brain.'

Either way, the physical exertion caused Brett to lose nearly six kilograms during his time in the water.

Ultimately, it was probably Brett's physical strength that tipped the scales in his favour, this despite him not possessing particularly extraordinary anatomical qualities. 'It's not possible for an untrained, relatively unfit person to swim non-stop for 28 hours and 30 minutes,' says Noakes. 'People with a greater body mass would have been able to float, but Brett is comparatively lean. He had that going against him.'

For a man of fifty, Brett was fairly fit, but not for swimming. 'Brett was working his upper body and most people have rather weak upper-body strength. His cycling fitness was therefore somewhat irrelevant. It's astonishing that his completely untrained-for-swimming upper-body muscles coped for so long. There's actually no sport that you can perform for that length of time if completely untrained for it. If we asked an athlete to cycle with his arms, even gently, he'd find it impossible to go on beyond two or three hours.'

Brett spent most of his time in the sea in a vicious storm, fighting for every breath.

'He's also a "sinker",' says Noakes. 'He can't float on his back. Great swimming athletes are natural floaters, so Brett's swimming action was drastically inefficient. A cross-channel swimmer might be able to swim 14 hours or so, but they are usually biologically superior. They have the physiology, they're trained for the event and already have a very focused mental attitude. We seldom ask humans to do what Brett did. He is one of those rare people who could adapt his body in these conditions.'

Physical aptitude aside, the key for endurance of any kind is mental fortitude, Noakes concludes. Getting one's mind around a goal requires a different kind of coaching and seeing the outcome is paramount. 'Brett's case shows just how powerful the mind can be. He had to decide whether to survive or not. Most of us would have quit. Despair would have overwhelmed us and we'd have drowned.'

Trudy Borain, a psychologist and specialist in post-traumatic stress disorder expands on what it takes mentally to survive as Brett did.

'When faced with life or death situations, we respond both biologically and psychologically,' she explains. 'We naturally go into flight, fright or fight mode. The sympathetic nervous system, part of the autonomic system that connects our brain stem with many of our vital organs, is triggered. It accelerates the heart rate and breathing, for instance, and increases the body temperature to provide energy to fight the threat or to escape it. It also connects to the digestive tract and warns the body against consuming too much energy, so functions like eating, drinking or even digesting become secondary. The body automatically goes into survival mode.'

In 'flight' or 'fright', some become 'paralysed' in dangerous situations, Borain adds, but Brett was almost constantly in fight mode.

'He is a highly functional individual and was fighting the water, raging against God, fighting death. His survival instinct was very strong and he constantly created life-affirming thoughts that were positive in his survival – that his "company" would keep him swimming, that his friends were coming to rescue him, that the hallucinations would guide him to his rescue. All the things connected with his rescue abandoned him, however. The *Naga Laut* left twice, the visions disappeared, the plane and other boat all moved off out of sight. He must have felt extraordinarily abandoned – as he must have done as the little boy who was unwittingly abandoned by his father due to his illness. In the water, as in life, Brett was able to keep those feelings in check.'

Even prior to this incident, Brett has been careful to maintain mental and emotional control. Although searching and questioning, his psychological state has, since childhood, been well organised and ordered. Critically, in the water, he was able to control his fear.

In a trauma, Borain explains, both our left and right brains are affected. The right brain stores all the implicit emotional, non-verbal memory located in the subconscious. This is where the memory bank is formed. The left brain, on the other hand, contains our explicit memory – all the things that we have learnt.

'We often operate on our implicit memory, when behaviour is strongly associated with something we feel, and often during a traumatic experience fragments of the emotional memory are activated. Brett was able to draw strength from both his implicit and explicit memory during his time in the water and was able to connect very well with both his body and mind. In fight mode, he could not feel fear. Had he started to feel that emotion, he would have succumbed.'

Brett used counting, tabulating, listing, singing all the songs on his iPod playlist and moving mentally through long obsessive sequences as a way of disassociating from the reality of his circumstances. Although entirely aware of what was happening to him, and remaining pragmatic and smart in the water, a side of his mind grasped certain things and fixated on them – he constantly counted his breaths and strokes and simultaneously slowly moved through a lifetime's memories. Whenever negative thoughts sneaked up, his mind would simply not let them flow, and his mix of punctiliousness and repetition was a way of getting through the nightmarish situation.

Also, by forming an imaginary 'company', with himself as the CEO, he could still maintain an illusion of control. Issuing orders and having colleagues answer back in 'support' of him was a delusional distraction, his mind's way of not accepting that he was entirely alone in the open sea.

Of course, such a traumatic experience brings with it an array of potential aftereffects.

After his ordeal, Brett set up the Brett Archibald Foundation and was invited to talk to various audiences – corporate, secular and charitable – about his fall overboard. A positive and dynamic orator, and comfortable in front of an audience, he soon found his way onto the South African and international talk circuits. Sharing his story was a chance not only to expurgate his experience, but also a way to raise funds for charities. His story has had a profound effect on his audiences, but Brett is the first to admit that there is much with which he still needs to engage. It took months for him to go for structured counselling, and the decision came only after a couple of alarming episodes.

During a mountain-bike ride on Table Mountain one hot summer's morning, he dived into a freezing cold lake to cool down. Shortly after completing the ride and enjoying a cup of coffee, his one arm went completely numb and his chest constricted in crushing pain. He was convinced he was having a heart attack and was rushed to hospital. While lying on a hospital bed, a drip in his arm and once again consciously counting to bring down his thundering heart rate, he had terrifying flashbacks to his time in the water. Tears streamed down his cheeks as he relived the anguish. He was unable to talk to a terrified Anita but begged that she stay with him in the hospital room.

On another occasion, while on a business trip to Johannesburg, Brett was driving through heavy traffic on a hot day in a car without air conditioning. He had a sudden overwhelming sensation that he was slogging through quicksand, and again he thought he was suffering a heart attack. Desperately trying to control the heaving in his chest and unable to drive, he pulled over to safety.

Both incidents were severe panic attacks, classic symptoms of post-traumatic stress. In each case, it took an hour or more to bring down Brett's heart rate and control the attacks.

Brett's visions have also proved tricky for him to unravel. The pillar of water, the Virgin Mary, the buoy with the clanging bell, the boys in the *perahu*, the 17th century sailing ship, and the images of his friends appearing at the back of the *Naga Laut* – these were, for him, incredibly vivid and real. Science would argue that they were the products of a body and mind under extreme stress.

In his book *Hallucinations*, the late American neurologist Oliver Sacks investigates visual and auditory hallucinations that arise from a variety of circumstances, including disease, drugs and deprivation. Now that scientists are more able to map the brain's electrical and metabolic activities, Sacks explains, they are better able to understand the specific cortical activity that corresponds with hallucinations. For example, visual hallucinations have been shown to correspond with the visual cortex. They can also occur if the frontal lobes, the seat of judgement and self-evaluation, are impaired by mechanisms such as dehydration and lack of sleep, as was the case with Brett.

Sacks discusses how the deprivation of normal visual input can produce hallucinations. Holy men who meditate in caves or prisoners who are held in isolation in dark cells have been known to experience 'the prisoner's cinema' – hallucinations produced by what has become known as 'sensory deprivation'. However, total darkness is not essential for this to happen, Sacks suggests. Visual monotony can equally cause hallucinations.

Research into sensory deprivation was particularly prevalent in the 1950s and '60s. Sacks cites a 1950s experimental study at McGill University where students were subjected to what was then described as 'prolonged perceptual isolation'. After an extended time in their monotonous environment, many resorted to self-stimulation – mental games, counting, fantasies – but eventually the hyperexcitability in regions of the brain from lack of normal sensory input caused visual hallucinations. They started off as initially simple visions, but developed later into more complex ones. Most often the hallucinations would appear without warning and with no control from the subjects.

Sacks goes on to describe another 1960s experiment where sensory deprivation tanks were designed 'to intensify the effect of isolation by floating the body in a darkened tank of warm water, which removed not only the sense of bodily contact with the environment, but also the proprioceptive sense of the body's position and even its existence. Such immersion chambers could produce "altered states" more profound than those described in the original experiments.'

Brett had to fight for his sanity in remarkably similar conditions. And it was no experiment.

Sleep deprivation, combined with exhaustion and extreme physical stress can also cause vivid hallucinations, Sacks tells us. Equally, auditory hallucinations can take place when someone is in a situation of extreme threat or danger. People have talked about 'hearing things' in such instances, with the most common auditory hallucination being the hearing of one's name – either in a familiar or else in an utterly foreign voice. He distinguishes this from the 'inner speech' that many of us are familiar with ('Now where did I leave my keys?').

In extreme situations, mostly when there's a threat to life, he cites how his patients describe hearing 'another voice, often strong, clear and commanding'. High-altitude mountaineers, for instance, have recorded hearing voices that steered them down a mountain in a blizzard or testified to seeing a figure, a 'guardian angel', in their peripheral vision climbing or trudging with them when they thought they were alone. A frequently recorded phenomenon in climbing, solo-sailing and polar-explorer circles, this has become known as The Third Man Syndrome.

As with visual hallucinations, a prolonged silence or auditory monotony can cause auditory hallucinations, which subjects characterise as being extremely clear and unusually detailed. Brett's visions – the ringing bell on the buoy and the men talking on the 17th century sailboat – were both visually and audibly evocative.

For Brett himself, definitive answers to his experience of these phenomena remain elusive. All the same, they have served to heighten his questions around his faith, spirituality and the continuation of the spirit after death.

'Part of the processing of a trauma is to create meaning out of the experience and how you bring that meaning into your life,' says Trudy Borain. 'Those constructs are very important for the processing of the trauma.'

The Renaissance Florentines described the final journey of death as 'entering the great sea', but Brett Archibald miraculously emerged from that sea.

Like many other tales of heroism, this is a simple story, but it's also a life-affirming one. If there is a moral to this story, Lyall Davieson suggests, perhaps it is to encourage all of us to raise our awareness, to lift our principles and to become more loving and accepting. To be brave enough to stand out as a single, shining exception.

Brett agrees. 'If there were more men around the world with attitudes like Doris, the world would be a better place,' he says. 'On that morning, he went out of his way for me and encapsulated the spirit of nurturing life. People may say and think many things, but at the end of the day, *it's their actions that truly count.*'

THREE YEARS LATER

Every day since my rescue in the Mentawai Strait, I say a quiet prayer of thanks and gratitude to all those involved – my family, the guests and crews of the *Naga Laut* and *Barrenjoey*, the captains and crews on the support boats who selflessly went out in search of me – as well as to all those who rallied to my cause during that time. The publication of *Alone* was eventually timed to mark the three-year anniversary of my ordeal and it serves as testament to everyone who played a part in bringing me home, no matter how small. If nothing else, I have learnt the value of the human spirit and the good that exists in the world, together with the importance of acknowledging it regularly.

The seed to write this book was planted during the ten days that I stayed on in the Mentawais to complete the surf trip. On the day of my rescue, I spent close on seven hours with Doris and the nine Aussie blokes aboard the *Barrenjoey*, during which time I occupied a good few hours writing down everything I could remember during my time in the water. I was then reunited with my mates on the *Naga Laut*, and over the next ten days we spent many, many hours sharing the stories and recounting our feelings, emotions and thoughts around the time that I was missing in the ocean.

I soon came to the realisation that there were a number of uncanny comparisons between our trip and that of the lads on the *Barrenjoey*. We were nine mates on a surf trip to celebrate a fiftieth birthday; they were too. Our trip had been dogged by a number of mishaps; theirs had too. It seemed to be a tale that was meant to be told.

On arriving back in Cape Town I faced a barrage of media and quickly came to comprehend the extent of the coverage this story had generated around the world. There soon followed a trip to Australia courtesy of *60 Minutes Australia*, when I again got to spend time with Doris and the guys from the *Barrenjoey*. I knew then that I wanted our story to be penned.

My main objective has always been to document my ordeal for my young children, as I knew that the enormity of what had happened to all of us was beyond their comprehension at the time. I wanted the full, detailed story to be available for them to read as they grew up.

And so the journey began.

I had delusions of having the book written and available in print before the first anniversary following our ill-fated trip. During that year, Anita and I lived through the ordeal time and time again, and on the first anniversary she penned notes to all involved, the most poignant being to Doris in which she wrote:

> Today is one year since Brett was found.
>
> That it is also Good Friday is no coincidence. Today is a celebration in our lives. I hope your heart is warm, because we have talked about you and thought about this time last year with such a sense of awe and gratitude.
>
> Not a week goes by without me thinking about how this could have ended for my family. And we have you to thank for that. Now we don't take one day for granted.

At that stage, we were not even halfway through the first manuscript! The trials and tribulations I was enveloped in at the time were sometimes so daunting that on occasion I was ready to throw in the towel. I was dealing with a failed business, a further diabolical investment into another business, the implosion of a friendship and business partnership with someone I had held near and dear to me, together with a multitude of emotional undercurrents from people who had been involved in the rescue who believed they had been wronged in some way or another. I was also deeply disappointed by some of those nearest to me.

Fortuitously, I had been introduced to a writer with whom I felt an immediate connection, and over the course of a year I spent many mornings at her house exploring the nuances and depths of my memories and arranging for her to conduct interviews with all the people involved. Not only was an honest and complete re-creation of the story a complex task – involving many people based around the world, each with their unique memory of events – but the process itself was a form of extended therapy for me. Fortunately she kept things on course.

Reliving my experiences in the finest detail was time-consuming and deeply moving. It was also, at the time, mostly subjective. It was only on reading the completed manuscript some twelve months later that the entire picture unfolded for me and I came to grasp the full magnitude of what had transpired during my time in the ocean. The inexplicable unity of people from around the world who had prayed for me or sent wishes via the 'Searching for Brett Archibald' Facebook page blew me away. Over the past three years, I have gone on to learn of countless amazing stories from people all over the world, many of whom I had never previously met, who played some role in this crazy drama. They all affected me and contributed to my comprehension of the experience.

Coming to terms with what happened to me is an ongoing

process; one, I imagine, that will take many more years before it's fully realised – if it ever will be. From my perception, there is simply no way that a person can spend 28-and-a-half hours knowing he is going to die, but not knowing how or when, and then surviving by the slimmest margin, without gaining a completely new perspective on life. I get to contemplate this thought every day.

I am often asked the question, 'How has this changed your life?' To say that it was a life-changing experience would be an epic understatement. In an incredibly short space of time following my return to Cape Town from Australia in late 2013, I was catapulted onto the local and international speaker circuit, and I have shared our story across the globe with some of the most amazing people I have ever met. But, of course, the most profound changes go far deeper than that.

Initially, I would often break down during my talks, specifically when sharing my lowest moments or on seeing a picture of my children on the big screen. During those 28-and-a-half hours in the ocean, I very quickly came to appreciate how fleeting life is and how quickly it can be taken away from us.

Never take anything for granted.

This is one of those life lessons that we're all aware of to some degree, but one that we don't necessarily take cognisance of or apply to our daily existence. Please believe me when I tell you that you don't want to wait until you're surrounded by a hundred kilometres of ocean on all sides to truly understand its importance!

Living through this experience has also been truly complex.

The lows were as deep and dark as I believe it is possible to go. The gut-wrenching and heartbreaking emotions that consumed me when I first came around in the ocean, having fallen from the *Naga Laut*, have been described in depth in these pages. In reality, though, I have not found any words that can truly convey my feelings when I *knew* I would never see my wife and children again. Of course, one's wife, children and family are important – you assume you know this and live it every day. However this experience has crystalised in exquisite detail for me just what that really means.

I am blessed to have such amazing friends in my life. I may have thought my time was up, but I also knew with complete conviction that my buddies on the *Naga Laut* would come back to find me. Staying alive until that moment became my only goal. To have had them come so close after twelve hours of hell and for them to sail away again without seeing me was the most harrowing moment I have ever suffered in my life.

But then again, the highs have been astonishing: the moment I saw the mast of the *Barrenjoey*, that small black crucifix of redemption, and the relief in that instant when I knew that they'd spotted me; the exhilaration of getting through such a physical and mental ordeal once I was on board; the elation of being reunited with my friends on the *Naga Laut*; and, of course, the absolute and unbridled joy of confounding that initial low – seeing my wife, children, family and friends again.

The highs may have triumphed, but being so close to death brings changes. Like many survivors of such experiences, I have been left with profound and haunting questions.

In compiling this book and building up the layered pictures of my experience, I have gradually been forced to take stock of the physiological and psychological effects of my extremely close call. This has led me to plumbing the fundamental questions in my life – exploring my personality, understanding my identity and delving deep into my soul. I have embarked on a spiritual journey that brings with it its own nuances, questions and challenges at every turn.

I know without a shadow of a doubt that God was with me during that time; that He has always been with me and that He will always be with me on my life journey. My church is the ocean, the place I find solace and peace. I am embracing this renewed journey with my Maker and each new day with Him in it is a blessed and enriching one. I have learnt much about forgiveness, compassion and understanding.

I am a firm believer in synchronicity. Each and every time I reflect on the many seemingly trivial occurrences during those 28-and-a-half hours, I am amazed at how the universe came together to facilitate my rescue. These days I allow my intuition to guide me and I try to embrace the positives and ignore the negatives that so often pervade our lives.

Through all I have learnt, both during my ordeal and since then, I find myself constantly returning to my initial learning: how precious our lives are and our time is, how we can't take any of it for granted, and that we need to spend it doing the right things with the people who are important to us. Of course, that is easier said than done, and I continue to grapple in my attempts to understand the weight and significance of an experience that took me right to the edge and brought me back again.

From this notion, however, I have identified three specifically important areas in my life. They are what I call my three 'F's:

Faith
Family
Friends

I know that if I manage to find a balance between those three, then everything else has a way of falling into place. The rest is all peripherals!

As we launch this book on the third anniversary of that near-fateful day, I continually strive to find a moment in every day where I give thanks for the richness of my life and all of those in it.

Psychiatrist and best-selling author Scott M Peck wrote this opening line to his book *The Road Less Travelled*: 'Life is difficult.' That it is, without a doubt. However, it is also most certainly full of choices, and it is in making those choices that we as individuals are able to define our future paths in life and create our own destiny.

I have read and re-read the manuscript of *Alone*, parts of it so many times that I can recite them verbatim. I will, however, continue to read it often to remember what this experience has taught me and to warm my heart, and as a reminder to say thank you to so many.

I hope that this book makes your heart warm too – thank you for reading it.

Always believe in the impossible! And never, ever give up!

CAST OF CHARACTERS

In the water
Brett Archibald (Arch or Jetman)

Brett's imaginary Board of Directors
Bob: Brett's mouth; operations director
Emily: Brett's left nostril; sales director
Hilary: Brett's right nostril; marketing director

Brian Archibald: Brett's father
Rob de Beer: died the week before the surf trip

The Naga Laut
Passengers:
The team who made up 'The Ten Green Bottles Tour'
Anthony Singleton (Tony): trip organiser
Niall Hegarty
Craig Killeen
Mark Ridgway (Ridgy)
Mark Snowball (Snowman)
Jean-Marc Tostee (JM)
Benoit Maingard (Banger)
Weyne Mudde
(Ed Pickles: didn't make it on the trip because of a cancer scare)

Crew:
Skippy: Brett's nickname for the captain
Yanto: the only English speaker of the Indonesian crew; the all-round fixer, first mate and surf guide
Jaipur (Baz): engineer
Boi: boat's chef

Anton: Skippy's son and cabin host – with a smattering of English phrases

Back home
Family & friends at Fiskaal Road, Camps Bay:
Anita Nicolopulos (Neets): Brett's wife
Zara Archibald: their nine-year-old daughter
Jamie Archibald: their six-year-old son
Loni and Paula Nicolopulos: Anita's parents
Helene Planting: Anita's younger sister
Andrew Planting: Helene's husband
Karmen and Luke Thomsett: Anita's cousin and her new Australian husband – just married the previous weekend
Zenda and Joe Stravino: Anita's aunt and uncle, in town for the wedding
Lettie Marondera: the family's housekeeper
Louise Killeen: Craig's wife
Lulu Ridgway: Mark Ridgway's wife
Gaby Grieveson: Anita's close friend
Wayne Grieveson: Brett's close friend and Gaby's husband
Katya Laspatzis: Anita's friend
Ari Laspatzis: Katya's husband
Kirsten Horn: Anita's friend
Dudley Horn: Kirsten's husband
Tessa Tostee: JM's wife
Barbara Singleton: Tony's wife

In Hermanus:
Chantal Malherbe: tour operator who booked the trip on the *Naga Laut*
Gideon Malherbe: Chantal's husband
Gigs Cilliers: former world kneeboard champion and Brett's friend

Brett's family in the Drakensberg:
Greg Archibald: Brett's brother
Joanne Archibald: Greg's wife
Shirley Archibald: Brett's mom
Terence Archibald: Greg and Joanne's oldest son
Nicholas Archibald: Greg and Joanne's son
Megan Archibald: Greg and Joanne's daughter
Irene and Mike: Joanne's parents
Sandra Archibald: Brett's sister
Neil Fourie: Sandra's son

Brett's friends who were constantly in touch with Anita during his time in the water:
Gary Knowles: Brett's close friend who lives in Australia
Chris Joseph (CJ): Brett's close friend who works in Singapore
Andre Crawford-Brunt: Brett's friend who lives in London
Ray Cadiz: Brett's friend who lives in Cape Town

The Barrenjoey
Crew:
Tony 'Doris' Eltherington: skipper; Australian expat captain of the *Rajah Elang* and one-time Gold Coast surfing legend
Aroziduhu 'Elvis' Waruwu: crew member
Wilson: crew member
Aneraigo 'Anas' Laia: crew member
Adek: crew member

Passengers:
Lyall Davieson: designated trip organiser
Dave Carbon: first man to reach Brett in the water
Simon Carlin: second man to reach Brett in the water
Colin Chenu: third man to reach Brett in the water
Justin Vivian: urologist who monitored Brett's health on the boat
Jeff Vidler

Pete Inglis
Gary Catlin
Mark Swan

Doris's contacts:
Steven Sewell: charter captain from Western Australia, on a 127-day run in the Malacca Strait
John and Belinda McGroder: owners of the *Barrenjoey* and residents of the Mentawais. Live on their private boat *Amandla*
Martin Daly: owner of three other boats, *Indies Traders I, II & III* that he offered to the search
Suley: captain of the *Huey*

Tony 'Doris' Eltherington's family:
Denise: Doris's older sister who taught him how to surf
Kerry: Doris's sister
Dawn: Doris's mother
Kim (Bowie): Doris's older brother
Lesley: Doris's first wife
Taryn: Doris's daughter
Suzanne: Doris's second wife
Jarrah: Doris's daughter
Madeline: Doris's daughter
Dave Kinder: Doris's best friend who died the day before Brett went missing – and perhaps part of the inspiration to find Brett

PUBLISHER'S NOTE

The timeline and versions of events in this book were re-created from the first-hand accounts of the many people involved. Where exact times were unknown or conflicting, best estimates have been used.

ACKNOWLEDGEMENTS

Heartfelt acknowledgements are extended with sincere gratitude to the following.

My beautiful, amazing, mind-blowing wife Anita! You are my best friend and the rock in our family. You are my sun, my moon, my stars, my universe. Your unconditional love makes my heart burst with happiness every day. Thank you for talking to me the whole way through those 28-and-a-half hours. You never gave up on me; I heard you and that kept me going. You rock my planet, lady! I love you more!

My two beautiful, quirky and amazing children, Zara and Jamie. Together with your Mom, you gave me the strength to keep fighting, to never ever give up, and to believe that I would see you again, despite the many times that I felt I just couldn't carry on. I pray that I will live to a ripe old age to watch you grow from the incredible children you are now into the beautiful big people I know you are going to become.

My boys on the *Naga Laut*: JM, Tony, Banger, Craig, Ridgy, Niall, Weyne and Snowman. My mates who never gave up. I am convinced that your time on the *Naga Laut* during those hours was worse than my time in the sea. You had no idea if you were looking for a live person or a body. Searching a boat for someone who had vanished, contemplations of a suicide and long weary hours of staring into a tumultuous ocean took its toll on each of you. Ridgy, to have got the boat to within 100 meters of me after twelve hours in that storm was nothing short of miraculous. JM, your quick thinking and communications role kept my family and the world informed. Thanks to you all for your recollections of events and the sharing of your own personal moments. Through these and the letters you all wrote me I have a vivid and rich collection of stories to share with my children. Boys, I would go into battle with you any time. What a team. Thank you for everything!

To my very special friend Ed Pickles. You shared with me how hard it was for you in Dubai while I was missing. I am so grateful for your wishes and concern during that time. I look forward to many surf sessions in Jeffries together.

The crew of the *Naga Laut*: Yanto, Skippy, Baz, Boi and Anton – you are special people. The care and nurturing you provided me for the rest of the surf trip was exceptional.

Tony 'Doris' Eltherington. There are no words that can adequately thank a man for saving your life. Please know that your steadfast commitment to search for me, no matter what the consequences, will always be remembered. You saved a son, a husband, a father, a brother and a friend and I, as well as all my loved ones, are eternally grateful. Thank you also for the hours that you gave us towards creating this book. You are constantly in our thoughts and prayers and we will give thanks to you forever. You are a legend!

The lads on the *Barrenjoey*; Lyall Davieson, Jeff Vidler, Justin Vivian, Simon Carlin, Colin Chenu, Dave Carbon, Pete Inglis, Gary Catlin and Mark Swan. Aussie Aussie Aussie! Thank you for giving up the last two days of your surf trip to find me. Particular thanks go to Lyall, Simon, Jeff and Colin for retelling your sides of the story with insight and integrity. Meeting you all changed my life in so many ways. I hope that you know how much it means to my family and me.

The entire crew of the *Barrenjoey*; Elvis, Wilson, Anas and Adek. Thank you for spotting my bald head in that vast expanse of ocean. You guys are my superstars!

Lou Killeen, Lulu Ridgway, Wayne and Gaby Grieveson, Karmen and Luke Thomsett, Helene, Paula and Loni Nicolopulos, Zendi Stravino, Kirsten Horn, Katya and Ari

Laspatzis and Letwin Marondera who were Anita's 'A Team' throughout my ordeal. What a group of people. Wayno – you were the proverbial calm in the storm. Thank you, all.

My incredible mother, Shirls. I am deeply sorry that you had to endure such a traumatic event in the twilight years of your life. I know you suffered many tormented hours believing that you were going to become one of those parents who loses a child. You are an angel on this earth, and though many people do not see your halo or your wings, I do. I love you very much.

My Dad, Brian Archibald. Although long since passed, you were my constant companion in the ocean and we had many conversations. I am glad we made our peace before you left us. You were a unique man who was tormented and afflicted by a tragic illness through no fault of your own. I want you to know that you taught me many valuable life lessons when I was a young boy that have always stood me in good stead. Thank you for that. Rest in peace.

My siblings and their families; Sandy, Kim, Brian, Zack, Neil, Greg, Joanne, Terence, Nicholas and my little Meg. Thank you for your support over the past fifty-odd years of my life. Although we live many miles apart, I think of you all constantly. I love you guys.

Paula and Loni Nicolopulos. You are the best in-laws a man could ever ask for. Your unwavering commitment, loyalty and the unconditional love that you bestow on our little family is extraordinary. You make our world a better place.

My Eleni Mou and blister-in-law Helene. Thank you for the support you gave Anita during those dark hours in her life. You were her rock and confidant. Your firm belief that it was not my time and that there was no way I was going to die in that blaze of publicity, but that I'd pass away peacefully in my sleep in old age, brought much relief to an otherwise very sombre house. You are da bomb!

The rest of our Lutz clan. The Stravinos and Skrabls. 'Die Kants and die ander Kants'. Joe and Zendi, Luigi and Philippa, Paolo and Jeanne, Giulia and Luke, Lillo and Manfred, Claudi and Grant, Karmen and Luke. What a family to be a part of! Luigi and Paolo, thank you for all your efforts in trying to scramble your flying connections; it will always be appreciated.

Gary Knowles and Chris Joseph, my brothers from other mothers. It could not have been any more coincidental that at that exact time you were both in Indonesia. Synchronicity at its finest. Thank you for being Anita's ears on the ground in a foreign country and for doing everything that you did to help. Being there to meet me in Singapore on my way home was the best thing you have ever done for me! That moment was poignant and will stay with me forever. The 'Three Musthavebeers' being reunited after my ordeal was more meaningful than you will ever know.

Gary and Di, thank you for travelling twice across Australia to spend time with Anita and me. GK, being there for me meant so much and gave me the opportunity to truly sob and expunge much angst from my system.

The Plantings, Steyns, Grievesons and Horns for being at the airport to welcome me home and being my shield against the media barrage. Together with Lou Killeen, Sarah and Terence Craig and Ivor and Pauline Goetsch for being at Fiskaal Road to welcome me home and subsequently spend one of the best days of my life with me. Home, safe in my family's arms and surrounded by close friends.

Ute Latzke, my other sister. Thank you for the spiritual journeys you take me on. You were also a constant companion in the ocean. We have discussed our many philosophies on the spiritual realm; I look forward to many more in the future.

Steve Griessel, for giving me the opportunities that you have. You provided me with a platform to truly understand and push myself. You introduced me to the concept of synchronicity and it has been a major part of my life ever since. We have travelled down a long and winding road together and emerged stronger, wiser and more fulfilled.

Nick Christellis for being my mentor and continually helping me over life's many hurdles. I have so much to thank you for.

Coralie Trotter for being my life coach over the past eighteen years. You have given me insight in to what makes me tick and how my personal psyche works. You have unravelled so many complexities that had burdened my soul for so long. The journey has been real.

My brother-in-law Andrew Planting and Estelle and Pierre Tostee for your immediate response in galvanising prayer groups in Cape Town and Durban respectively, which mushroomed across South Africa and the globe. There were many moments during my ordeal when I felt I had nothing left, yet I know that I was lifted on the wings of prayer and angels in whatever form or manner they manifested themselves. Estelle, thank you for your constant prayer during that time, especially for 'Bring him, Jesus, bring him, Jesus, bring him, Jesus', and sharing the passage from Isaiah 48:15 with me when you opened your Bible at that moment: 'Yes, I have called him, I will bring him, and he will succeed in his mission.' You were certain I was alive and retired to bed, slept soundly and awoke to hear the joyous news of my rescue. That alone has had such a profound impact on my life and helps me every day on my spiritual quest.

Joe Stravino, Ray Cadiz, Andre Crawford-Brunt and John Spence. Your immediate and unconditional offers of financial assistance in order to get aircraft and boats mobilised were mind-blowing. Although the inclement weather prevented any of these from being used, I will remain forever grateful.

Chantal and Gideon Malherbe and Gigs Cilliers. Your role in being the link between the *Naga Laut*, *Amandla*, *Barrenjoey* and Martin Daly, together with your knowledge of that part of the world and leveraging every one of your connections, was phenomenal. Chantal, thank you for being at the airport to meet me on my return; it was an emotional moment.

John, Belinda, Fynn and Duke McGroder. The fact that your charter had been cancelled and the *Barrenjoey* was in port on stand-by is the embodiment of synchronicity. Had it not been, how differently this story could have unravelled. Meeting you and hearing the full story from your perspective was emotional and liberating. Duke, what a way to celebrate your birthday; you reminded me so much of my little Jamie. Thank you for all those hugs on the evening of my rescue. John and Belinda, thanks also for log-book details, elements from your article "Rocket Science With Uncle Doris" in *White Horses* and other fact-checking of this story. Your family will always hold a special place in my heart.

Shelly Henn. Thank you for launching the Facebook page 'Searching for Brett Archibald'. Your inspiration in creating this not only provided a platform for thousands of people to come together, but also provided me with an insight in to how much goodwill there is in the world. Through this I have been given new faith in humanity, and I have a collection of stories and messages that will bolster my spirits forever.

Jenny Handley. You got me on the road to getting this

book made – I am indebted. Also, to my good friend Gary Green, author extraordinaire, who kept at me to complete *Alone* on the many occasions that I was ready to throw in the towel. I hope you enjoy the read.

Kirk Willcox, director of marketing and communications for SurfAid, for your background information on the Mentawais, surf charter operations and the surfing scene in general in Indonesia; and for your insight into the character of your friend Doris Eltherington.

For historical and anthropological information regarding the Mentawai Island Regency, we are indebted to the fieldwork website, journal and articles of mentawai.org compiled by Australian anthropologist Glenn Reeves.

For information and details around the Australian surf scene in the 1960s and '70s, and for certain details in parts of Doris's history, thanks go to journalist Matt George for his article about Doris in *The Surfer's Journal*.

For additional details of Doris's life and character, and for her generous hospitality provided to the writer during her trip to Australia – and 'the world's best prawn sandwiches' – thanks go to Doris's daughter, Taryn Eltherington.

For her sensitive editing and all-round advice, an enthusiastic thanks to Alison Lowry.

For the vivid and realistic production of the *Miracle At Sea* documentary, my thanks go to Nick Greenaway and Charlie Wooley of Australia's Channel Nine *60 Minutes* team. Your genuine concern for my family during our stay in Australia was much appreciated.

For the simple understanding and clear explanation of the physiology behind my survival, together with the time he offered, thanks to Professor Tim Noakes of the Sports Science Institute of South Africa.

For explaining the psychological aspects associated with this story, Cape Town psychologist, with a keen interest in post-traumatic stress disorder, Trudy Borain.

For correspondence and permission to use information from his book *Hallucinations* (Picador, 2012), the late Oliver Sacks.

To Tim Richman for graciously leading me through the complex labyrinth of publishing a book. Tim's father passed away as we finalised the manuscript and layout – what a terrible blow, yet he remained stoic and strong during that tough time. Deep respect, my friend. Always remember our conversations and the importance of mourning properly. And to everyone else at Burnet Media and Jacana, including Liz Sarant and Francesca Bourke – thank you.

And crucially, to the wonderful woman who wrote this book but who, sadly for me, has chosen to remain unnamed. My confidant, CB. Your interpretation and weaving of so many pieces of extraordinary information into this exceptional retelling of our story has been nothing short of amazing. Thank you for allowing me the space to share, talk, cry and laugh about this traumatic event in my life. I have shared more of my life with you than with any other person on this planet except Anita. I am honoured to have embarked on this path with you. A special thank you goes to your husband and your two boys for their unfailing support and love for you during the many hours that this book took you away from them.

To all the friends I have made on my journey through life, who reside both near and far. Your support and the messages sent to my family and me during that horrific time are unparalleled. I am blessed to know you all. You know who you are! I am grateful.

This book is dedicated to my 3 'F's.

Faith
To God, for testing me beyond all belief; for making me look into my core and realise what in life is really important.

Family
My wife and soulmate Anita, my delightful daughter Zara and my special son Jamie, who make me whole – together with my extended family who complete my existence.

Friends
My inner circle of friends, a special group of new Aussie friends, and those thousands of people out there in the world who never stopped believing I would make it.

If it weren't for you all, your prayers and belief, I would not be here today.

For more images and footage of Brett's rescue see

www.brettarchibald.com